The Limits of Interpretation

The Limits of Interpretation opens a window onto unexplored dimensions of Wilfred Bion's thought, presenting essays that illuminate both familiar and lesser-known facets of his work. It guides readers through complex notions such as visible-invisible hallucinations, bizarre objects, and a radical reframing of the Oedipus complex – shifted from incest and parricide to arrogance and the desire for knowledge.

Taking various of Bion's key works in turn, Civitarese explores what is unique about Bion's thinking on essential topics such as projective identification, infantile development, and intuition, to shed light on the continued importance of Bion's early work, in particular for contemporary psychoanalysis. By focusing on Bion's Kleinian-phase essays, this volume highlights their pivotal role in comprehending his entire theoretical landscape and how far they extend beyond traditional Freudian and Kleinian frameworks. It even poses the question: was Bion ever truly a Kleinian?

Offering a close reading and clear interpretation of Bion's sometimes dense writing, this is essential reading for any psychoanalysts or psychotherapists wanting to understand Bion's work better.

Giuseppe Civitarese, MD, PhD, is a training and supervising analyst (SPI, APsaA, IPA). He lives in Pavia, Italy. His books include *The Intimate Room: Theory and Technique of the Analytic Field*; *The Violence of Emotions: Bion and Post-Bion Psychoanalysis*; *Truth and the Unconscious*; *Sublime Subjects: Aesthetic Experience and Intersubjectivity in Psychoanalysis*; and *Psychoanalytic Field Theory: A Contemporary Introduction*.

NEW LIBRARY OF PSYCHOANALYSIS
General Editor: Anne Patterson

The *New Library of Psychoanalysis* is published by Routledge Mental Health in association with the *Institute of Psychoanalysis*, London.
  The purpose of the book series is:

- to advance and disseminate ideas in psychoanalysis amongst those working in psychoanalysis, psychotherapy and related fields
- to facilitate a greater and more widespread appreciation of psychoanalysis in the general book-reading public
- to provide a forum for increasing mutual understanding between psychoanalysts and those in other disciplines
- to facilitate communication between different traditions and cultures within psychoanalysis, making some of the work of continental and other non-English speaking analysts more readily available to English-speaking readers, and increasing the interchange of ideas between British and American analysts.

The *New Library of Psychoanalysis* published its first book in 1987 under the editorship of David Tuckett, who was followed by Elizabeth Bott Spillius, Susan Budd, Dana Birksted-Breen and Alessandra Lemma. The Editors, including the current Editor, Anne Patterson, have been assisted by a considerable number of Associate Editors and readers from a range of countries and psychoanalytic traditions. The present Associate Editors are Susanne Calice, Katalin Lanczi and Anna Streeruwitz.
  Under the guidance of Foreign Rights Editors, a considerable number of the *New Library* books have been published abroad, particularly in Brazil, Germany, France, Italy, Peru, Spain and Japan. The *New Library of Psychoanalysis* has also translated and published several books by continental psychoanalysts and plans to continue the policy of publishing books that express as clearly as possible a variety of psychoanalytic points of view. The *New Library of Psychoanalysis* has published books representing all three schools of thought in British psychoanalysis, including a particularly important

work edited by Pearl King and Riccardo Steiner, *'The Freud-Klein Controversies 1941-45'*, expounding the intellectual and organisational controversies that developed in the British psychoanalytical Society between Kleinian, Viennese and 'middle group' analysts during the Second World War.

The *New Library of Psychoanalysis* aims for excellence in psychoanalytic publishing. Submitted manuscripts are rigorously peer-reviewed in order to ensure high standards of scholarship, clinical communications, and writing.

For a full list of all the titles in the New Library of Psychoanalysis main series as well as both the New Library of Psychoanalysis 'Teaching Series' and 'Beyond the Couch' subseries, please visit the Routledge website.

The Limits of Interpretation

Essays on Bion and Field Theory

Giuseppe Civitarese

Routledge
Taylor & Francis Group

LONDON AND NEW YORK

Designed cover image: Getty: Andrey_A

First published 2026
by Routledge
4 Park Square, Milton Park, Abingdon, Oxon, OX14 4RN

and by Routledge
605 Third Avenue, New York, NY 10158

Routledge is an imprint of the Taylor & Francis Group, an informa business

© 2026 Giuseppe Civitarese

British Library Cataloguing-in-Publication Data
A catalogue record for this book is available from the British Library

ISBN: 978-1-041-03768-2 (hbk)
ISBN: 978-1-041-03125-3 (pbk)
ISBN: 978-1-003-62524-7 (ebk)

DOI: 10.4324/9781003625247

Typeset in Bembo
by codeMantra

Contents

Acknowledgements

Chapter 1 is based on "Experiences in Groups as a Key to 'Late' Bion." *International Journal of Psychoanalysis* 102:1071–1096 (2021)

Chapter 2 is based on "The Limits of Interpretation. A Reading of Bion's 'On Arrogance'." *International Journal of Psychoanalysis* 102:236–257 (2021)

Chapter 3 is based on "Invisible-Visual Hallucinations in Bion's 'Attacks on Linking'." *International Journal of Psychoanalysis* 104:197–222 (2023)

Chapter 4 is based on "The Concept of Time in Bion's 'A Theory of Thinking'." *International Journal of Psychoanalysis* 100:182–205 (2019)

Chapter 5 is based on "Intuition and We-ness in Bion and Post-Bionian Field Theory." *International Journal of Psychoanalysis* 105:13–39 (2024)

Chapter 6 is based on "Bion's O and His Pseudo-Mystical Path." *Psychoanalytic Dialogues* 29:388–403 (2019)

Introduction

The first four chapters of this book are devoted mainly to Bion's writings from the pre-Kleinian and then the Kleinian period. I refer, on the one hand, to the essays on group psychology collected in the volume *Experiences in Groups* (1961) and, on the other hand, to some of those collected in *Second Thoughts* (1967). These essays are notable not only because they were reprinted at a time when Bion, having published three of his major monographs, had become, so to speak, himself – having developed his most original and ground-breaking theses – but also because they are followed by a commentary written in 1967. In this way, Bion looks back on them, and the dialectic between old and new is extremely interesting for the reader.

In the last two chapters, on the other hand, my analysis introduces an additional dialectical level between the ideas of the "early" Bion and the subsequent developments in his thought from the early 1960s onwards, as well as in the post-Bionian theory of the analytic field. My aim is not only to link the most innovative ideas present in this book on groups and in the essays from the Kleinian period to the so-called "second" or "late" Bion, but also to what I believe to be the most vibrant paradigm in the contemporary psychoanalytic landscape, which goes under the name of post-Bionian theory of the analytic field. My work is therefore in no way that of a historian of the discipline, something I am happy to leave to others, but rather a way of looking back in order to better understand the present and to refine the tools of everyday clinical practice.

The order of the chapters generally reflects not the chronological order in which I wrote them, but the order in which Bion's papers were written. In this way, I facilitate the reader's task of understanding how his most original thoughts gradually take shape. What follows is a brief outline of the content of each chapter.

In order to understand the "late" Bion, i.e. his production from *Learning from Experience* onwards, the most difficult and controversial, it is worth rereading not only the essays in *Second Thoughts*, but also *Experiences in Groups*. The hypothesis I develop in the first chapter is that Bion spent his life as a scholar – probably without being fully aware of it, since he never talks about it – translating his theory of groups into his theory of individual psychoanalysis. To illustrate this thesis, I will systematically compare some of the principles of the two. The return to group experience is useful for another reason. Bion revolutionizes theory but still works as a Kleinian. Despite brilliant suggestions, he does not fully develop a new technique. To have a toolbox that everyone can use, we have to wait for the analytic field theory, which is an original development of his thinking. In this model, the analyst does not see the analytic pair as two isolated subjects interacting, but as a group. There is no "fact" of analysis that cannot be heard as unconsciously co-created. Here, then, the emphasis on the group inspiration of Bion's late work helps us to grasp the meaning of this technical principle, which is so easily misunderstood, and vice versa.

The second chapter is devoted to a rereading of "On Arrogance", a very short paper written by Bion in 1958, which reveals its extraordinary topicality. It can be seen both as a commentary on Sophocles' *Oedipus Rex* and as an essay on the "disease" of psychoanalysis. In both cases, lying at its centre is the triad of curiosity-stupidity-arrogance that drives us to know the truth "at any cost". In this work, Bion redefines the crime of Oedipus (and therefore of psychoanalysis) around the epistemic instinct and no longer around sexuality; he exposes the objectifying attitude of the analyst; he revolutionizes the understanding of negative therapeutic reactions. The "psychosis" of the analyst (or of psychoanalysis) is expressed in the phenomena of wanting to become a psychoanalyst, of wanting to be "scientific" (as opposed to gaining a hermeneutic understanding), of wanting to tell the patient what he thinks is the truth, and finally of looking "down" on his patients and colleagues. Anticipating the themes of *Transformations* (1965) and *A Memory of the Future*, "On Arrogance" lays the groundwork for a cogent critique of the ideology of psychoanalysis and an effective ethical re-foundation of the discipline.

In Chapter 3, I deal with "Attacks on Linking" (1959). In this chapter, it is as if Bion had listened to his former analyst. In a lecture on technique given the previous year, Melanie Klein had expressed the wish that someone would write "a book about linking [...] one of the essential points in an analysis" (2017, 110). Later taken up and commented on in *Second Thoughts*, "Attacks on Linking" has become perhaps Bion's most famous paper and, apart from Freud, one of the most cited papers in the entire psychoanalytic literature. In this short and dazzling essay, Bion presents the enigmatic and fascinating concept of invisible-visual hallucination (IVH), which seems never to have been taken up and discussed as such by other scholars. I therefore propose to reread Bion's text starting from this concept. In an attempt to give as clear a definition as possible, a comparison is made with those of negative hallucination (Freud), dream screen (Lewin), and primitive agony (Winnicott). Finally, I formulate the hypothesis that IVH could give us the model of what remains at the origin of any representation, i.e. a micro-traumatic inscription of the trace of stimuli (which may, however, turn out to be traumatic) in the psychic fabric.

A complex and subtle theory of time is at the heart of Bion's text "A Theory of Thought" (1962a), the subject of Chapter 4. The central point is the distinction between "conception" and "thought", psychic elements that are born in the infant out of experiences of satisfaction and frustration, respectively. These mnestic inscriptions should be understood as being in dialectical relationship with each other. It is from this matrix, within which the original temporality is established, that lived time derives, but only when it is inserted into the symbolic order through the function of language, which gives access to the "concept". Our sense of time is therefore based on the rhythm of presentation of the breast and thus on the primary relationship with the object, as well as on a broader symbolic network. The meeting of a preconception of the breast with the mere absence of the breast is not capable of generating a "thought" and establishing time.

This is why Bion distinguishes between the absence of a breast or non-breast and nothing (*noughtness*), a state of nameless fear. Bion's concept of time provides an empirical idea, based on clinical cases, in which the destruction of time is observed, of both the origin of time and what Heidegger called – in contrast to "linear" or objective conceptions of time – the ontological structure of temporality.

"Intuition" is among the most frequently used concepts in all of Bion's writings. In order to understand its role in his thought, however, it is essential to give it as clear a definition as possible. The thesis of Chapter 5 is that by intuition Bion means a "specific" psychoanalytic concept. It is thus possible to extract intuition from the vague and mystifying reading of it by some authors, which runs the risk of falling into an empty "intuitionism". For Bion, intuition is a psychoanalytic function of the analyst, the main factors of which are the various expressions of dream-thought and insight.

Furthermore, within the framework of the post-Bionian theory of the analytic field, I propose to add to these factors the use of the "we" vertex (or we-ness), i.e. to regard virtually every fact of analysis as co-created. The aim is to make the concept of "field" itself more accessible. Compared to the metaphor of the analytic field, the concept of we-ness has both greater clinical versatility and greater pregnancy at the metapsychological level. Indeed, it reflects more directly a radically social conception of human subjectivity: what is known in contemporary speculative thought – in J-L. Nancy, for example – as the "ontology of the we".

In the chapter that concludes this book, I explore Bion's concept of O, which, like few others, is both essential and elusive. Its ambiguous nature gives rise to the most disturbing interpretations and many misunderstandings. One of these is the idea of opening up a "mystical" psychoanalysis. In order to refute this thesis, I propose a reading, which is certainly personal and sometimes even impervious, but which aims to place this concept in a theoretical framework that is as clear, logical, and coherent as possible. The meaning of the concept of O is only defined in relation to other key concepts (mainly transformation, invariant, and at-one-ment). It will therefore escape us if we do not take into account the dialectical tension that arises from this fruitful interplay, and if we do not pay attention to the ever-changing discursive contexts in which it is found. Above all, however, it is important to realize that the concept of O is also peculiar in comparison with other, more clearly specified and circumscribed concepts of Bion. In fact, it is itself a constellation of concepts, as many names or partial definitions.

1

EXPERIENCES IN GROUPS AS A KEY TO "LATE" BION

In my experience as a Bion scholar, I have long tended to leave aside certain important aspects of his thinking that I considered marginal or abstruse. These include the role played by the grid (Bion 1963), the Dodgsonian mathematics of *Transformations*, and his book on groups. I have noticed, however, that I am not alone in this respect. Later, I did, as it were, attempt to settle my accounts with the grid in an article I wrote a few years ago (Civitarese 2013a); however, I cannot say that I really understood it until connected it with Bion's concepts of regression and his symbol of "in search of existence" (Civitarese 2020a, 2021a). Then, my investigation of this link between the grid and Bion's imaginative geometry prompted me to go back to *Experiences in Groups* (Bion 1961).[1] In fact, the grid is the conceptual radar we can use to pick up the changes in the emotional climate that occur in the therapeutic relationship between patient and analyst. The crucial point, though, is that we should be able to see these two people not in isolation but as members of a group. This would mean reading what happens between them in the light of group theory.

Little by little I came to realize, in short, that in order to understand Bion, it is essential to take a circular path through his work. As in the rhetorical figure of the *hysteron proteron*, in which the chronological order between two events is reversed in order to highlight their particular relationship, so EG is not only the anticipation of ideas that will be developed later; but it is also their fulfilment.

DOI: 10.4324/9781003625247-1

My aim here is double. First, I try to demonstrate that the idea of psychoanalysis we find in the "late" Bion is but the transposition of his group theory – which probably happened without his being fully aware of it, since (as far as I know) he never talks about it. To develop my point, I compare some concepts we find in EG with some concepts of "late" Bion's theory of individual psychoanalysis. In this way, I also hope to shed some light on some of the most difficult to grasp among them – for instance, negative capability, O, reversible perspective, containment, and transformation. I will let Bion himself speak as much as possible, and even when I do not make it explicit, for the sake of brevity, I hope it is clear from the context that each time I propose to see what he says about the group as poured into his concepts concerning individual psychoanalysis, as these have been received and reinterpreted by post-Bionian analytic field theory (FT).

In fact, my second aim here – directly related to clinical practice, and not only to the history of ideas – is, by trying to validate my first hypothesis, to give a more solid theoretical foundation to the technique, already sketched in Bion, but fully developed by FT, of virtually listening to *any* narrative that enters the analytic conversation as co-created on the unconscious level by a group-of-two made by the analytic dyad. Therefore, at the end of the paper, I will discuss a short clinical vignette to show what new we gain from postulating a "jointly created unconscious", and not just "two distinct unconsciouses [that] affect each other" (Gerson 2004, 74).

Why Reread *Experiences in Groups*?

My reception of Bion's thought started from the angle of FT, the theory that attempts a radical interpretation of the current paradigm of so-called intersubjective psychoanalysis. That is to say, it is the model of psychoanalysis that considers the analyst's unconscious participation in the process of analysis in a very inclusive manner. In doing so, it follows to the letter the principles that Bion sets forth in *Transformations* (1961) and that some critics find "scandalous": the analyst should "forget" the patient's past and concrete reality in order to focus as sharply as possible on what happens in the session. In FT, this becomes listening to virtually anything that is said (no matter by whom) as being produced, at the unconscious level, by the *system* formed by the two distinct unconsciouses in contact, and as reflecting its constant and more or less successful activity of trans-forming raw sensoriality into images that have meaning.

I have never found it easy to explain this principle. Even the particular way of illustrating it proposed by the exponents of the so-called Pavia School[2] has always seemed somewhat misleading to me. Indeed, sometimes we give the impression of reverting to a relational/interpersonal model that looks at the mere interaction between two separate subjects and not at the system (or field) they give birth to. This is why I began to think more and more often of the group as the model of the two-person therapeutic relationship and to feel the need to reread EG carefully. I realized that while it is easy to get the concept of a subject whose functioning is power-fully influenced by a group feeling, it is almost impossible – who knows why – to think of two people who are close enough to func-tion unconsciously as a small group. Not unlike ultrasound and ul-traviolet rays, if compared with intuition based on the senses, the group-of-two entity and its properties seem to fall outside the range of our theoretical intuition.

Let us imagine a group therapy situation. We think it is self-evident that the therapist should pay attention to the emotional transformations that permeate the group and that would not even dream of explaining them simply by considering the biography of its single members. As Bion writes, "we are not concerned to give individual treatment in public, but to draw attention to the actual experiences of the group, and in this instance the way in which the group and individual deal with the individual" (80).

Or again, let us think of Bion and Rickman's experience in Ed-inburgh of using groups to select officers (the so-called "Leaderless Group Project"; Trist 1985). They organized a setting and let the spontaneous evolution of the group dynamics bring out its leader-ship functions. But is the analytic session very different if seen as a group-of-two that has to let the *agency* functions of the group itself emerge – and, in parallel to them, those of the individuals who make up the group?

A third case concerns the famous (or infamous) notion of O, which Bion regards as the only thing that counts in the session.[3] If we think of it as the basic assumption of the group-of-two (this is my proposal), it will stop sounding like an obscure concept.

From these examples, it is clear that thinking of the two-person relationship as a group brings us closer to some of Bion's most elusive concepts. We need to make the guess, I repeat, that for him the project of a lifetime was to pour the wine of his group theory into the glass of the therapeutic couple relationship. Like child psychoanalysis, group psychoanalysis has never been considered "true" psychoanalysis. Bion tried to do as the Greeks did when they gave the Trojans a wooden horse. He hid a group soul inside his theory of individual psychoanalysis. This is both evident and scotomized. It is "evident" because it seems obvious. It is like reinventing the wheel. It is "scotomized" because it has taken me years and years to regain possession of it, and I must say that I have come across a surprising blindness to it even in colleagues who value the contribution that Bion has made to the study of groups.

Here again, we have to be careful. I am not talking about a *generic* influence of EG's theory on "early" and "late" Bion, in other words, on Kleinian Bion and "Bionian" Bion. I always used to think that what interested me more than anything else was the latter, but eventually – going at a crab's pace – I realized that running from EG to *A Memoir of the Future* (1991), there is a stunning continuity between the two sets of respective concepts. One could indeed say that EG is the memory of the future of "late" Bion.

A New Look

Why did Bion take an interest in groups? We can presume, on the one hand, that his experience as an officer in the First World War was of fundamental importance, as was, on the other, his encounter with Rickman, his first analyst. Rickman had been in analysis with Freud, Ferenczi, and Klein and was interested in community therapy. Together they developed a document that became known as the Wharncliffe Memorandum. Wharncliffe was the name of the hospital where Bion joined Rickman in 1940 to start a pilot community therapy project. As Pines recalls, "in the sense of making systematic use of the happenings and relationships in the hospital, it was the first time the concept had been formulated" (1985, 6).

Later, in 1942, they devised the Northfield Experiment, "perhaps the first and prototype reflective institution" (Hinshelwood 2000, 8). Although it only lasted six weeks, the experience in the selection of officers was crucial in giving a direction to Bion's thinking. It was there that what we can call his intersubjectivism – in other words, his theory of the radically social nature of the subject – came into being.

4

When, in 1943, Bion and Rickman published in *The Lancet* an article entitled "Intra-group Tensions in Therapy: Their Study as the Task of the Group", the future first chapter of EG, they aroused the enthusiasm of a French analyst, Jacques Lacan, who was little known at the time and who travelled to London with the specific aim of meeting the authors. He later wrote:

> I find in their work something of the miraculous feeling of the initial stages of the Freudian elaboration: that of finding in the very impasse of a situation the vital force of an intervention ... [the article] will mark a historic date in psychiatry.
>
> (1947, 15)

Lacan also painted a portrait of the two extraordinary personalities he had met:

> Thus, I am going to try to present these two men for you *au naturel*, men of whom it can be said that the flame of creation burns in them. In the first [Bion], this flame is as if frozen in a motionless and lunar mask accentuated by the thin commas of a black moustache ... one of those beings who remain solitary even in the utmost commitment ... In the other [Rickman], this flame scintillates behind a lorgnette to the rhythm of a verb burning to return to action ... with a smile which makes his fawn brush bristle.
>
> (1947, 15)

He had the impression, he explains, that they were "pregnant with a birth of sorts that is a new outlook opening upon the world" (1947, 19).

Learning from Experience

Bion describes candidly where his interest in groups came from. When at the Holywell Mental Hospital in Birmingham he came in charge of the rehabilitation ward, the experience I already mentioned above as "the Northfield Experiment", he soon found that he could no longer concentrate and study in peace because he was assailed by a thousand requests from all the patients and staff members that were constantly milling around him. After a couple of hours, he decided that what was needed was a bit of discipline and so he started studying the problem. He soon realized that he could solve it if only he stopped seeing it as a problem regarding the individuals and instead treated it as a "disease" of the community – the fact that 20% worked and 80% did nothing. He asked himself how he could persuade the group "to tackle neurotic disability as a communal problem" (14).

One of the most striking things about EG is how Bion develops his discourse as if it were the account of a trip or a report on an experiment. The empirical, and not only theoretical, aspect has been part of psychoanalysis from its very beginnings (Freud's *Junktim*), but since Bion radicalizes the idea that in order to understand a phenomenon one has to observe it carefully, one can say that experience plays an even more central role in his thinking. "Learning from experience", then, is not only the title of one of his most important books but has also always been his guiding principle. Learning from experience requires a workshop. You have to come up with a suitable space.

What does Bion bring out? He accepts the proposal, made by most of the members of the group, of a "dancing class" (!). Basically, a game, he explains, a "quite impractical idea, quite contrary to any apparently serious military aim, or sense of social responsibility to the nation at war" (20).

The Imaginary Space

Here, for the first time, we see Bion outlining the need to find a new setting and to develop a new theory of how to observe ("a system of patient observation"; 19) – as we know, an insistently repeated call in *Transformations* (1961). He then devises an "imaginary space" (15), "as if it were a framework enclosed within transparent walls" (14) in which patients could move as they wished. The idea was to observe what was happening and to have "a means by which the progress of the patients could be indicated" (14). "As the patient's progress", he writes:

> was seen to run along one or other of these paths, so his 'assets and liabilities' … could be assessed with reasonable objectivity. As his progress appeared to be towards one or other of the possible exits from this imaginary space, so his true aim could be judged.
>
> (15)

What we see at work in this passage is the original insight of the grid, the instrument that Bion was to introduce in *Elements of Psycho-Analysis* (1963), as a three-dimensional space pervaded by continuous perturbations or emotional vectors. It is a kind of reality show, like *Big Brother*, but with the difference that here the observer too is inside the house; or rather, both inside *and* outside. The two perspectives work as a kind of binocular vision or like the ground/figure in Gestalt relationship.

However, there is a hierarchy between the two. In the foreground are the tensions that develop between the observer and the other guests in the "imaginary space" (15). As Bion notes, "At this point the conversation seems to me to indicate that the group has changed its purpose ... [settled on a] new course" (31); the group was "in the process of changing course"; an "improvement ... has taken place in the atmosphere" (32). The thematic and emotional variations within the group reflect its attitude. Their importance stems from the fact that they powerfully influence both the conscious and unconscious behaviour of the group as a whole and of its individual members. In short, *the analyst has the task of following in real time the transformations that originate in the group*. In this way, the analyst can make reasonable predictions about what the "weather" will be like in the immediate future. There are climatic conditions in which one can work and others in which this is not possible. Sometimes the only sensible thing to do is to prepare for the worst and to protect yourself.

Reversible Perspective

The analogy of the transparent home/room is then developed in the Necker cube (although Bion does not mention its author). This is the ambiguous two-dimensional representation – a so-called "impossible object" – of a cube where it is not possible to decide by logic which side is closest to the observer. Spontaneously, we are led to choose the lower right-hand side (marked with D) as closest to the observer; it is as if we prefer to see the cube *from above*. However, it would be equally possible to consider the lower left-hand side (marked with B) as being closer to the observer, as if we choose to see the cube from below (Figure 1.1).

Let us assume we take the lower right-hand side (D) as that closest to the viewer. Let us imagine that it depicts a room with a person standing in the middle. If we reverse the perspective by taking the

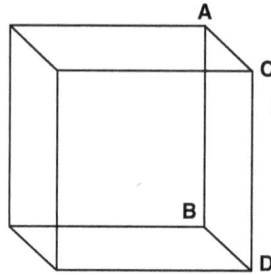

Figure 1.1 The Necker cube (Bion 1961, 86)

lower left-hand side (B) as that closest to the viewer, the same person who was previously *inside* would now be *outside* the house. The "floor" would disappear under his feet forcing him to take a perspective on the house from the outside. In analysis, the game plays out between material reality and psychic reality, between external perception (or sense-based intuition) and internal perception (emotion/representation or intellectual intuition), between waking and dreaming, and between "conscious" and "unconscious". As one of the perspectives is obvious and visible, the problem is always what technique to use to make visible the non-obvious or non-visible perspective. Bion's solution is to use the phenomenological method of focusing on the object by setting aside what is already known about it as much as possible. With FT (Civitarese 2008, 2015; Ferro 2009), this will become listening to everything *as if* it were a dream dreamt together by the analytic dyad.

The image proposed by Bion helps us remember that what we *do not* see is precisely the group's basic assumption, in other words, the unconscious – but also that the unconscious is an intrinsically social or group phenomenon. We can give meaning to our emotional experience as subjects only intersubjectively, i.e. by sharing a common language, a medium that is not yours nor mine, and that nobody can completely control. Doing analysis means (1) counteracting each time the force of gravity of the mind that puts the "lower right-hand side" of past and material reality before us and instead (2) reversing the perspective in order to be able to see the "lower left-hand side" of psychic reality, that is to say, the basic assumption that is active at any given moment or, as it were, the percentage saturation of emotional "oxygen" in the air. Performing this operation requires a certain amount of mental work.

On the first point, Bion is as usual precise and straightforward: "I believe the ability to shake oneself out of the numbing feeling of reality that is a concomitant of this state is the prime requisite of the analyst in the group" (149). Shaking off "the numbing feeling of reality" or "mourning reality" (Civitarese and Ferro 2018) is the analyst's first duty. FT takes this systematic change of perspective to be a basic principle. On this point, it agrees with Bion when he affirms that "in a group, the total of what is taking place remains the same, but a change of perspective can bring out quite different phenomena" (87) or when he gives the example of the Necker cube and the game between side B and side D. To this, thus valorizing also the aspects of theory that in Bion was much ahead of his way of working with patients, FT adds the possibility of translating them into precise tools of technique.

Is the Group a Matter of Numbers?

In essence, FT achieves its radical change of perspective by theorizing that the analytic couple is already a group. Some famous quotes from Freud (1921, 115) come to the mind, for example the one in which he assimilates the hypnotic relation to "a group formation with two members [*eine Massenbildung zu zweien*]" or the other in which he observes "The contrast between individual psychology and social or group psychology, which at a first glance may seem to be full of significance, loses a great deal of its sharpness when it is examined more closely" (1921, 69). It must be acknowledged, however, that he never deepened the intuition of this equivalence. Otherwise, it would not make sense to say that Freud's psychoanalysis is based on a one-person psychology.

Coming to Bion (8), he writes: "I am impressed, as a practising psycho-analyst, by the fact that the psycho-analytic approach, through the individual, and the approach these papers [collected in EG] describe, through the group, are dealing with different facets of the same phenomena". So, he seems to concede that two people already form a group. At the beginning of EG, though, Bion writes that "The minimum size of the group is three. Two members have personal relationships; with three or more there is a change of quality (interpersonal relationship)" (26). Now, my take is that Bion spent the rest of his life revolutionizing classical and Kleinian psychoanalysis – and in effect contradicting himself on this point. In fact, as early as in the second chapter of EG, we find two lines of correction:

> Anyone who has employed a technique of investigation that depends on the presence of two people, and psychoanalysis is such a technique, can be regarded, not only as taking part in the investigation of one mind by another, but also as investigating the mentality not of a group but of a pair.
>
> (62)

We understand that the "mentality" of a pair transcends that of the single members of it. Later on, Bion clarifies that:

> no new instinct is brought into play—it is always in play. The only point about collecting a group of people is that it enables us to see just how the "political" characteristics of the human body operate. ... the individual cannot help being a member of a group ... the psycho-analytical situation is not 'individual psychology' but 'pair'.
>
> (131)

And further:

> no individual, however isolated in time and space, can be regarded as outside a group or lacking in active manifestations of group psychology, although conditions do not exist which would make it possible to demonstrate it. ... a group is more than the sum of its members.
>
> (132)

It can be said that at this point, towards the end of EG, Bion increasingly equates individual with group psychoanalysis, at least if we accept to see the "pair" as a group. Indeed, he writes that "the pair relationship of psycho-analysis can be regarded as a part of the larger group situation" (166). So, we do have the impression that in EG, Bion gradually corrects the dry definition given at the beginning and does seem to embrace the idea that two people already form a group.

This is a point on which it is worth staying for a while, widening the view. If we search the entry "group" in the Merriam-Webster

Dictionary (2021), among a few definitions we find "two or more figures forming a complete unit in a composition", "an assemblage of objects regarded as a unit"; "two or more atoms joined together or sometimes a single atom forming part of a molecule". As we can see, the emphasis falls on the *function* and the *perspective* from which various objects (two or more than two) are observed. All the more so, from the point of view of psychoanalysis, if we admit that a communication from unconscious to unconscious takes place, what would be the *quid* that would be added if instead of two, we are dealing with three people? What sense would it make to say, as is currently done, that the father-as-third (or function) is always already present in the primary mother–infant relationship?

At the beginning of EG, Bion distinguishes "personal" relationship from "interpersonal" relationship, but it is not clear on what basis. The burden of proof should be reversed. Whoever objects to seeing a group already in the couple would be able to demonstrate the difference? On the contrary, all the concepts of "third" or "field" that have been developed by various authors clearly strive to conceptualize a group functioning of the pair.

Bion's own reference to the concept of field in physics is very precise (and here, obviously, he is talking about individual psychoanalysis):

> According to Heisenberg, in atomic physics a situation has arisen in which the scientist cannot rely on the ordinarily accepted view that the researcher has access to facts, because the facts to be observed are distorted by the very act of observation. Furthermore, the *field* in which he has to observe the relationship of one phenomenon to another is unlimited in extent, and yet none of the phenomena 'in' that *field* can be ignored because all interact.
>
> (1965, 45, emphasis added)

And further:

> A patient who, in my view, is displaying projective transformation and requires the use of Kleinian theories for comprehension, also uses a *field* which is not simply the analyst, or his own personality, or even the relationship between himself and the analyst, but all those and *more*.
>
> (1965, 114, emphasis added)

11

Thus, if we can credit Bion for having first introduced in 1943 the concept of field in psychoanalysis as derived from physics, Madeleine e Willy Baranger, for their part, clearly see no difficulty in seeing the couple as a group:

> a melody is not the sum of the notes or that a group is not the sum of its members; in other words, we are emphasizing the existence of a 'gestalt' in the analytic situation and we define this gestalt as our specific field of work.
>
> (2008, 807)

We could take this to extremes. There is also an extensive literature on the concept of "internal grouping" (Kaës 2005), on which I cannot dwell for reasons of space. The fact is that nowadays we would tend rather to say that the minimum group comprises *one* person. Taken per se, the subject consists of an internal group of voices in constant dialogue with each other.

In an adult and mature person, the internal group usually works well enough to solve the problems it has to face instant by instant. But when the capacity of the internal group is overwhelmed, then it is necessary to get in touch with another mind (or several minds) to be able to perform the same task of giving personal meaning to experience. Since each person "wears" a public identity or "mask" (in Latin, "persona" is "mask"), which is constantly negotiated within the social sphere, this meaning will always be not only personal, but also "impersonal", i.e. always political by nature (Esposito 2015).

Intersubjectivity and the Unconscious

Being a subject means having a subjectivity that relates dialectically with an intersubjectivity (Civitarese 2021b). In the monadic subject, the group is present first as instinctual or pre-reflexive intersubjectivity and later as linguistic or reflexive intersubjectivity. Human beings come into the world already endowed with "valences", as Bion calls them, borrowing the concept from chemistry, where they indicate the spontaneous ("instantaneous, inevitable, and instinctive"; 153) inclination of elements to establish links and consequently to make up more complex units. The existence of psychic valences explains the formation of the basic assumption, whose benign equivalent in the sophisticated group is on the other hand the ability to work together towards a common goal. We cannot say that the subjectivity of the subject emerges from the "intersubjective" or transpersonal layer of being, nor the other way round. We must necessarily think that there are always two poles in dialectical relation with each other. Therefore, the group is the necessary and sufficient condition for there being a subject and vice versa. Psychic illness does not arise from the dialectical relationship per se but from the crisis of this relationship.

In order to understand what can happen, let us use an image. If subjectivity and intersubjectivity are the two indivisible sides of the coin that is the subject, the figure on one side can nonetheless wear down to such an extent that it is no longer clearly identifiable. At that point, we will have either a mass-individual, and this is the case of the group with a basic-assumption activity, or, at the other end of the continuum, a psychotic person suffering from hallucinations and delusions, i.e. someone who has broken most of their ties with the group. Indeed, Bion amends Freud's opposition between individual and group:

> It is possibly for this reason [he writes] that Freud's description of the group, and still more that of Le Bon, whom Freud quotes with some approval, reads somewhat strangely to me when I compare them with my actual experiences in a group. For example, when Freud quotes Le Bon as saying "Groups have never thirsted after truth. They demand illusions and cannot do without them" ..., I do not feel able to agree with that description. ... I think one of the striking things about a group is that, despite the influence of the basic assumptions, it is the *W* group that triumphs in the long run.
>
> (134–135)

In essence, it is as if Bion had said that Freud, befuddled by his Cartesianism, had no clear idea about the intersubjective nature of the fabric of the ego. The individual not only may *lose* but also *find* themself in the group. Freud is well aware that the psychology of the individual is affected by the individual's relationship with the group but does not see the group as the flesh and blood of the subject. It is for this reason that even though his conception of the unconscious must necessarily allow for the intersubjective fact of language (thing-representations become conscious only when they are linked to word-representations), he nevertheless essentially confines it within a monadic ego.

In other words, while Freud always sees the group (and the unconscious) as regressive, for Bion, it can be both regressive and progressive. For the latter, one of the group's specific tasks is to manipulate the basic assumptions so as to ensure that they stop hampering the group. Freud sets up an opposition between the ego and the group, subjectivity and intersubjectivity, *distinctiveness* and *indistinctiveness*. Bion, in contrast, sees the first term as necessary to the second and vice versa; and, if anything, he asks himself what might alter the harmonious functioning of the individual in the group and the group in the individual. By doing this, he transcends the caesura between subjectivity and intersubjectivity. It is not the existence in itself of the group but the group in its basic assumption – in other words, a particular type of functioning – that erases the individuality of the members. It is clear that when we say that Bion put emotion back at the centre of psychoanalysis as the H/L/K (hate/love/knowledge) "link"; that is, as a function of a relationship, it would be more accurate to say that the decisive step is taken in these pages of EG where the emotion related to a given basic assumption is seen as the decisive factor in determining the fate of the relationship itself.

Unconscious Emotional Experience (O) as the Basic Assumption of the Analytic Dyad

Bion argues vehemently that the only thing that counts in the session is the unconscious emotional experience shared by patient and analyst in the here and now.[4] He calls this the O of the session. In his work, this concept takes on a plurality of meanings (Civitarese 2019a, 2020b). Nevertheless, from a practical point of view, it is sufficient to keep in mind the equation O = basic assumption.[5] This formula instantly reminds us of the postulates that underlie the FT technique: seeing the couple as a group, investigating "the basic assumption" of the two-person group, aiming each time to give back a "work group" structure to the analytic dyad.

When interpreting these principles of Bion's, we could say that, for the analyst, each time it is a matter of preparing a weather report of the situation and determining what action to take. By "weather" I mean what he calls "emotional situation" (44), "group mentality" (50), the "prevailing atmosphere" (51) experienced by the group, "group mental life" (54), "group culture" (57), "the unanimous expression of the will of the group, an expression of will to which individuals contribute anonymously" (59). Bion always puts these unconscious expressions of the life of the group in opposition "to the avowed aims of the individual members of the group" (50). The basic hypothesis is to see "a group mentality as the pool to which the anonymous contributions are made, and through which the impulses and desires implicit in these contributions are gratified" (50). The adjective "anonymous" here is very precise: the unconscious as "third" is not only anonymous because it cannot be known directly, but also because it is the result of the merging of two distinct unconsciouses. According to Lacan, it is "a third term ... that part of concrete discourse qua transindividual, which is not at the subject's disposal in reestablishing the continuity of his conscious discourse" (1966, 214).

The concept of basic assumption is equivalent to that of repressed representation (Freud) or unconscious fantasy (Klein) of the group. Bion identifies three of them: fight–flight (*baF*), pairing (*baP*) and dependence (*baD*) or "symbiotic relationship" (82). Each corresponds to emotions that condition the behaviour of individuals in the group and the group as a whole. If we transpose these concepts onto the level of individual therapy, we realize that they correspond to the H, L, and K bonds, respectively. What prevails in *baF* is hatred of the "enemy", in *baP* love as a feeling of self-idealization and therefore as a defence against hatred, and in *baD* a type of pseudo-truth or pseudo-knowledge that is not born from experience. Every time Bion refers to the "group", we must therefore understand it to mean "intersubjective unconscious" ("We all live in groups, and have plenty of experience, however unconscious, of what that means"; 64); every time he mentions the leader, the "individual", we must translate it into "the ego" or "consciousness".

The basic assumption generates emotions that hinder the pursuit of the conscious objective, in other words, "the idea of a group met together to do a creative job, especially with the idea of a group met together to deal with the psychological difficulties of its members" (64). The way Bion describes how a leader with marked paranoid traits can be chosen by a group to represent a *baF* is reminiscent of the way in which FT talks about the emergence of "characters" in the analytic discourse. It is as if they resulted from the images that the couple's waking dream thought puts together to transform raw emotions and sensations into images or alpha-elements. As a whole, the analytic dialogue expresses the basic assumption active at a given moment in the couple group; therefore, not the emotional state of just one of the individual members, but that of the system or dyad. In fact, as Bion points out, changes in basic assumptions or "culture" may occur in the group and the analyst can

> use these changes, to the benefit of ... clinical observation, in much the same kind of way as scientists in other fields are able to use changes of wavelength to obtain different photographic appearances of the object they wish to study.
>
> (73)

Authenticity and Vitality in Analysis

We always come back to the same paradox that lies at the basis of self-consciousness and therefore of humanity or being: with Hegel (1807, 108), to the "*I* that is *we* and *we* that is *I*". In Bion's words, "man is hopelessly committed to both states of affairs. In any group there can be seen the man who tries to identify himself wholeheartedly with the basic assumption, or wholeheartedly with the sophisticated outlook" (90). The psychic life of the individual and the group consists in finding a balance in the continuous oscillations (which are the only way to find a balance) between feeling persecuted by "arid intellectualism" or by the pressure of emotions. However, within the group, Bion observes, it is easier to cooperate in basic-assumption group mode than in work group mode. The same applies to the "internal group" of the individual, to "those aspects of his personality that constitute his 'groupishness'" (131). There is always the idea that the process of subjectivation implies work. This should not be understood as distancing the individual from the group but as a parallel process of differentiation of the individual *within* the group, in other words, both the individual *and* the group to which they belong.

When they are in the basic group, the individual feels more vital ("his capacity for co-operation is emotionally most vital in the basic group"; 90). How can this fact be explained? By definition, the group in basic assumption is made up of emotions, and emotions are the most *immediate* translation of the state of reactivity/energy/ sensitivity and the most immediate and massive activation of the instinctual defences that are primarily dedicated to physical survival. Only in the group does the individual discover that they possess certain abilities. Consequently, Bion notes, one must think that the group "is more than the aggregate of individuals, because an individual in a group is more than an individual in isolation" (90).

If this capacity is manifested only in participation in a group, we must also think that the very purpose of the group, its natural tendency, is to function according to construct as much as possible emotional links. In a group in basic-assumption mode, so to say, these links take centre stage. Far from being always a dysfunctional phenomenon, then, basic assumption in some cases becomes a powerful saving device. If anything, once the group has also created a structure of rationality, the two can work as a pair and thus respond flexibly to stimuli.

As a way of describing the harmonious functioning of individual and group we can use Bion's reference in EG to the Augustinian concept of the City of God: "a feeling of vitality could only be achieved by the dominance of the basic assumption, notably the *baF*" (130). Perhaps, he means that the basic assumption ensures the individual's reimmersion in the "God", which, according to Husserl (Zahavi 2001), is the community or transcendental intersubjective, which is not only intellectual or linguistic (spirit or "verb"), but also instinctual and carnal. Bion goes on to write:

If a group wishes to prevent development, the simplest way to do so is to allow itself to be overwhelmed by basic-assumption mentality and thus become approximated to the one kind of mental life in which a capacity for development is not required. The main compensation for such a shift appears to be an increase in a pleasurable feeling of vitality (159).

Bion prompts us to reflect on the fact that vitality, authenticity, fullness of life, agency depend on the affective threads that connect the individual to sociality. As usual, the point is not to think in dichotomous but rather in dialectical terms.

Who or What to Treat?

The task of the psychiatrist or group leader is to take care of the group's maintenance. Each time the group slips into a basic assumption, he has to do the "job". He has to reorganize a group that works, in other words, one that relates to reality effectively. Bion writes:

17

It is almost as if human beings were aware of the painful and often fatal consequences of having to act without an adequate grasp of reality, and therefore were aware of the need for truth as a criterion in the evaluation of their findings.

(100)

If the group is more than the sum of the individuals that comprise it, it makes no sense to take care (only) of the individuals. *It makes more sense to restore in the group the climatic conditions that are favourable to the joint development of the group and the subject.* If, when two individuals come into contact, they are influenced by the emotional field that is generated, there is no point in acting as if it did not exist. Relationship *is* the main therapeutic factor, but then we need to look not only at what takes place on the *piano nobile* of conscious interaction between the two subjects; we also need to pay attention to what happens on the intersubjective (indistinct) level of the cellar.

What applies to the group applies to the group-of-two. One could tell the whole story of psychoanalysis in terms of the progressive discovery of the subject's intersubjective background and the creation of tools to include, to an ever-increasing extent, the analyst's unconscious participation to the analytic process (from transference to countertransference, from projective identification to enactment, from the various concepts of "third" to the analytic field). The question to answer should always be: "what description best clarifies the situation" (60)? Bion notes that:

"The individual feels that in a group the welfare of the individual is a matter of secondary consideration—the group comes first, in flight the individual is abandoned; the paramount need is for the group to survive—or the inter—not the individual"

(64).

Transposed into the sphere of individual therapy, this annotation would imply that when the group-of-two is in basic-assumption mode ("when the weather is bad"), someone is "abandoned", usually the weaker subject.

This said, we see why Bion thinks that precisely in the case of a small therapeutic group, the treatment should not concern the individual but the group (not the intra- or the inter-, but the trans-personal; not contents but functions or linkings). In this context, he mentions the "exasperation" of the individual who comes to the group expecting attention to be

18

dedicated to their own personal difficulties. If the analyst has the strength to resist the temptation to engage with the personal difficulty of one of the members of the group, they will be able to deal with the group's tensions, basic assumptions, and all the rest. In this way, the analyst does not work "against the group" but "manages to use the group" (80).

If the psychiatrist colluded with this request, explains Bion, and acted "as if he were carrying out individual treatment in public", he would soon realize "that he is working against the group, while the patient is working together with the group" (80). What does this mean? It means that while the patient is involved in a given basic assumption and the emotional climate associated with it, the analyst is not taking the common or group unconscious into account. Then the analyst is treating the patient as a subject detached from the group. Bion adds that when the analyst does not collude with the patient's conscious expectation, frustration is caused not so much by the fact that the analyst is unable to direct everyone's attention to his problems, "as by the exposure of difficulties the patient has not come to discuss, and in particular his characteristics as a group member, the characteristics of group membership, basic assumptions, and the rest of it" (80).

This sentence sounds ambiguous. Bion is thinking of the patient, but the very same resistance could be ascribed to the analyst. For both, the difficulty is to deal with the shared unconscious of the couple or the group-of-two. The analyst who makes the mistake in group therapy of conducting himself as if they were doing "a psycho-analysis in public" (81) is like the analyst who in individual therapy treats the patient as an isolated subject and not as a member of the group to which both belong. It is therefore not true that the analyst who makes such a mistake in a group would never make it in individual psychoanalysis. In fact, if they do not adopt an intersubjective perspective, in all likelihood they will make *the same* mistake. Renewing psychoanalysis, for Bion, consists in seeing the individual's neurosis no longer as transference neurosis (the old infantile neurosis, this time with the analyst in it) but as the basic assumption of the pair-as-group.

The Purpose of Cure

Bion points out that:

the individual in a group is profiting by his experience if at one and the same time he becomes more accurate in his appreciation

19

of his position in the emotional field, and more capable of accepting it as a fact that even his increased accuracy falls lamentably short of his needs.

(45)

Now, the idea that it is important to get an accurate idea of the *emotional position* the patient is occupying in the analytic field seems a well-chosen expression to characterize the purpose of therapy. Meltzer (1984) says that, unlike Freud, Bion expounds the first convincing theory of emotions in psychoanalysis. The emphasis he puts on emotion may have been dictated by his experience of war, a situation where emotions play a fundamental role. In Bion, it is no coincidence that military metaphors are omnipresent. He explicitly equates the activity of the rehabilitation ward with that of regiments engaged in combat (see 27). His idea of a work group is that of a unit in combat. It is clearly a matter of life and death. The atmosphere of trust and collaboration, a "good group spirit" (25), and "morale and good fellowship" (32) are essential elements. The leader should have "the outlook, and the sort of intuitive sympathetic flair, of the good unit commander" (22).

Good group spirit is made up of a number of ingredients: a common purpose; awareness of the group's "ties"; flexibility in acquiring new members or losing others; the absence of subgroups, unless they are important for the functioning of the main group; observance of the group's rules of evaluation and freedom of movement; insight; the capacity for self-care; the ability to deal with negative emotions within the group.

The objective of the group leader is to bring about the somato-psychic integration of the group:

> The problem of the leader seems always to be how to *mobilize emotions associated with the basic assumptions* without endangering the sophisticated structure that appears to secure to the individual his freedom to be an individual while remaining a member of the group. It was this *balance of tensions* which I previously described in terms of equilibrium between group mentality, group culture, and individual
>
> (78, emphasis added)

We would say something very similar if we were seeking to illustrate the Winnicottian concept of "personalization" (Winnicott 1945).

The problem that Bion addresses in this passage, and that we have already touched upon when discussing the concept of vitality, is the same issue that Heidegger (1927a) deals with when he asks how the individual can avoid merging into the mass and lead an authentic life. It is the theme of the normativity of the group (of the "many") that can crush the individual (the "one"). The German philosopher's answer lies in the concept of being-towards-death, in other words in the individual's ability to think about their radical loneliness and the finitude of life. Bion's answer is that an essential harmony should be maintained between group and individual, unconscious and conscious, intersubjectivity and subjectivity, affect and intellect; in short, the aim should be to ensure, in short, that the individual is able to "mobilize" the strength of the group's emotions, and that their freedom is not in opposition to the group.

This point is relevant, therefore, because it helps us avoid falling into an easy and misleading dichotomy between basic assumption and rational structure. It is interesting that Bion also calls the rational or work group a "sophisticated group". The term denotes something that is now some distance from what is simply "natural", and in this it proves to be wise (or not naive), but also, if the distance from nature is too great, there is the risk that it might taste wrong or be "corrupted". From the technical point of view, the problem is what to do in order to take the "vertex" of emotions into account − without letting the vertex of rationality collapse on top of them.

Maintaining the rational (or "sophisticated") structure of the group implies *work*. In itself, the force of gravity of the emotional life of the group always tends to drop from the differentiated rational structure into less differentiated states in which basic assumptions activate. Now, the very fact of seeing what the individual group member says or does *not say as their private expressions but as expressions of the group's life* is a technique that helps render visible what is invisible about group mentality or basic assumptions, and then tries to influence it. What the analyst practises is a "reversal of perspective" (Civitarese 2008), which is precisely what Bion means to illustrate with the example of Necker's cube.

Everything we have said so far can be transposed onto the plane of the two-person relationship. "Good team spirit" is equivalent to *at-one-ment*. Traditionally, psychoanalysis has mainly sought attunement on the level of discourse and content. Emotions have only served as handmaidens to this kind of understanding. They have never become true protagonists. For Bion, this is not the case. Tuning one's instruments must take place both on the level of effects, and thus of procedural schemes, and on the level of abstract contents. On the level of individual development, the former comes first, even if it is always couched in the words available to one of the members of the couple who helps generate the analytic field.

Emotional Oscillations, Inert Materials of Absorption, and Attunement

Bion points out the instinctual tendency of the individual to enter "into combination" (116) with the group "on levels that can hardly be called mental" (116). These are the same levels he postulated using the concept of the proto-mental system, in essence the pre-human plane of intersubjectivity. Human beings obey something similar to "tropism in plants" (117).

Having understood this dynamic, Bion changes attitude, stops giving "supposedly psycho-analytic interpretations" (117), and merely emphasizes that certain behaviours of group members seem to go in the direction of strengthening *baD* or *baF*. However, he immediately realizes that even these interventions of his addressed to individual issues (as it were, translating the unconscious into the conscious) sound like true "expressions of disapproval" (118). The effect is to cause the group to become puerile and thus to further reinforce the *baD* (cf. 127).

The leader's goal, instead, should be to create an environment conducive to development and growth (134). This process is generated when, faced with emotional tsunamis that risk destroying the mind of the individual or group, another mind or group absorbs the shock. In the group (or in the internal group of the individual), these destructive forces stem from conflicts of opinions and views that are too different from each other. The tension arising from excessive difference lacerates the body of the mind or of the mind of the group.

In some cases, Bion observes, the distance is such that oscillations of great amplitude and frequency arise because it is hard to imagine two views more widely separated than a belief that the leader is mad and the belief that he is the dependable person on whom you rely for your welfare – then the oscillations have to be both rapid in time and large in excursion (125).

The group (mind) is in danger of shattering. So, a search for other external groups is launched in the belief that the most urgent thing is to find inert material that can absorb the shock wave and bring it to a halt.

I find this metaphor extraordinarily suggestive. It gives us a plastic image of what emotion means as a force that is not enclosed within the subject but that is *directed towards the other*:

> The result is that the group can no longer contain the emotional situation, which thereupon spreads with explosive violence to other groups until enough groups have been drawn in to absorb the reaction. ... The object of this drawing in of other groups is not, as I at first supposed it to be, revenge on the psychiatrist for discomfort—though that may be there, and damage to the psychiatrist or group may be the result—but to bring in so much inert material in the way of outsiders from the group, who do not share the emotional situation, that the new and much larger group ceases to vibrate. There is no longer the violent and disagreeable mass oscillation.
>
> (125)

Finally, we understand better the meaning of the concept *at-one-ment* or attunement as a process of patiently working to diminish the violence of these urges. In an individual or group setting, the instrument that can reduce the explosiveness of emotions is interpretation, meant both as intervention made to the patient and just as being receptive to the unconscious meaning of discourse. Interpretation puts the basic assumption in contact with the work group. It is a way of becoming aware of what is happening here and now.

Universal Language and the Limits of Interpretation

Sometimes we make an interpretation "Without quite knowing why" (33). In such a case, it is easier to have doubts ("it is not at all clear to me that my observation, however correct, is really the most useful one to make at the moment"; 34). The point, however, is to try to sense whether, after it has been given, the field becomes more or less organized ("But I have made it, *and prepare to watch what follows*"; 33, emphasis added). Bion recounts in a vignette that the "emotional state of the group" provoked by an interpretation judged to be correct untimely is one of "discontent" (33). He fears then that the increase in tension may even question the existence of the group. The "discontent" could provoke "disruption of the group" (35). We see *the importance of constantly consulting the session's* "weather bulletin". Once, Bion recalls, he was actually removed from the group; alternatively, it may happen that the exclusion takes place *within* the group.

The interest aroused by these pages lies in the fact that they antic-ipate the theory of transformations (which Bion discusses at greater length in *Transformations*; 1961) as climate changes that can produce development or regression. Moreover, with respect to interpretation, they contain one of EG's most bizarre and at the same time brilliant ideas. The group tends to interpret in its own way what the leader tells it – it is like saying that the tools to communicate "are extremely weak". So:

> one might almost think that it would be less misleading if each individual member of the group spoke a language unknown to the remainder. There would then be less risk of assuming that we understood what any given individual said.
>
> (38)

After remarking that the conversation "becomes more and more desultory" (38), Bion tries to get it back on track by suggesting the elimination of what seems to him to be the main disturbing factor – nothing less than semantic meaning.

The suggestion is paradoxical: since we are struggling to under-stand each other, let's not bother trying in the first place. Bereft of (abstract) meaning and reduced to sense, communication might show up in a clearer and more direct way. So the idea is not silly. We will find it, for example, in the essay "On Arrogance" (1958a), where Bion equates the analyst's stupidity with Oedipus' and attrib-utes it to the impulse of wanting to know the truth "at any cost" (Civitarese 2021c).

Respecting the limits of interpretation would instead require the analyst to realize that communication is not only verbal but also non-verbal and that the two should not be separated.

Revolution

Before Freud, the attempts to advance the study of neurosis were largely *sterile because the individual was considered to be an intelligible field of study*, but it was when Freud began to seek a solution in the relationship between two people, the study of the transference, that he found what was the intelligible field of study for at least some of the problems that the neurotic patient poses, and problems that had hitherto defied all attempts at solution began to have a meaning

(104, emphasis added).

By analogy, Bion proposes the small therapeutic group as "an attempt to see if further results can be achieved by changing the field of study" (104). In this circumstance, he appears to us as a scientist who is proposing to use a more powerful microscope. Indeed, we could read this sentence as not only aimed at justifying the use of the small therapeutic group, but also as revealing a maybe still obscure project to be realized years later, namely of "changing the field of study" (104) of individual therapy.

Bion is aware that he is talking like a fire-raiser. Rhetorically, he acknowledges that the first fire-raiser was Freud. To him we owe the "revolution" of transference, the conceptual device that shifts treatment from mere knowledge onto the analytic relationship. However, Freud would only have grasped this up to a certain point:

It appears to me that *Freud is in some ways failing to realise*, in his discussion of groups, the nature of *the revolution he himself produced* when he looked for an explanation of neurotic symptoms, not in the individual, but in the individual's relationship with objects.

(134, emphasis added)

Bion therefore presents himself as Freud's authentic heir, the person called upon to carry on and complete his work. How? By establishing the group as a new field of study: "The whole point about looking at a group is that *it changes the field of study* to include phenomena that cannot be studied outside the group. Outside the group as a field of study, their activity is not manifest" (134, emphasis added). I would suggest a very similar idea, but with respect to Bion himself. He too failed to fully realize the extent of the revolution he produced in re-shaping individual therapy as group therapy. My point is that thanks to the developments brought about by FT we do get some clarity about what we obtain from changing again the field of study.

Bion claims to have extended the scope of what we are given to observe in the domain of psychoanalysis: "*The group, … reveals some-thing that is not otherwise visible*" (134, emphasis added). Among these "invisible" things, there is the feeling of disbelief I mentioned earlier:

> *the apparent difference between group psychology and individual psychol-ogy is an illusion* produced by the fact that the group provides an intelligible field of study for certain aspects of individual psychol-ogy, and in so doing *brings into prominence phenomena that appear alien to an observer unaccustomed to using the group.*
>
> (134, emphasis added)

Clearly, he is already following the principle that will state in *A Memoir of the Future* (1975, 190): "If serious psycho-analytic discus-sion cannot take place in the domain which Freud found adequate, it must be enlarged".

What Kind of Listening?

In another vignette of EG, the group rejects some interpretations, but Bion says:

> However, I do not propose to consider this point just now, but rather to take perfectly seriously the statement made by these members of the group who seem to represent the whole group very fairly in denying any feeling of hostility. I feel that a correct assessment of the situation demands that *I accept it as a fact that all individuals in the group are perfectly sincere and accurate* when they say they feel no hostility towards myself.
>
> (46, emphasis added)

We could take the expression "perfectly sincere" as the distinctive mark of a way of listening to the discourse of the unconscious that seeks to go beyond the *you/I* split and to reset it as *we*. This is likely to remain the most valuable legacy that Bion's study of groups has bequeathed us. The reason is that he provides us with the tools to work with the unconscious meant as alpha-function or as a device designed to "digest" the emotional experience. For Bion, Ogden writes, "dreaming (which is synonymous with unconscious thinking) is the principal psychological form in which this work is performed" (2008, 24).

Bion (1962b, 89) conceptualizes dreaming and the unconscious as a "psychoanalytic function of the personality". In so doing, he gives us the possibility to move away from an idea of the unconscious as an "evil other" (Terman 2014), "chaos, a cauldron full of seething excitations" (Freud 1933, 73), or "a mob, eager for enjoyment and destruction" (Freud 1932, 221), which comes into the open in the "immorality of … dreams" (Freud 1900, 620): all visions from which derives what Ricoeur (1970) called a "hermeneutics of suspicion".[6]

In fact, if I listen in terms of the O of the or "dream" of the session, I allow myself to read the possible unconscious meaning that even *the telling* of historical and concrete events may have here and now. Then, if I take this meaning as if it were created by the common (intersubjective or third) unconscious, I move beyond the split between *you and I*. I *trust* what *you-and-I* (together) feel because it is what *we* feel, *I take it to be true for us*, as it is already *the result of an intersubjective negotiation within the couple*. I consider it as the best we have been able to do as authors, actors, and dramatists in the improvised drama that each time is a session. That is why Bion's main principle is that of "transformation", rather than Freud's of "distortion" (Civitarese 2018).

It is an effective way to validate the other, or rather to lay the foundations for the conscious and unconscious experience of mutual recognition that constitutes a moment of *at-one-ment*. I rediscover the other in me, and myself in the other. I have the chance to re-establish a healthier dialectic between subjectivity and intersubjectivity. One grows if the other grows and vice versa. Listening in terms of field or *we-ness* implies the renunciation of a position of power, domination, and arrogance. The mediation of power never leads to recognition and positive reciprocal intersubjectivity (Mancini 2019). This can only be done by a relationship that reaches the level of equality at which the logic of *Liebeserfahrung* ("the experience of being loved"), which Freud (1920, 130) mentions in a footnote to *Civilization and its Discontents*, is established.

The COVID-19 Pandemic and Immunodepression

Now, in order to give an example of why, to my eyes, it is relevant to consider the analytic dyad as a group and what kind of radical change of perspective it entails, precisely the issues I discussed in the previous paragraph, I will present a brief clinical vignette.

A., a patient, tells me she is afraid of the COVID-19 epidemic. In particular, she is worried about the fragility of her partner, who is immunodepressed. She works in a hospital and could easily be the one that brings home the virus. The analysis still takes place in presence, we both use masks and there is a certain tension in the air because of the real possibility of infecting each other. It is a calculated risk and for the moment I do not think, it is appropriate to switch to Zoom sessions, also because A. would hardly accept it.

At first, I grasp the realistic aspect of A.'s observation, and the conversation continues on other topics. Later in the session, however, it comes back to me in a completely unexpected way. I wonder what it might mean for us from the unconscious point of view. What "immune fragility" was A. talking about? Hers? Mine? *Ours?* The answer changes according to the theoretical vertex I would choose to use. I could see in it an aggressive impulse towards me, and the consequent sense of guilt, perhaps because she feels I am distracted by my fear of the actual contagion. I could interpret A's feeling as a transference, a projection that has attached itself to a detail that was actually something that belonged to me at this moment, at least in terms of its intensity. In fact, in thinking this, I would be supported by knowledge of her past history. She had suffered from similar relationships with her parents. Actually, consciously, I do not feel at all that I am disinterested in her. In short, I would be inclined to think, and maybe to interpret to A., that she sees me in a distorted way; that basically she misunderstands how things really are.

From the following dialogue it emerges that A. thinks that I may find sessions with other patients much more pleasant. Basically, her aggressiveness, which makes A. think that I am so vulnerable, would derive from jealousy, that is, the feeling that someone is taking away from her something precious that belongs to her. So, in the end, this would be the "virus" that risks producing emotional turbulence in the therapeutic relationship (the COVID-19 disease). Listening in this way, I would maintain the perspective of two separate subjects interacting, each of which, even if partially influenced by the other, gives meaning to the experience on its own.

However, I might draw on a different concept of the unconscious, this time conceived as a joint psychoanalytic function. When I "wake up" to the possible unconscious meaning of A.'s discourse, I might see in her narrative a transformation of proto-emotional and proto-sensory elements (beta-elements) into images and concepts (alpha-elements) that are the result of an unconscious work not exclusively of the patient but of the couple or group (as it were, of a joint or shared alpha-function). From this other point of view, the emotions that I can infer from the patient's story, but which I actually see only as the spokesperson of a process in which *we* both are involved, would no longer derive from transferential projections or projective identifications, so to speak, one-way. On the contrary, they would reflect the creative and transformative capacity of that kind of common unconscious (or dynamic Gestalt or field or inter-subjective third) that inevitably forms when two people are close enough to each other.

On the plane of this unconscious writing of the text of the session, it is impossible for us to determine what the relative participation of patient and analyst is: first, because by definition, it is anonymous; second, because, the result of their coming together constitutes a field, something that is more than the sum of its starting elements. This is what we mean when we speak of symmetry on the unconscious level of the relationship. It logically follows that the emotion that has been narrated (mainly fear and anger likely linked to a sentiment of jealousy) is not only of the patient or only of the analyst and is not the result of any misunderstanding. On the contrary, it expresses the *truth* that has been already and, so to say, automatically negotiated unconsciously. It is what is *really* going on and needs to be contained. I no longer listen to what A. says in a suspicious manner. If anything, I *trust* the poetic-poietic capacity of our unconsciouses. I give confidence to what they enact, albeit with varying success. Eventually, by trusting the group we are, I also trust each of us separately. As all of our patients lack a safe place inside, I see this as the main therapeutic factor.

The consequences of seeing the analytic pair as a group are remarkable: instead of anger from misunderstanding for my alleged disinterest (my "immunodepression"), I consider that *really* the emotional function that binds us at a given moment is a shared feeling of fear and anger. I repeat, this is because *really* the air is saturated with these emotions; *really* there is an immunodepression in the field, that is, a lack of vitality that leads not to building bonds and expanding the mind but to destroying bonds. In my role, I have *consciously* to take responsibility for what is happening, for my own "jealousy", fear, and anger. Even if I am not able to give myself a reason about what their cause is, it becomes urgent to change this climate. It goes without saying that a first change, and *possibly the most relevant*, already takes place when by interpreting in this way I inevitably modify my profound affective attitude towards A. and I open the possibility for authentic recognition, that is, neither sentimental nor voluntaristic.

I listen from the angle of a hermeneutic of trust or "faith" and not of suspicion. This does not mean renouncing interpretation, in the same way that we could give infinite readings of a poem but not necessarily thinking that there is something behind it to be deciphered. It is evident that I can listen in this way, that is, I can allow myself to read no matter what kind of narrative, even relative to concrete facts (the immune-depressed partner, A. working at the local hospital, the coronavirus, etc.) as if it were a kind of dream dreamt together with A., that is, "forcing" myself to ask *why this? why now?*, only if, on the one hand, I use the technique of putting concrete reality in brackets – moreover, something that any analyst should do if we agree that our compass is the concept of unconscious – and, on the other hand, if I use this compass primarily to explore not the intrapsychic structure of the patient, but the way we function as a group. The "immunodepression" becomes the character or affective hologram of the couple, what Bion calls the O of the session, and which in my view, as I have argued all along in this paper, corresponds to the basic assumption of a group.

Jealousy, then, in our vignette, with all that it entails of anger and persecution, is not (only) in the patient's infantile neurosis, nor (only) in her affective relations outside analysis, nor (only) in her as a patient who exchanges things with the analyst in the therapeutic relationship, but at the level of the *common* unconscious. The "virus" is the dangerous character in a fictional story that metaphorizes the potentially destructive H-bond (*hate*) that is prevalent at any given moment. The analyst should know how to deduce that because, if it lasts long, such a situation risks producing not development but *regression* (Civitarese 2020a).

Listening to the analytic conversation always by privileging the common unconscious meaning represents a "hyperinclusive" and "centripetal" technique. It is "hyperinclusive" because there is no tale of reality, nor dream, reverie, action, feeling, and sensation that virtually cannot be seen from this point of view (in fact, it is more a matter of letting yourself be surprised by the rekindling of this point of view). It is "centripetal" because of the effect it has of taking things seemingly far away and making them close. *But what is close to us interests us more.* The analyst, again, in the same movement ceases to be suspicious and restores vitality to the analysis. Rediscovering, each time with amazement, that he is deeply immersed in what is happening, sharpens his senses. This already favours a type of understanding based on experience (the Bionian transformations in O) over a type of understanding more based on abstract knowledge and grids of interpretation. For the kind of emotional attitude of trust or "faith", it produces in the analyst, and for the radical assumption of responsibility, it implies with respect to the facts of the analysis, in my opinion it could be *the decisive factor* for the creation of links that is at the heart of the analytic process. If we identify intellectual knowledge with K, then we can say that the main aim of treatment is fostering the development of functions more than transmitting knowledge. This is what Ogden (2019) portrays as the shift from an epistemological psychoanalysis to an ontological psychoanalysis.

Within this theoretical frame, by "interpretation" (Ii = *implicit*), I mean above all the analyst's ability to be receptive to the discourse of the unconscious as a way to know the reciprocal position in the field and foster moments of mutual "recognition". According to the model of the mother–child relationship (Bion 1962a), the mind grows through moments of recognition (*at-one-ment*, emotional attunement, etc.). Then, by "interpretation" (Ie = *explicit*), we can also mean what the analysts tell the patient. This can vary greatly: from silence or just banal comments to very sophisticated and "saturated" interventions. To me, what is more important is that ideally whatever we choose to say or not to say, *it reflects our implicit reading of the emotional state of the field.*

In the example we have just seen, it might promote such a moment just telling A. something trivial, but which would convey to her the fact that I take responsibility for the lack of vitality or immune-depression that *is* there (it would be the same with more burning feelings: if, for example the narrative was about a linking of reciprocal abuse; the analyst would trust this "truth" an ask how they (he) *are* "abusing" each other). For example, I could say that, yes, it is true that if somebody at home is more likely to catch the virus, then you can easily think that you may hurt him and feel guilty, and that it is very frustrating when this situation extends over time. *Just naming the emotions.* Then of course, I would wait for other signals from the field that may help me to see how unconsciously this was taken by A. or, rigorously I should say, by *us*, and how the emotional climate changed or not after my conscious attempt to influence it positively.

Bion adumbrates this two-step process when, years later, he writes in *Attention and Interpretation* a passage in which overtly he talks about individual psychoanalysis through the lens of his group theory:

> the prevalent emotional field is one of rivalry and hostility such as I have described, in group situations, as peculiar to the fight-flight basic assumption. The individual is similarly affected by the *group* emotional situation. It is, therefore, impossible to give correct interpretations, save by accident, unless that *situation* is assessed.
>
> (1970, 4)

I hope it is clear that (1) listening in this way does not imply in the least to disregard what the pandemic produces concretely in our lives, etc., even if, strictly speaking, an analyst were so afraid of infecting or being infected they would have to close the "theatre" of analysis, as they would no longer be able to maintain a correct analytic attitude; and that (2) the problem of distinguishing at this level what is the patient's and what is the analyst's does not even arise because it would contradict the basic postulate from which the technique is derived. For example, it would make no sense to ask whether a reverie (sensation, feeling, action, idea, etc.) is rather a countertransferential reaction because *the theoretical framework is no longer that of two isolated subjects, in the same way in which Bion stopped seeing a group as a simple aggregate of individuals.* It would be like wanting to impose, as it were, on Italians to speak French in their own country.

Instead, by definition, at least as long as we are talking about the unconscious, all the elements that present themselves on stage belong to the field, that is, they are seen as unconsciously produced by the group-of-two. *It is on the conscious level, instead, that we regain difference, separateness, individuality and asymmetry.*

As we know, we cannot prove the goodness of a basic postulate per se, not even in mathematics. It is more a matter of seeing what we get if we make use of it, to say it again in Bion's (73) words, "in much the same kind of way as scientists in other fields are able to use changes of wavelength to obtain different photographic appearances of the object they wish to study".

Notes

1 From now on I will use the following abbreviations: for *Experiences in Groups and Other Papers* (1961): EG; for pst-Bionian Field Theory: FT. All quotes indicated only by the page number refer to EG.

2 Authoritatively, Kernberg (2011), Elliott and Prager (2015), and Seligman (2017), among others, have listed FT among the main currents of contemporary psychoanalysis. Since the majority of authors who developed it live in Pavia, which is the seat of a very old university, it is legitimate to use this denomination. Unfortunately, I do not have the space to outline the principles of FT, and I must assume a minimal familiarity of the reader with it and with Bion's thought. On both topics, there is now a very extensive literature, to which I refer. We can no longer think that it is something esoteric or restricted to narrow and marginal circles. For example, see Levine and Civitarese (2016).

3 See Bion (1965, 48–49): "In psycho-analysis, any O not common to analyst and analysand ... is incapable of psycho-analytic investigation; any appearance to the contrary reflects a failure to understand the nature of psycho-analytic interpretation". See also Bion (1992, 380): "Psychoanalytic 'observation' is concerned neither with what has happened nor with what is going to happen, but with what is happening".

4 See Bion (1965, 48): "In psycho-analysis, any O not common to analyst and analysand alike ... may be ignored as irrelevant". And later (1992, 381): "The only point of importance in any session is the unknown".

5 For a broader discussion of this point, here I can only refer to my other works mentioned above.

6 See Nissim Momigliano (1991, 792–793): "This is what I call *respectful listening* instead of *suspicious listening* ... a way of listening which is particularly carefully attuned to what the patient says in response to the analyst's interventions. The analyst must refrain from immediately judging any criticisms, refusals, or 'lack of confirmation', to be negative therapeutic reactions or arrogant or envious attacks, and must ask himself if they might not be a contribution to better understanding".

See also Orange (2009, 396): "Traditionalism, unfortunately, can take the form of a 'hermeneutics of suspicion,' ... 'This attitude views the patient, if not as an enemy, as a trickster, demanding our constant vigilance. A critical, skeptical stance is then mistaken for neutrality'".

2

THE LIMITS OF INTERPRETATION. A READING OF BION'S "ON ARROGANCE"

"On arrogance" (1958a)[1] is one of Bion's most important essays. That said, in the literature, there is almost nothing that deals specifically and in detail with it. There are only dispersed and generally rather superficial hints. It is as if it had been set aside. This is all the more astonishing if we consider that in many ways it anticipates "Attacks on linking", Bion's most popular and cited article, and that, conversely, in this same paper, Bion dedicates a paragraph to the issues he deals with in "On arrogance". Moreover, in 1967, in *Second Thoughts*, he adds a very intriguing commentary, one as long as two-thirds of "On arrogance", now to be read as an integral part of it.

Although in the original *The International Journal of Psychoanalysis (IJP)* formatting it accounts for just over three pages, in the short essay, Bion develops a refined play of mirrors in which they are reflected in each other, and gradually become clearer, themes like the discovery of a "new" psychotic syndrome and its specific symptomatological triad of curiosity arrogance and stupidity, the new concepts of "obstructive object", the possibility of an alternative interpretation of the Oedipus complex (and therefore of the role of sexuality in the aetiopathogenesis of psychic disorders), the related epistemological problem of the concept of truth, the training of analysts, and the life of psychoanalytic institutions.

My reading, which is not intended to give the "true" meaning of "On arrogance", being inevitably personal, nevertheless fills a gap. The key aspect, among others, that I would like to illustrate is

DOI: 10.4324/9781003625247-2

how in "On arrogance", and starting from the clinical problem of the impasse that is generated with certain pseudo-neurotic patients, Bion starts to carry out that sharp criticism of a certain aspect of moralism or ideology of psychoanalysis that we will find in all his later work, especially in *Transformations* and in *A Memoir of the Future*. Therefore, the "arrogance" we are dealing with here has nothing to do (at least not *directly*) with the character trait (neither Bion's nor anyone else's), but, I repeat, with a certain epistemological attitude and a certain "ethics" of care linked to a notion of truth understood as to be achieved "at any cost", for example a positivist notion of truth. This of course does not imply that a certain way of conceiving what is considered "true" cannot then result in a particular institutional climate or individual attitude.

The solution that I think Bion proposes, but, as it were, between the lines, is to develop theoretical instruments that can better take into account the subjectivity of the analyst-observer and highlight what his or her "arrogance" (again, in the epistemological sense of *hýbris*) may consist of. What I attempt here is a close reading that brings out the ambiguities of the text, then shows how in the commentary added in 1967 they essentially disappear, and makes it clear what the future developments of Bion's thought will be. Because of its complexity, "On arrogance" is not of immediate comprehension. That is why, in my view, an account that examines its rhetoric, that is, how it is constructed and how it "works", and therefore any hidden inconsistencies and potentialities, can help the reader to rediscover and appreciate it.

A Wrong Story

When Bion included "On arrogance" in *Second Thoughts* (1967), he numbered the paragraphs from 83 to 91; it is as if he were dreaming a text of arithmetic precision that at the same time had become canonical and had therefore been provided with an index. The opening is ambitious but at the same time subdued, perhaps so as not to seem excessive. Bion communicates that he has identified a new syndrome. This is no small thing. He announces to the world that there is a certain category of patients unknown until the present day. Apparently neurotic, they in reality use psychotic mechanisms on a massive scale. How can they be recognized? It's not easy. They present, but in a scattered way, references to the triad of arrogance, curiosity, and stupidity (what he would call, a "constant conjunction", which of course does not concern the mere use of these words but the very things they designate). Bion makes clear the meaning he wants to give to arrogance as a malignant degeneration of pride due to the prevalence of death instincts. We should note the psychiatrist's attitude[2] he assumes at this point; as we will see, the paper takes aim at the detached and scientific approach of the analysts towards the patient. At first, the target may be difficult to make out, but gradually, it becomes ever more clearly defined.

When they appear, these symptoms are "evidence" that the analyst is facing a "psychological catastrophe" or a "psychological disaster". The proof that a disaster has occurred lies precisely in the "lack of evidence of any relatedness" (144) between the three elements of the triad. Here already, the duo of evidence/lack of evidence seems to allude to the capacity/incapacity of the analyst as a diagnostician to realize the true nature of the problem he is facing. Pervading the whole essay is an effective rhetoric[3] of blindness and vision whose origins cannot be in doubt. In fact, the "triad" suggests that, for these patients, the "disaster" is no longer only their past or present outside the analysis, but also the "disaster" of psychoanalysis when it proves inadequate to treat them.

Indeed, in the second paragraph, Bion speaks only of "a disaster", without an adjective, stripping the expression of any specificity. He thus insinuates into the reader's mind the idea that he is implying not only the patient's "psychological disaster", but also the negative course that treatment takes when the analyst does not truly realize who the patient is (for example, along the dichotomy neurotic/psychotic). The patient's arrogance begins to re-echo in a certain "arrogance" intrinsic to the discipline that should "treat" it: *two* "disasters" and not just one, each a mirror image of the other. Needless to say, by now, we want to know more and our curiosity as readers is well and truly piqued.

Regarding the "psychological disaster" of psychosis, Bion writes that arrogance, curiosity, and stupidity appear as the "ruins of the psyche" (144). The image suggests the architectural elements of a post-apocalyptic scenario: here a column, there an arch, further on a piece of wall. So the analyst faces the problem of how to put the pieces back together again so as to create a coherent picture of what might have happened. But in the paragraph in "Attacks on linking", dedicated to the triad curiosity-stupidity-arrogance, Bion takes the archaeological metaphor further: with these patients, the catastrophe that destroyed the ancient civilization has not passed, but is still *active*. It is like saying that while we are excavating in Pompeii, Vesuvius is still erupting lava. This situation is due to "the destruction of a capacity for curiosity and the consequent inability to learn" (Bion 1959, 311). The patient cannot ask himself the "why" of things, given that "'why' has, through guilt, been split off" (Bion, 1959, 312). In other words, asking "why", for the patient, would be tantamount to discovering cause–and–effect links and therefore having to assume a burden of responsibility that he could not bear at the moment. Consequently, the patient does not ask why he is there with the analyst, nor what he is doing. What Bion says here is illuminating. He clarifies that, unlike arrogance and stupidity, curiosity is not necessarily a negative element. It becomes one only when, after the "psychological disaster", it becomes split and is accompanied by surviving links that "are perverse, cruel, and sterile" (315).

Oedipus Reinvented

To begin to make sense of the disaster that severed the links between the elements of the triad and then dispersed them, Bion proposes the "selected fact" of the Oedipus myth. But first, a note about style. As usual Bion strikes a serious and solemn tone, the tone of someone who is dealing with important matters. This is a style of his that can easily pass for arrogant and assertive in itself, as in fact Meltzer (1978, 30) says: "the reading of the paper 'On Arrogance' at the Paris congress struck many people as a shocking display of the very 'hubris' Bion was describing". Bion often sounds military and dogmatic; "his ideas are marked by a certain 'tankishness' at times" (Souter 2009). However, this should not prevent us from seeing neither how compelling this style is, on the one hand, so much so that it is difficult to paraphrase it, nor the value and originality of the concepts it expresses. Meltzer himself, who criticizes Bion's idiosyncratic and "rather exasperating" style and emphasizes its "high level of abstraction", in the short notes he dedicates to Bion's essay, significantly compares its reception to the equally negative ("shocked and hostile") one that welcomed the first performance of Beethoven quartets.

Indeed, Bion oscillates between cautious assertions ("may escape detection", "may seem", "may be supposed", "wish", "suggest") and more assertive statements ("should be taken...as evidence", "the lack of evidence of any relatedness is evidence"). Evidence of what? That pride, instead of becoming self-respect, has degenerated into the malignant form of arrogance; in other words, to repeat, the instincts of death have prevailed over the instincts of life.

Let us not forget that when, in 1957, Bion presented this paper at the 20th IPA Congress in Paris, he is still absolutely not only in the Kleinian tradition, but also well aware of introducing new ideas that do not precisely represent mainstream psychoanalysis. It is understandable that he should sway between caution and recklessness, and that he should try, if possible, to avoid (as we saw, unsuccessfully) appearing arrogant. This is perhaps the reason that prompts him to make some concessions to the vocabulary and metapsychology of the time. What is clear, however, is that everything revolves around the idea that "it's a disaster not to realize that ...". We should allow ourselves to read this sentence in a deconstructive way, preserving all its ambiguity. In this way, we can appreciate the fact that in the text, it could simultaneously refer to several layers of discourse. In any case, it is easy to imagine that, in the historical context of the time, Bion's ideas can sound as a bit of a provocation. After all, he is saying that in order to understand the essence of the new syndrome, we need to put aside the Oedipus Freud has acquainted us with, and he offers a version of it that seems innovative even if compared with Klein's. Although in some way Bion maintains the centrality of the Oedipal complex and grafts the Kleinian element of epistemophilic instinct onto it, this point would still be a matter of debate today. It is as facile to picture what Bion's answer would be: "If serious psychoanalytic discussion cannot take place in the domain which Freud found adequate, it must be enlarged" (1991, 176).

At the heart of the Oedipus story, Bion proclaims, is not the sexual crime, but "the arrogance of Oedipus in vowing to lay bare *the truth at no matter what cost*" (144, emphasis added). Let us examine his choice of words: the verb "to vow" borders on metaphysics – one of its etymological roots points to the meaning of "to offer a sacrifice" – and thus here it seems to allude to missionary dogmatism. The giveaway (assuming there was any need for one) is the expression "at no matter what cost": a principle of fanaticism that refuses to respect limits. In the context, it is clear that Bion's reference to Oedipus has no ornamental value at all. The expression "truth at no matter what cost", on the contrary, lies at the heart of his subject.

That is why we need to invest in a few words about the myth and the new reading.

Opting to discuss the Oedipus myth, Bion indirectly reveals where he drew inspiration for his paper. In *Oedipus Rex* and *Oedipus at Colonus* "arrogance" translates *hýbris*.[4] As the Choir recites: "arrogance insatiable pride/breed the tyrant/feed him on thing after thing blindly/at the wrong time uselessly/and he grows reaches so high/nothing can stop his fall" (Sophocles 1978, 62). Then again, at the beginning of *Oedipus at Colonus*, immediately after coming on stage, Oedipus talks of the "masters" that keep him alive, mentioning not only age and suffering, but also "pride" (γενναῖον). Although the Greek term translates more precisely as "noble origins" or "nobility of soul", the word "pride" correctly renders the meaning. By choosing this term, Sophocles neatly indicates the transformation that has taken place in Oedipus from one play to the other – incidentally, "On arrogance" could be read not only as an essay on the theory and technique of psychoanalysis, but also as a separate commentary on Sophocles' *Oedipus*.

Harking back to the myth of Oedipus has at least two meanings, but in this case, they overlap each other. The first general meaning concerns the myth itself as a narrative form that expresses a certain idea of truth that is irreducible to any technocratic or "scientific" concept. The very fact that it has an infinite number of variants is an indication that each myth symbolizes first and foremost the impossibility of knowing reality as it really is. In a myth, it is never possible to identify the first cause, the origin, the culprit. In this context, this essential characteristic of myths in general relates closely to the meaning of the Oedipal scene as Bion suggests interpreting it. What he does, it seems to me – otherwise we would not understand Meltzer's comment – is to question the universally explicative value (the ultimate truth) of the Oedipus myth in psychoanalysis. Bion is being very cautious, but what we can infer from the text is that, to his eyes, arrogance or the (utterly "unnecessary") "violence" of interpretation lies in the "sacralization" of the Oedipus complex (or, for that matter, of any other concept).

Again, let us focus on the style. Bion's first move is to emphasize the fictional dimension of the myth. He writes: "I shall rehearse the Oedipus myth". It is as if he were saying: "I will stage the myth (the tragedy) of Oedipus"; or, literally, I will put the Oedipus myth to the test, we will rehearse it in the theatre. So, not only will I test the concepts that we can glean from the Oedipus myth, but also my own text will be a recital/performance/personal staging of the Oedipus myth. But "I will do it", he continues – and here we come to the second move – from *my* point of view. Alone, the assertion that in this context there can be *several* points of view has enormous theoretical import and may come across as challenging. This is why Bion tones down the thrust of his brave proposal. He rectifies the classical interpretation of the myth but veils it behind the claim that it is only a "shift of emphasis". The sex crime remains on the scene, albeit it as a "peripheral element". Front and centre now is the confrontation between Oedipus and the Sphinx. Bion emphasizes its fictional character twice more, speaking of it each time as a "story".

As on the first page of a play script, Bion provides the list of characters. Surprising, disturbing, evocative, the list itself is an example of the effectiveness of his skills as a writer: the Sphinx, who challenges travellers to solve the riddle and then kills herself when this happens; Oedipus, who solves the riddle and becomes the new king, but then blinds himself and goes into exile; Tiresias (the one "who possesses knowledge"), who disapproves of his intention to question the oracle in order to know why the plague has come upon Thebes; the oracle, who pushes for the investigation. The elements of arrogance, stupidity and curiosity, which are found scattered and unconnected in patients, are in this story instead *linked* together in a coherent and intelligible way. For this reason, the myth can serve to suggest by analogy what may have brought about the psychological disaster of psychosis.

At this point, the curiosity of any reader who readies herself to witness the tragedy is even more alive. The "riddle" of the Sphinx is reflected performatively in the riddle that textual rhetoric sets before her sagacity. Bion hints at the possibility of discerning the scattered elements that identify "a certain class" of patient when brought together in the "triad". In such patients, psychotic mechanisms are "active". Each of them must be seen as "a significant event demanding investigation" (144). Like a tightrope walker on a wire, Bion keeps up the paradoxical game of affirming and denying the meaning of the investigation or of curiosity. Only a thin line separates a good from a nefarious curiosity, just as rightful pride can turn just like that into arrogance.

The myth of the Sphinx symbolizes how narrow this dividing line is. We have no choice but to live with myth, just as we also have to tolerate the ambiguity of existence and the paradox intrinsic to human nature. So what does it mean to solve the riddle and thus provoke the Sphinx's suicide? It may mean making do with false knowledge, abstract, or split-off knowledge; deluding ourselves that the answer is not contained in the question, but that there is a "real" answer. In the act of "vowing" himself to abstractly discover the truth, Oedipus shows himself to be arrogant, immoderate, and lacking in the true respect for the sacred that Tiresias had requested from him; he "consecrates" to himself, not to the gods; he reduces the myth to an enigma, to a problem that admits of an intellectual solution, in other words, a partial solution – a non-solution. Science solves (its) riddles but in fact can say nothing about the most important questions of existence, which have to do with the ineffable (Bion's concept of "O"), the sense that cannot be converted into meaning.

The enigma *cannot* be solved. It immediately comes back in other forms. The suicide of the Sphinx is an enigma, just like the incest that will soon follow and like the earlier plague at Thebes. Oedipus and the Sphinx belong to two different spheres. The first is a human being, the second a supernatural being. The disregard for measure that the tragic hero shows by accepting the challenge reflects this irreducible distance or the disparity in their nature that is present from the outset. Oedipus does not respect the limits that the gods have given men. But could he avoid the task? Certainly not. His destiny is to represent the need both to question and to fail – or is perhaps only a temporary and partial success that will soon have to face a new plague, a new question.

Oedipus has dialectics on his side, but the Sphinx belongs to another – or *Other* – dimension, that cannot be known through language. In itself, the enigma ("veiled talk"; Di Noia 1978, 439) is structured like a metaphor or a fable, which is to say that it is intrinsically ambiguous. Wishing to resolve its ambiguity would be like emptying the sea with a bucket. This is clear, on the one hand, from the banality of the riddle and, on the other hand, from the fact that the new riddle represented by the suicide of the Sphinx (can a demon[5] really die?) takes gestural-behavioural rather than oral form. In essence, no one can defeat the Sphinx, just as *lógos* can never claim *to say* all that is real. Those who think it *can* are deluding themselves. It seems to me that Bion's target is human *hýbris* when man pretends to know what *cannot* be known – even within the perimeter of psychoanalysis of course.

On another level, achieving and maintaining the awareness that any knowledge is illusion could also be expressed as tolerance for aesthetic conflict (Meltzer 1986). Instead, in order to defend himself against the frustration of not being able to know *everything* about the object, Oedipus also deprives himself of the gain (the thought) that he would receive from tolerating the ambiguity of the enigma, or rather of the (enigmatic) object. Having eliminated the aesthetic conflict – or, to put it another way, having denied the dark side of the object's inaccessible intentions – Oedipus has had the way paved for him towards incest, which here is a figure that stands for total knowledge and for his subsequent blinding and exile.

In the text, Bion skilfully weaves together a series of references that may easily escape the notice of the reader. For example, how can we not see the parallel between Oedipus who must reveal the identity of Laius' murderer (i.e. himself) and the analyst who must reveal the psychotic elements active in apparently neurotic patients ("have to be analytically uncovered"; 144)? What if the outcome in both cases is, precisely, a "disaster"? That's what Bion brings out. Apart from the triad of symptoms (arrogance, etc.), one characteristic of these patients is that they typically suffer from negative therapeutic reactions. The more the analyst investigates, understands, and provides insight, the more the patient regresses ("the very act of analysing the patient makes the analyst an accessory in precipitating regression and turning the analysis itself into a piece of acting out"; 144). In addition, he reacts with "stubborn resistances" to the analyst's attempts to investigate the nature of the "ruins". This is the same stubbornness (but turned on its head) that Oedipus[6] shows in wanting to solve the riddle, or the analyst shows in self-righteously insisting on explaining the events of the session through the patient's past and invariably within the context of the sexual "crime". What emerges is the need to review the very notion of negative therapeutic reaction, as well as the link with the death drive, which Bion himself had initially presented as a fact.

There is no way round the question and Bion puts it very clearly. The analyst's curiosity (which we now know always goes hand in hand with stupidity and arrogance) mirrors the curiosity that produced the catastrophe of psychosis. It is in itself a form of "psychosis". The analyst's obstinate curiosity to know reinforces the patient's resistance to *not* want to know (which is simply the negative form of primitive arrogance) and induces further regression. This is a decisive step. It is here that Bion relates regression not to improvement or the death drive, but to a precise attitude of the analyst. The point is that, just like Oedipus when he is about to receive proof that he is the parricide, they both look to the past ("What is the worry that has made you turn about and speak these words?" [*Ποίας μερίμνης τοῦθ' ὑποστραφεὶς λέγεις*], Jocasta asks him [Sophocles 1994, 399], reflecting the image of Oedipus tired out and with his gaze directed backwards). Thus, there is a kind of short circuit between two different but somehow symmetrical forms of arrogance, each bearing a shadow of the opposite sign.

From this angle, the analytic process itself becomes "an acting out", Bion writes. Can this problem find a solution? Can this development be avoided? "Yet I have not been able to see how this can be done", Bion (144) admits. Had he written that he had "found" it, he would have given the impression that he himself was being presumptuous. In the absence of solutions, it is better to make the best of a bad job: to deal with the patient's regression and turn it around – in Bion's terms, "to accept the acting out and regression as inevitable, and if possible to turn it to good account"; where "the acting out" consists in the fact that "the analytic procedure itself is precisely a manifestation of the curiosity which is felt to be an intrinsic component of the disaster" (144).

Making the Best of a Bad Job

Granted, but how? Bion does not back down and throws in a sentence that contains all the most creative developments of his thinking. He talks about giving "detailed interpretation of events that are taking place in the session" (144). It is perhaps only nowadays, in light of the controversy over the role of trauma and reality in the analytic discourse, that we can comprehend the significance of this formulation – essentially, although not exclusively, its focusing on the here-and-now of the session – and the path that has taken us to this point. We could rephrase it by saying that it is impossible for the analyst to stop being curious and investigating; however, he should no longer be curious about the past but rather about the present; and not only about the patient but, as shown by Bion's equation Oedipus = analyst, also about himself. Tolerating not knowing is in itself a wiser way of knowing, since it is not only abstract, but also affective and pragmatic.

44

In this phase of analysis, continues Bion, transference is peculiar. It is addressed to the analyst *qua* analyst, that is to say, to his function, in that he is one who is curious and who investigates, not in that he reminds the patient of aspects of his parents because of the role they played in his childhood neurosis. I would read it as another way of saying that we have to look at the specific (current) elements of the analytic situation; at the analyst in terms of how he is and not how he reflects the patient's *imagos*; at the inevitable, intrinsic, and objective acting-out component that characterizes the relationship *vis-à-vis* the triad of curiosity, arrogance, and stupidity (in fact Bion adds that both patient and analyst become "blind" and "suicidal").

The analytic process itself (significantly, Bion does not write "process" but "procedure") becomes perverted and turns into an acting out in the form of destructive attacks launched against the ego in both the patient and the analyst, in the same way as Klein describes the child's fantasies of attacking the breast. Integration does not lead to a stable reconstruction of the ego but to further disintegration. The patient takes one step forward and two steps back. There is evidence to suggest, Bion writes, that, as the ego reorganizes itself, the cause of the attacks may lie in the increasingly evident reappearance of the "sexually orientated" Oedipal scene. But here Bion swerves again. Actually, he writes, an even more important role can be played by arrogance. As readers, we feel that the moment is approaching when he will finally give us the solution to the riddle he formulated at the beginning by confronting us with the unknown (X) represented by the strange triad of stupidity, arrogance, and curiosity. Here is the key section:

> Briefly, it appears that *overwhelming emotions* are associated with the assumption *by the patient or analyst* of the qualities required to pursue the truth, and in particular a capacity to tolerate the stresses associated with the introjection of another person's projective identifications.
>
> (145, emphasis added)

The point seems to be that if patient and analyst demonstrate the qualities that are necessary for the pursuit of truth – in particular, the ability to accept each other's projective identifications – then they find themselves forced to withstand the pressure of overwhelming emotions. The conflict that emerges is then between knowing the truth and avoiding the truth: "the implicit aim of psycho-analysis to pursue the truth at no matter what cost is felt to be synonymous with a claim to a capacity for containing he discarded, split-off aspects of other personalities while retaining a balanced outlook" (145).

In other words, the implicit aim of psychoanalysis to pursue the truth "at no matter what cost" (it is worth noting that in the first sentence we find "pursue the truth" and in the second "pursue the truth at no matter what cost") is interpreted by the patient as the analyst's claim to be able to absorb projective identifications while maintaining a balanced (imperturbable) mental attitude. But then the analyst appears arrogant in the eyes of the patient, who evidently feels bereft of that very capacity, and for this reason, falls prey to explosive feelings of envy and hatred.

Now, as perhaps we can see better in the clinical vignettes discussed in "Attacks on linking" (my impression is that they are the same patients in both papers), the explanatory formulas that Bion uses in accordance with tradition are an example of the (involuntary, unconscious) "moralism" that he himself denounces in "On arrogance": envy and hatred, "evil", primary aggression, destructivity are all and always *in* the patient. They are not read as signs of the psyche being in a state of exhaustion; nor are they of the *group* of two, and *not* only of the patient. The analyst does not wonder if by chance his investigation is too demanding on the patient and arouses emotions in him that he is not able to contain.

Said differently, there is some ambiguity in Bion's discourse, which persists throughout the text of "On arrogance", and only unequivocally dissolves in the 1967 commentary: being able to absorb the patient's projective identifications can be understood as a synonym of emotional availability to take on his anguish; instead, "claiming" to remain in balance can be read as a denial of the previous point. True, the analyst should at the same time empathize with the patient, be pervaded by his emotions or be in unison with him, but he should still exercise a certain stewardship over things, without letting himself be overwhelmed. Equally, however, this assertion would seem to disprove the need to experience moments of crisis, to go through the schizo-paranoid position, or, in Bion's language, to stay in a state of "madness" ("a sleep akin to stupor"), as of someone who is about to hallucinate (Bion 1970, 47). One might therefore suppose that what causes the violent outbursts of

46

envy and hatred in the patient is the analyst's claim to maintain a certain imperturbability, which in the patient's eyes is a symptom of a *real* unavailability (that would be a different explanation from transference, unconscious phantasy, or death instinct). He would look like an analyst who was putting himself not at the service of the patient's maturation but, in an abstract sense, at the service of the truth *at any cost*. The dichotomy Bion is anticipating is between transformations in −K (*minus* knowledge) and transformations in O; between abstract, intellectual transformations, and transformations that also pass through the body and emotions.

So arrogance seems synonymous with −K. For Bion, incest as a sexual crime allegorizes epistemic crime: a form of intrusive, greedy, predatory, and ruthless curiosity that replaces the knowledge that comes from the ability to live through an emotional experience and in fact inhibits it. But something that is not animated by emotions does not live and does not grow.[7] The "invisible" fabric of an arrogance that takes on the guise of moral superiority is envy. Those who suffer from envy despair of ever being able to receive the nourishment they need and for this reason they hate those who have it, and destroy it so that no one can have it. Judgement is used to kill the truth. In the end, though, the desert spreads evermore. In *Learning from Experience*, Bion will term the condition of deprivation of those who suffer from envy as "without-ness". I quote this paragraph here to remind how the issue of "moral superiority", either on the side of the patient or the analyst, is central for him:

> It is a super-ego that has hardly any of the characteristics of the super-ego as understood in psycho-analysis: it is "super" ego. It is an envious assertion of moral superiority without any morals.... The most important characteristic is its hatred of any new development in the personality as if the new development were a rival to be destroyed. The emergence therefore of any tendency to search for the truth, to establish contact with reality ... is met by destructive attacks on the tendency and the reassertion of the "moral" superiority.
>
> (1962b, 97–98)

Bion now feels the need to return to some clinical material. It is significant that he mentions negative therapeutic reaction as a fourth element to supplement the triad. The clinical vignette he presents describes a patient with such traits. He mentions how he has offered the patient insights but that these insights have produced only further madness. With the passage of time, the patient loses the ability to demonstrate the insight he had previously possessed. He regresses further and begins to show psychotic features. Evacuative projective identifications, confusional states, and depersonalization all mount, as explained by Klein, Segal, and Rosenfeld (other triads, stylistically speaking). In light of the way the patient performs in the session, Bion even wonders how he manages to lead a life outside the consulting room, which as far as he can tell is no worse than before. For us, this annotation is also a clue. It is as if between the lines he was telling us that the madness is not in the patient but rather in the couple and the way it works in the session.

In more general terms, I think that what Bion is talking about here is the limits of a psychoanalysis based on a psychology of the isolated subject, which veers too far towards the epistemic side of representation and not enough towards the ontological side of affect (Ogden 2019). The analyst Bion is describing (the himself he was some years before, in the guise of a detached observer) is one who offers many insights (far too much light) but seems insufficiently able or willing to receive projective identifications, non-verbal communications, and emotions. Unheeded, these can but multiply. From projective identification as the "normal" way of communicating and building up a mind, we get then to the kind of excessive projective identification that leaves the subject severely impoverished.

The Frustrated Couple and the Obstructive Object

Since on the level of symptoms the question remains mysterious, Bion, instead of looking through the theoretical lens of transference, now tries to reformulate the problem in terms of the internal object. What we notice is a characteristic oscillation between a one-person and an intersubjective or "group" perspective. This is one of the reasons to reread "On arrogance": to get an idea of how Bion strives to gradually detach himself from a Kleinian paradigm of psychoanalysis. The "psychotic" material appeared in sessions in which the patient spoke in an incoherent and ungrammatical manner. He was able to put a name to significant objects but without pronouns or verbs, or he used verbs but without subjects or references to the location of the action. Verbal communication seemed almost impossible, to the point that they formed what Bion termed "a frustrated couple" (145). On one occasion when he was particularly clear-headed, the patient himself commented that communication seemed so "mutilated" that no creative work and no progress were possible. Interpretations of this behaviour in a sexual key were certainly not unknown to the patient, Bion comments, but they had no effect. His anxiety, instead of diminishing, increased.

Nevertheless, Bion senses that there must have been some change or progress. So he looks out for clues to confirm this. Illumination was not long in coming. One day, "in a lucid moment", the patient says he wonders that Bion can "stand it". Bion assumes that this means there is "something" he *is* able to stand but that the patient *cannot*. He then speculates that this may have been the change-inducing factor, this very ability on his part to stand "something". This amounts to saying that, *despite* the impasse, the concomitant ability to tolerate such a burdensome situation had promoted change. The patient, however, had already observed that there seemed to be a factor hindering him in his attempt to enter into creative contact, and that this was not only mutilating verbal communication; also that this "obstructive force" seemed to be sometimes in himself, sometimes in the analyst, and sometimes in an unknown place – and that he had no control over it. The next step, says Bion, is when the patient (here, we see a glimpse of Bion's future concept of the patient as "the best and most highly qualified collaborator"; [1977] 2018, 91) tells him that *he* (the analyst) is the "obstructive force" (or "the persecuting object"), and that his "outstanding feature" is that he cannot "stand it".

To recapitulate: on the one hand, in the eyes of the patient, the analyst is the one who is able to tolerate "it" or "something"; on the other hand, he is sometimes identified with the obstructive object that is unable to stand "it". These passages are full of ambiguities. It is difficult to tell whether the patient is accusing Bion of not tolerating being the obstructive object or whether he identifies him with the obstructive object that cannot stand "it". And indeed, Bion admits that it is not at all clear to him what this "it" refers to.

The turning point, though, is intriguing. For the third time, the accuser moves over to the side of the accused, just as in *Oedipus the King*, where the protagonist discovers that not only is he guilty, but that he is guilty of not one but two crimes: parricide, but also incest. The first time was when Bion admitted the unfortunate complication of curiosity that is intrinsic to both the analytic attitude and the psychological disaster of psychosis; the second time was when he pointed out another complication in the search for truth "at no matter what cost" as an implicit goal of psychoanalysis. The solution to the riddle now seems close at hand. All that remains is to grasp what this "it"[8] is, the "it" the analyst cannot bear and which makes him "the obstructive object". Identifying it with a creative couple that arouses envy and hatred, he writes, led nowhere. So for the umpteenth time, Bion sets aside the primary scene, and with it, on a theoretical level, the parental couple of Freud and Klein.

Vision as a Method

In the meantime, we must once again emphasize the effectiveness of the expressive technique that Bion demonstrates in "On arrogance". He is writing an absorbing psychological thriller. By now we might have expected a final denouement, delivered by a born storyteller who has mastered all the tricks of the trade, but Bion delays it and in so doing increases the tension: "Before I discuss this problem [of the nature of the obstructive object] further, I must mention ..." (146). However, he expects that the digression will serve to better understand the next step. In this period, he specifies, the references to arrogance, curiosity, and stupidity mounted and appeared more and more interconnected: "The stupidity was purposeful, and arrogance, not always called by that name, was sometimes an accusation, sometimes a temptation, and sometimes a crime" (146).

We have here again an observation that seems contradictory. If arrogance, stupidity, and curiosity increase, this means that the direction of analysis is certainly not going towards "evolution"; however, the fact that the ability to see them as related to each other grows would suggest the opposite. *What then?* It is as in the case of "something" and "it". We must not think of a linear and unidirectional process. It may well be that the analyst's "arrogance" produces a certain effect, and his ability to tolerate the situation another. At all events, the phenomenon described above leads Bion to hypothesize that the triad of "symptoms" is closely associated with the obstructive object. The point I have made so far is that, more or less obscurely, Bion is coming to conceive the idea that they should be considered not only unilaterally as the result of the patient's past/internal "disaster", but also as the result of a couple's problematic way of interacting.

50

At this point, however, Bion takes a step towards a much more explicit formulation: it is the obstructive object that is stupid, arrogant, and curious. Having been witnesses to the scene in which the patient identified the analyst with the obstructive object, we now realize that we are possibly facing a complete reversal of perspective, a real twist. I say "possibly" because there still remain the chance to say that this was not what *was* happening, but only what the patient *felt* that was happening. But let us read the passage:

> it became clear that when I was identified with the obstructive force, what I could not stand was the patient's methods of communication. In this phase my employment of verbal communication *was felt* by the patient to be a mutilating attack on *his* methods of communication. From this point onwards, it was only a matter of time to demonstrate that the patient's link with me was his ability to employ the mechanism of projective identification. That is to say, his relationship with me and his ability to profit by the association lay in the opportunity to split off parts of his psyche and project them into me.
>
> (146)

So, Bion says that *it is the patient* who thinks the analyst is the obstructive force that does not accept his projective identifications; and that *it is always the patient* who *feels* that Bion's use of verbal communication is a mutilation. But couldn't the use of verbal communication actually be the result of accepting the patient's projective identifications? The fact is that basically, in "On arrogance", on an explicit level Bion does not deviate from the Kleinian view that if the analyst accepts projective identifications and gives "good" things to the patient, he increases their envy. But at the same time, he talks of obstructive forces, illustrates the patient's point of view, is ambiguous on many points, refers several times to the couple, emphasizes the symmetrical problem of curiosity and arrogance, and identifies Oedipus with the analyst and his guilt with an idea of absolute (for the analyst: positivist) truth.

If we read all of this paying attention not only to the text, but also as it were to the subtext, it seems to me that it is sustainable to claim that we are facing a paradigm shift in psychoanalysis: from the isolated subject to the relationship, and from the relationship to the group-of-two or intersubjective field. Seen from this perspective, the passage looks noteworthy, as in no way "suspicious". It is "re-spectful" of the patient, his perceptions, sensations, and emotions and also of his sincerity and ability to connect to the other as he can, and not as he should. If anything, it is the analyst who is the one who is out of tune with the only mode of communication that the patient actually has available in order to create a "link" with him. Instead, he insists on imposing his own modality. He continues to make a phone call to someone who at the moment can only send him smoke signals. This emotional distance further deprives the pa-tient of the ability to communicate:

> What it was that the object could not stand [and by "object" we must now understand the description of a function of the couple-as-a-system or as a synonym of "frustrated couple"] became clearer in some sessions where it appeared that in so far as I, as analyst, was insisting on verbal communication as a method of making the patient's problems explicit, I was felt to be directly attacking the patient's methods of communication.
>
> (146)

Again: the patient "felt". But this time, we have "I, as analyst, *was* insisting on verbal communication". The concept that Bion comes to understands at this point is that a lack of attunement on the level of communication that can be defined as non-verbal, emotional, semiotic, bodily – in other words, at the level of the aesthetic and in-tersubjective constitution of the individual (Civitarese 2016a, 2017a, 2019b) – places on the patient the overwhelming burden of having to deal with an excessive and emotional pressure. This happens es-pecially when "supposed" truths – as they are not shared, but com-ing only from the analyst's mind, eminently conceptual or mainly related to content – take on the tone of a "moralistic" accusation against the "demon" that in the unconscious guides the patient's actions.

I don't want to be misunderstood at this point. The word "arro-gance" here must once again be written in quotation marks: it means to think you can know the truth at any cost. I am not talking about anything that is not unconscious or involuntary and, if anything, it stems from a well-intentioned desire for knowledge and from a wish to help. However, my impression is that the Freudian conception of the unconscious as hell, and a certain way of interpreting to the patient how he systematically misunderstands the reality of things and the analyst's attitude, lends itself easily to convey a devaluing meta-communication to the patient and, moreover, gives life to an ideological relationship. Let us think for a while of terms such as envy, manipulation, seduction, resistance, misunderstanding, attack, hatred: they all have a negative flavour and easily take on an accusatory tone. The analyst behaves like the police officer who Freud (1932) sees as having to hold back the wild and joyful crowd of the unconscious. Of course, this does not prevent the development of genuine caring relationships. The point is rather this: can we refine the ear to the elements of ideology that can infiltrate the analysis? We may or may not like it, but this is the black beast Bion fights against in this essay and also throughout *Transformations* and *A Memoir of the Future*.

But let us go back to the text. The patient feels that his "communication systems" (i.e. his ability to think) is under attack, even if it is reduced to the non-verbal, and the attack is mutilating. Bion infers from this that the patient's projective identification should no longer be described as yet another attempt to manipulate or control the analyst, etc., but as the sole desperate resource left to him if he wants to maintain a bond. In actual fact, there is still a certain indecisiveness about the two perspectives. The reason is clear. Bion has spent his life reinterpreting individual psychoanalysis in terms of group psychoanalysis, but I would venture to say, without being fully aware of it. Otherwise, in *Experiences in Groups*, he would not have said, in my opinion mistakenly (although he later "corrects" himself), that the "minimum size of the group is three" (1961, 26).[9]

The fact is that Bion is moving from "suspicious" to "respectful" listening (Nissim-Momigliano 1992); and from the model of two separate subjects to that of two joint minds – long before he met Klein, he had *it* in his blood – committed to doing the best they can in a difficult situation. If nobody else can do it, then at least the patient's ability to keep open a non-verbal channel provides him with the rewarding experiences of being able to evacuate negative psychic elements and of giving them to others so that they are preserved. It is "a primitive form of communication" (146) on which, Bion explains, purely verbal communication also depends. In essence, he no longer sees projective identification as an instrument to colonize the other, but as a way to communicate and to weave the intersubjective fabric of the ego. We are reminded here of the passage in

Experiences in Groups (1961, 38) where he writes that it would be "less misleading if each individual member of the group spoke a language unknown to the remainder". In this way, no one would be presumptuous enough to think that they had "understood" what anyone else had said.

Bion's short essay ends on a real firework. He has finally figured out what the obstructive object is. It is the arrogance of thinking that it is possible to heal such a primitive and severe disaster by imposing the false truth of abstract understanding, by using words as vehicles of meaning and not so much of sense – which he roughly identifies with classical transference and "deep" interpretation. To put it in extreme terms, for the sake of expositive clarity: Bion sees these technical devices as a way of exercising a cold, scientific curiosity that operates (or may operate) at the expense of the ability to receive the patient's projective identifications. The analyst's pre-constituted knowledge of the patient, which has not been achieved through moments of sharing, becomes "destructive and mutilating attacks, largely through varieties of stupidity, upon his capacity for projective identification" (146). The arrogance, the curiosity imbued with *hýbris*,[10] lies in claiming to be able to translate into words that which is not translatable insofar as it is non-verbal; the stupidity lies in not realizing the vanity of the enterprise. To use a different jargon, transformations in –K (knowledge) easily become a manifestation of the analyst's "stupidity", in the sense of non–intelligence about things – "how dreadful it is to know when the knowledge/, does not benefit the knower!", says Tiresias (Sophocles 1994, 355), and as such prevents transformations in O. More appropriately, the latter can be termed "becoming". This is why Tiresias discourages Oedipus. One cannot claim to know what O, *being, becoming,* is. O "cannot be known but must be 'become'" (Bion 1965, 155).

But we can say all this only in hindsight. In "On arrogance", we cannot really state that the case is clearly and completely solved. For this, we will have to wait at least for the commentary. It is true that the conclusion of the article seems to confirm that the essay is, above all, about the epistemological arrogance of psychoanalysis: "the denial to the patient of a normal employment of projective identification precipitates a disaster through the destruction of an important link" (146), and soon after: In addition, what is formed is "a primitive superego which denies the use of projective identification" (146). But, again, here Bion could be referring to the original

54

patient's "disaster" (denial → cruel superego), and *not* to a denial or a superego that appears in the analytic field. Paradoxically, in order to avoid a new disaster as much as possible, the analyst should ignore this hypothetical truth about what happened in the past. This is what Bion will tell in the commentary arguing against the causal way of thinking. Why? Because if the analyst, plausibly enough, tells himself that the disaster must have happened in the primary relationship, this same "arrogant" thought may act as a shield against the possibility that he might play the same role as the object from the past.

As readers, we are left in the uncertainty of not understanding precisely what this "denial" means. It would seem correct to affirm that it has both a conscious side and an unconscious side. The two sides, however, are not separate from each other. The more our theory is capable of self-scrutiny, the more likely it is that it can also keep unconscious "obstructive objects" at bay. On the conscious side, this can easily be explained. Bion's idea, developed mainly in *Transformations*, is that above all else we have to "cure" the analysts' superego, which leads them to barricade themselves behind causal theories of what happens in analysis. This is the way the "moralism" of psychoanalysis manifests itself: thinking that one possesses the truth and insisting on explaining verbally to the patient the nature of his problems without taking sufficient account of the knowledge of the body and its intentionality.

The model of care should not be the mother-child relationship but the mother-*infant* relationship, in other words, the mother with the child who is not yet able to understand the meaning of words. This minimal clarification has a considerable theoretical effect. It instantly immunizes us against the virus that makes us value cognition over affection. It goes without saying that it would be naive to place any non-verbal exchange between mother and infant outside the field of the symbolic in the broad sense, and therefore outside language.

Bion states a paradox. Careful observation of the facts of the analysis helps us to discover new constant conjunctions and ultimately to bind them together by making new links, which can also be of the cause-and-effect type. This implies, however, setting aside already known connections. His position is, therefore, not an *absolute* refusal to investigate causes. Our minds are instinctively impelled to think by forging cause-and-effect links. However, he greatly narrows things down to include only that which seems acceptable to him: "the 'causal link' has apparent validity only with events associated closely in space and time" (Bion 1967, 163).

The criterion of proximity or immediacy is therefore essential. We come back to Husserl's concept of things that are "under the eyes", "things themselves", or "things in the flesh" (*leibhaftig*). We should not be too surprised. Who would argue that listening to a symphony in a concert hall or in the foyer of a theatre is the same thing? As we can see, the difference lies in introducing a radical and rigorous phenomenological principle into the theory of observation in psychoanalysis, which could be summed up in the expression "vision as a method" (von Herrmann 1981, 23).

A Qualified Pseudo-Analyst

That "On arrogance" is more, or at least as much, an essay on the limits of psychoanalysis as on the madness of his patients can also be seen from the invaluable comments that Bion adds in *Second Thoughts* (1967), and which – it is worth noting – come after *Transformations*. Bion reiterates the idea, already expressed by Klein, that psychotic mechanisms are found in all analysands. As "evidence", he cites the case of the aspiring analyst (!). Choosing this professional path would seem to fulfil the desire to avoid dealing with one's own madness. The effect of qualifying as an analyst – actually, as Bion adds with subtle perfidy, becoming "a qualified pseudo-analyst" (1967, 162) – would be to have his mental health certified by experienced colleagues. But the high point is yet to come. Bion sees acquiring the qualification of psychoanalyst as tantamount to becoming capable, thanks to the flux of projective identification ("in which he does not believe", and that therefore we must think of as in action but inverted, as directed from the analyst to the patient; Ferro 1987), of preening "himself on freedom from the psychoses for which *he looks down upon* his patients and colleagues" (Bion 1967, 162, emphasis added).

After a century of structural analysis of texts, critical theory, feminism and deconstruction, and disciplines to which psychoanalysis has given a decisive impulse, it should not seem weird to us the idea that the "truth" of "On arrogance" may be contained in this postscript and that what Bion seems to refer to only some is instead to be extended to himself and to all. But what fascinates me about this very brief writing of his is precisely that it is evidence of the ability that psychoanalysis has to "cure" and renew itself.

I do not know if there is another passage in all Bion's work in which he expresses so clearly and corrosively his criticism of the "moralism"[11] of psychoanalysis that is usually mystified into familiarity with the psychic mechanisms of the unconscious-as-hell or prison: translating from the unconscious into the conscious, allying oneself with the "healthy" part of the patient's ego and looking "down upon his patients and colleagues" for madness. This happens not because analysts are worse than other human beings, but rather precisely because they *are* human beings, and therefore also fragile and frightened. Basically, it is an epistemological issue, not a characterological one, but the first can pave the ground to the latter.

Moralism is not ostentatious. On the contrary, the analyst is normally very keen to maintain a non-judgemental attitude – in psychoanalysis, a precept one absorbs with one's mother's milk. At times moralism exudes pedagogy, interpretation that looks for culprits, self-indulgence, misplaced sense of superiority and confidence, sharp-eyed and hyperalert suspiciousness, ruthlessness rationalized as anti-sentimentalism, etc. However, these factors should not be generalized. Even though they make up part of the landscape, they have little probative value. Personality factors certainly play a role, but mostly moralism is disguised as "science". This is why it is insidious and treacherous. Bion's denunciation of the arrogance of psychoanalysis would remain an extemporaneous and generic observation were it not substantiated by the robust criticism of the use of causal ("scientific") theories in psychoanalysis that Bion develops notably in *Transformations*, and later, in another register, in *A Memoir of the Future* (Civitarese 2017b). In this sense, the 1967 commentary on the conclusions of "On arrogance" makes the link between moral superiority and causalism very clear:

> I regard the idea of causation [I read this as: "explaining the obstructive object with the disaster that happened in the past"], implicit throughout the paper, as erroneous; ... The "causal link" has apparent validity only with events associated closely in space and time. The fallacious nature of reasoning based on the idea of "causes" is clearly argued in Heisenberg, *Physics and Philosophy* ... the psychoanalyst does not allow himself to be beguiled into searching for, and proposing, except in conversational terms,

57

"causes" ... The discovery of "cause" relates more to the peace of mind of the discoverer than to the object of his research.

(Bion 1967, 163)

Elsewhere he explains:

But, good heavens, what would happen to us if I couldn't blind myself [as we know, Oedipus becomes a true "seer" only when he blinds himself] to sidereal space or space time when I want to tell my time by my watch? ... If we are to translate our thoughts and feelings into physical or corporeal fact, there has to be a certain focusing of our mental apparatus as a prelude to action. That very act seems to me – putting my thoughts into verbo-visual terms – to involve putting other elements out of focus [he does not say that they do not exist, but only that for a while they should be put out of focus]. It is difficult in practice to de-focus – peripheralize – the irrelevant without falling in to the opposite error of permanent insensibility; blindness, deafness, repression. That is why I talk of the "opacity" of memory, desire, understanding.

(1991, 232)

What we note in this passage is the conflict between attention to subjective or inner experience ("my time", intuition as internal perception, the reasons for action) and thinking geared to action (external perception, the causes of action). If you want to bring out one side, you have to peripheralize the other. For the purposes of analysis, Bion sets the value of the analyst's intuition as internal perception against the search for causes. This is why he develops the concept of the analyst's transformations in hallucinosis (Civitarese 2015). The point becomes how the analyst can hallucinate in order to grasp the patient's hallucinations, that is to say, how he can put himself in a state in which he can have "sensuous experiences without any background of sensuous reality" (Bion 1967, 163). Or, put in more reassuring terms, how he can acquire the ability to "intuit psychic reality which has no known sensuous realization" (Bion 1967, 163).

Again, in the first instance, it is worth paying attention to the textual game. Bion never stops reversing positions: not the psychotic patient who has delusions and hallucinations, but the analyst who must be able to hallucinate. Then, on another level, in order to free ourselves for good from the bias of "superiority", can we think of a more radical way to *symmetrize* the patient-analyst relationship than asking the latter to "hallucinate"? The circle closes: in his commentary to "On arrogance", Bion exposes a previous flaw of his and is proud of the progress he has made in the meantime. There was a time when he actively used to question memory and obey desire, whereas now he has come to theorize the concept of negative capability, or rather negative capability and faith (Civitarese 2019b). Everything goes through a personal transformation, that is to say, through experience (transformation in O): "I found more difficult when I was relying on memory to provide the links than I do today when I allow the analytic situation to evolve" (Bion 1967, 161). It is soon clear where he is heading: "I do not consider an interpretation in psycho-analysis derives from facts accessible to sensuous apparatus" (Bion 1967, 164).

This is self-criticism in its fullest form. It seems that from Bion's angle, the triad arrogance-curiousness-stupidity is the toxicity that arises from the non-observance of the principle of negative capability/faith – a principle that Bion overturns into the voluntary deletion of the triad of memory, desire, and comprehension. This is the way in which the analyst, in turn, blinds himself, like Oedipus when he comes to know his guilt, but which in *Oedipus at Colonus* is still not called real guilt because it is involuntary. Thus a dizzying game of mirrors is played out between the intolerance to frustration typical of psychosis and the intolerance of a psychoanalysis that has not yet arrived at the principle of systematic doubt and the value of the analyst's intuition-as-hallucinosis.

Obviously, Bion is not claiming that in order to get in touch with the analysand the analyst must "really" hallucinate. As usual, his way of defining his concepts is to shine the dim light shed by associations with concepts taken from other disciplines or fields of knowledge (in this case psychiatry), and to season them with a touch of provocation. Here, he wants to summon up, on the one hand, the particular state of mind, so well described by Jaspers (1913), which in the psychotic individual anticipates the emergence of delusions or hallucinations; and on the other, if metaphorically he uses the concept of hallucinosis – hallucination that occurs in an intact personality – metaphorically, what he is saying is that the analyst should pay as much attention as possible to reverie, that is, to the incessant imaginative workings of the mind.

If we interpret Bion's statement correctly, we see that it is only another way of alluding to the dreaming activity that we experience even when we are awake. This is why he speaks of hallucinosis. Because the analyst knows he is in a similar state. Synonymous with this intuition is the Bionian concept of "evolution". The example he gives of this in the commentary is particularly clear: evolution is when a memory comes to mind without having been actively recalled.

Bion the Immoralist

Bion the "immoralist", then, is certainly not the same as Bion the "amoralist" – if anything, he is the opposite of an amoralist. The analyst rediscovers a true sense of ethics if he resists the moralism that emanates from the arrogant drive of a cruel superego understood as a true basic assumption of the psychoanalytic institution/group. It hinders the affective-somatic communication that takes place by projective identification because it is dominated by an absolute or abstract demand for knowledge, as it is for all those who idealize technique as an instrument of investigation of the inanimate world. Instead of an emotional stance of openness and hospitality, we find the "exaltation of a 'moral' outlook and lack of respect for the truth. The result is starvation of the psyche and stunted growth" (1965, 38). As we know, moralism rather allows space for abstract and preconceived ideas and thus shows little respect for human interest; rather, it rigidly observes norms to the detriment of humanity and vitality; it tends to transform people into robots, making them incapable of "feeling".

Faithful to himself, a few years after having written "On arrogance" Bion reiterated the equation psychosis = deficiency of the scientific method, and therefore, in a veiled way, also of a "scientific" approach in psychoanalysis:

We assume that the psychotic limitation is due to an illness but that that of the scientist is not. Investigation of the assumption illuminates disease on the one hand and scientific method on the other. It appears that our rudimentary equipment for "thinking" thoughts is adequate when the problems are associated with the inanimate, but not when the object for investigation is the phenomenon of life itself. Confronted with the complexities of the

60

human mind the analyst must be circumspect in following even accepted scientific method; its weakness may be closer to the weakness of psychotic thinking than superficial scrutiny would admit.

(1962b, 14)

Nothing less than that: weakness of scientific method = weakness of psychotic thinking. Until the end of his life, Bion would continue to maintain this position very firmly. Even through the lens of the subsequent developments of his thinking, we can get a sight of its deep meaning as a principle of the renewal of the analyst's internal setting. The stakes are neither merely abstract nor merely ethical. What matters is whether in the end the attitude that comes forth from a new ethical position is also substantiated by theoretical and technical principles. At issue is the very soul of psychoanalysis – and in my opinion its chances of remaining vital and surviving as a discipline.

Psychoanalysis contains within it both profoundly emancipatory and alienating features, suffice it to mention, among all, Kernberg's (1996, 2012) or Foucault's criticism (1976). Bion and the other authors who have expanded his ideas simply think that now we can see the latter with pinpoint precision. From this point of view, I hope that the meaning of my rereading of "On arrogance" is also clear. This was not meant as an academic exercise to repeat something that has already been said, but rather as a question asked of one of our forefathers for the purpose of shedding light on the theoretical issues we are passionate about in the present. If there is a point, it lies precisely in taking every occasion to turn the very legacy that has been handed down to us into a problem.

Notes

1 References to single pages, with no indication of the year, are to this article.
2 See Hinshelwood (2014): "Bion approached his subject in a particularly medical manner … This is unusual for Bion".
3 By the term "rhetoric" here and elsewhere I do not mean "empty rhetoric", but only the way the author structures the text.
4 Essentially *hýbris* means "violence" and non-observance of laws; as such it stands in opposition to *díke*, i.e. "rule", "use" or "justice" (Chantraine 1999, 1150).

5 See also Gross (2013, 51): "It is a bewildering fact that there are no representations, no illustrations of the Sphynx' suicide in classical Greek art!" And Yuan (2016, 53): "in Greek culture, the Sphinx constitutes an archetypal image of the enigmatic other, *an alterity par excellence: female, alien,* and *monstrous. It alters from divine to demonic … in a word, an evil spirit"*. In Greek mythology the sphinx is the daughter of Orthrus and Echidna, both Chthonian gods. See also von Hofmannsthal (1906, 106–107): "The demon, the hideous demon has familiarity with me!"

6 In his translation of *Oedipus the Tyrant*, Hölderlin qualifies Oedipus' curiosity as "angry [*zornige*]" and aimed at breaking down the barrier between humanity and the divine (Edmunds 2006, 101).

7 Meltzer (1984, 19) emphasized Freud's "virtual incapacity to form a theory of emotions", which he saw as being due to the fact that Freud viewed affects "as *manifestations* of meaning and not as *containers* of meaning".

8 The use of the impersonal pronoun is significant because it suggests a third mind, field or intersubjective plane.

9 Two people already form a group. At the beginning of *Experiences in Groups* Bion does not seem to think so: The minimum size of the group is three. Two members have personal relationships; with three or more there is a change of quality (interpersonal relationship)" (1961, 26). Bion spent the rest of his life revolutionizing classical and Kleinian psychoanalysis to deny himself on this point. Already in the second chapter of *Experiences in Groups* we find two lines of rectification:

> Anyone who has employed a technique of investigation that depends on the presence of two people, and psychoanalysis is such a technique, can be regarded, not only as taking part in the investigation of one mind by another, but also as investigating the mentality not of a group but of a pair" (1961, 62)

On the same page, then, he speaks significantly of the "basic assumption of the couple". Later, he clarifies that "the individual cannot help but be a member of a group … the psycho–analytical situation is not 'individual psychology' but 'pair' (1961, 131). And beyond that: "no individual, however isolated in time and space, can be regarded as outside a group … a group is more than the sum of its members" (1961, 132). It can be said that at this point, towards the end of *Experiences in Groups*, individual psychoanalysis actually becomes group psychoanalysis.

Today, we would rather say that the minimum group is given by a person. Taken per se, the subject is constituted by an internal group of voices in constant dialogue with each other. We express the same concept when we say that "the I is the Other".

10 The curiosity that Bion talks about here is different from the curiosity that is needed for development and that is destroyed by a primitive and cruel superego, as he describes in "Attacks on linking".

11 Terman (2014) attributes to classical psychoanalytic theory a "paranoid strain" or "gestalt" that takes on a "moral quality".

---------- 3 ----------

INVISIBLE-VISUAL HALLUCINATIONS IN BION'S "ATTACKS ON LINKING"*[1]

[T]here plant eyes, all mist from thence
Purge and disperse, that I might see and tell
Of things invisible to mortal sight.
(Milton, Paradise Lost, Book III, quoted by
Bion in Cogitations, 1992, p. 366)

His 1959 essay "Attacks on Linking" (hereafter referred to as AL; Bion 1959),[2] later taken up and commented on in *Second Thoughts* (1967), is perhaps Bion's most famous paper and, Freud aside, the fourth most cited article in the whole of the psychoanalytic literature.[3] Fame is deserved. In AL, Bion develops his model of the mother–infant relationship, sketches the concept of content/container, theorizes the eminently functional and emotional nature of linking, expands on the Kleinian theory of projective identification, and introduces the idea of a normal version of it.

It is as if Bion had listened to his former analyst. In a lecture on technique given the year before, Melanie Klein expressed the wish that someone would write "a book about linking ... one of the essential points in analysis" (2017, 110). The theme at stake is psychotic thinking, and excessive and therefore pathological use of projective identification as a defence in borderline patients. Defence consists primarily in attacks on linking. From the point of view of metapsychology, we can say that in describing the nature of the destruction, Bion identifies it with the instant in which the analyst has

DOI: 10.4324/9781003625247-3

the intuition that "events occurred in which the patient experienced invisible-visual hallucinations" (309).

This catastrophic event is followed by projective identification proper, a process whereby the minute fragments of the destroyed links are evacuated, and lastly by the reparative phase involving the formation of beta-screens of "bizarre objects". Thus, it can be said that the "strange" concept of invisible-visual hallucination (IVH), which here is mentioned only twice (three times if we also consider the expression "visual hallucinations of invisible objects" [310], and four if we consider all of Bion's works) is at the heart of the article.

I searched the literature for clarification or commentary specific to IVHs but could find none.[4] Given the reputation of the text, I found this surprising. The reason may be that, as is often the case with Bion, it seems to be a rather abstruse concept or more or less similar to others – but, for instance, it says much more than just "splitting". In order to give as clear a picture as possible, I discuss IVH in relation to Freud's concept of negative hallucination, Winnicott's of "primitive agony" (1974), and (tangentially) Lewin's (1946) of dream screen.

So, my first aim here is to shed light on one facet of Bion's theory that has somehow remained in the shadows and to give it the full dignity of a metapsychological concept. I also try to show that the dynamics of IVH can be understood differently from the way Bion sees it, that is to say, from a field point of view.[5] Instead, my broader goal in revisiting this classic and beautiful essay is to contribute to a finer understanding of the concepts of normal, pathological and reverse projective identification, and bizarre object. Finally, I offer some suggestions for a possible general theory of representation.

The Concept of Linking

First of all, we should clarify what Bion means by "linking". By using the verbal form (five times, including most importantly in the title), he clearly emphasizes not so much *what* linking gives rise to, referred to as a "link" (a word that recurs 30 times in the paper), but the psychic *activity* itself. The essential thing to bear in mind is that linking is mainly – but not, as we shall see, exclusively – an *emotional* function. Bion makes the point that it is "anything which is *felt* to have the *function* of linking one object to another" (308, emphasis added).

However, if we want to grasp the true nature of linking, we must admit that it could never be pure emotionality. There is no emotion or affection that, insofar as it is felt by a subject, is not inevitably touched by what makes self-consciousness possible, that is, by abstract thinking. In some cases, one of these two components, the more affective or bodily, may dry up. What AL and all the other essays in *Second Thoughts* try to theorize is the close link that exists between verbal thought, the apparatus of consciousness, image (ideogrammatic thought) and emotion. If this link is not grasped, it becomes difficult to understand why attacking on linking harms the ability to express oneself.

If it were not so, for Bion it would not make sense to say that in the psychotic part of the personality such links are, so to speak, consumed and appear to be "logical, almost mathematical, but never emotionally reasonable" (315). We can think of these frayed ties as having lost their emotional quality and having been reduced to abstract threads that still connect, but in a cold, mechanical way. But links that are impoverished of the qualities that make empathic communication between subjects possible can only give rise to reciprocal relationships of domination or imposition. They are "perverse, cruel, and sterile", Bion adds (315).

Emotion continually orients us in our existence. It expresses a constant tendency towards or away from an object. It goes without saying that the more intact – in other words, affectively *positive* – the bond is, the more effective is the ability of the conjoined terms to communicate via (normal) projective identification, and to be creative and mutually curious. If this function is lost, life itself becomes empty. In linking, two threads are intertwined: logical-linguistic and emotional-affective. In the subject, the two threads have different colours and are distinguishable, but their interweaving cannot be unravelled. Theirs is a relationship of co-implication. Both are necessary for self-consciousness and the feeling of existing. In psychic suffering, it is the affective thread that frays, the one factor of the linking function that comes powerfully into play in the most intimate relationships. For this reason, psychoanalysis deals primarily with this area. For the same reason, it has the problem of developing tools to influence the emotional life of patients, which obviously does not allow direct ways – to paraphrase Bion, does not allow logical or mathematical or just informational ways.

The term "linking" can look back on a long history. When we look at Bion's choice of noun and verb, which turns out to be particularly felicitous, it is easy to think that various ideas borrowed not only, as I said, from Klein, but also from Freud have played a part. In general, in his use of the German word *Bindung*, translated in the Standard Edition not as link but as "tie", Freud means an emotional, affective, libidinal, erotic bond or investment, essentially a "love relationship", or aim-inhibited sexual impulses. He often uses this word in *Group Psychology and the Analysis of the Ego*, an essay that could be read as if everything that is said about masses describes the inner group that constitutes the ego – i.e. as referring also to the separate subject.

According to Freud, the bonds that hold various individuals together to form a mass loosen as the result of a deep sense of fear that ends up generating panic. At that point, the mass falls apart. Should the ties hold, however, the mass lives a psychic life of its own. Bion disagrees with Freud on this point. In his view, the panicked group does not lose its cohesion, and panic is a manifestation of the fight/flight basic assumption. I suspect that they are referring to different stages of the process of the dissolution of the group – first regressing to a mass and then heading towards total fragmentation.

Such disagreement, though, is of no importance to our discussion. What matters here is the role assigned in theory to the concept of linking. Moreover, in illustrating Le Bon's thesis on the psychology of the crowd, Freud (1921, 78) takes up the idea, seemingly in its entirety, according to which the group

> is extraordinarily credulous and open to influence, it has no critical faculty, and the improbable does not exist for it. It thinks in images, which call one another up by association (just as they arise with individuals in states of free imagination).

What Freud gives us, therefore – to put it in Bion's terminology – is a new definitory hypothesis, namely the idea of a constant configuration that contains recurring features; in our case: an "image" as the bond that holds individuals together in a mass; a kind of "regressive" or "inferior" thinking (as it belongs to a lesser-abstract level) that is typical of this formation; and finally, a feeling of fear or terror that is a factor in both constructing the link and then, if it gets excessive, destroying it. For the purposes of elucidating our topic, we deduce from Freud's the view that when the *links* that hold the mass together dissolve, the *images* that allow it to "think" also disappear. This seems an anticipation of the concept of IVH.

In *Experiences in Groups*, Bion deals with Freud's essay at some length. It is probably the text from which he takes the series of elements mentioned above – in other words, the relationship between link, emotion, and image – before reassembling them in a personal synthesis. Transposing this model into the context of individual analysis, Bion identifies the factor that causes the attack on linking as the awakening of an intolerable feeling of envy in the patient due to innate and environmental factors.

For Bion, IVH describes an act of violent separation, fragmentation, or splitting of an image coupled with a certain quota of affect – otherwise, why would it have a visual character? However, when reading AL, we can easily get confused, as Bion uses the term *link* to indicate both the function and the objects that from time to time represent its factors. The issue becomes a little clearer if we think that attacking what connects two objects, ultimately, also means attacking the object. Bion variously indicates what is attacked and therefore represents the "link", as interpretation; oneiric or hallucinatory image; perceptive or psychic apparatus as a whole or one of its single functions (consciousness, attention, memory, judgement); the part of the personality that generates an awareness of external and internal reality; the ego; thought; the parental couple; and the relationship between internal objects, analyst and patient, infant and breast, sense impressions and consciousness or verbal thought. So, the attack can simultaneously refer to the intra- or interpsychic domain, and to the activity of representing, or to representation-as-content. In general, the focus is more on *function* than *content*. What properly binds is not so much the image but the underlying emotion. We can see in this an overturning of the centrality that Freud assigns to representation.

If we now ask ourselves what the types of linking we have listed have in common, we can answer that they all convey the idea that sense and meaning are social constructs. Indeed, again, they all presuppose *self-awareness*, which is based on the ability of the human subject to think, and ultimately, on language and concepts. As

Heidegger, in his typically icastic style, emphasizes, "Only when man speaks, does he think – not the other way around, as metaphysics still believes" (1954, 16). And later he states again in a very surprising manner that "receiving-perceiving is always language and jointly a saying of words" (1987, 200). For images to link beta-elements (raw sensory elements), they need to be "seen" by a *human* subject. In his own way, between the lines, Bion reiterates the constraint that binds image to language as a social product. In order to grasp the dual or hybrid nature of *link* (and *linking*), it is important to implicate the role of language.

Semiotic/implicit and semantic/explicit meaning are nothing other than emotional resonances poured into the "moulds" of language, networks of sensory-affective links in the guise of "touching images" or "transfigured emotions". Transforming information that reaches the body into the form of proto-emotional and proto-sensory stimuli involves simplification and generalization: meaning is that which is common to several objects, the result of a process of abstraction,[6] therefore becoming available for communication. Basically, linking means to abstract, as in symbol formation ("the ability to bring together two objects so that their resemblance is made manifest" [50]). In itself, any process of abstraction implies uniting on the basis of relations of similarity while disregarding differences. It happens in language, and Bion is well aware that consciousness is closely related to verbal thought. But it happens also by emotional attunement. The two modalities are distinct but not separate. There is a circular relationship between them.

Proto-sensoriality sediments mainly in image-bound links that are, however, not only visual. Their characteristic is that, before approaching a high level of closure in concepts and words – a quality that can never be absolute, because of the role played by verbal signifier – they are still quite ambiguous or *open* to a multiplicity of interpretations. Images are, so to speak, more "models" than "theories" of experience. So, even if Bion's concept of IVH assigns centrality to image, in the subject, image is always intertwined with affect and thought. It is true that the affective component of the bond is much more powerful than the merely logical one in defining the degree of intimacy of the relationship.

Knives and Daggers

In the first vignette recounted in AL, the patient, on a strictly cognitive level, accepts the interpretation given by the analyst. However, he immediately begins to stutter and emits sounds that give Bion the impression of "gurgling", as if he were underwater and about to drown. This happens in response to an intervention in which Bion emphasizes to the patient his mother's ability to cope with the "refractory child" he had been and, reciprocally, his love for her. The passage reminds me of a comparable case of a patient, who, in response to a similar observation on my part, said angrily "But you are my analyst and not my mother's!" We get the impression that Bion forced his truth on the patient and that the latter did not have the capacity to accept and integrate it. The visible result is the signs of fragmentation of the psychic container registered at a bodily level (stuttering and gasping as if drowning).

In the second vignette, "stuttering" as a crisis of bodily identity – what Bleger (1967) calls an "institutional" or "psychotic" layer of identity – "symptomatically" recurs in the expression "disjointed remarks" close to the beginning of the section. The adjective "disjointed" means something like "scattered" and reminds us of the moment at the end of Act I in *Hamlet* when the unhappy prince tells Horatio and Marcellus that "The time is out of joint". This is not a superficial association. It is impossible not to recall the compelling commentary that Derrida dedicates to this phrase in his *Specters of Marx* (1993a), which revolves around the theme of the non-absolute origin of temporality, but rather of its dependence on personal history. The fact that time (but also the temporality intrinsic to speech and to writing as a condition *sine qua non* of meaning) can leave its hinges and be out of order means that there has to be a device that has the positive function of hinging it. The association helps us understand that IVH also reflects the crisis of the matricial structure of the sense of time that the infant achieves in the primary relationship (Civitarese 2019c; Civitarese and Berrini 2022a, 2022b).

The patient complains that he cannot sleep. Bion interprets that he is afraid of the visions he might have if he dreamed. The patient disagrees and explains that he cannot dream because he feels "wet". Bion says to him that this is the same term he had previously used to express contempt for weak and sentimental people. It sounds like a transference interpretation. More precisely, Bion tells the patient that he is refusing the interpretation as a way of devaluing the analyst. Again, the patient disagrees. If we take a different listening stance, when he rejects the interpretation about fear of dreaming and says he is wet, we might also think that it amounts to saying that the analyst cannot expect a little baby to be able to do things bigger than him. However, Bion insists in his attitude of wanting to grasp some truth *about* the patient and links the word "wet" to expressions of contempt he has already heard him express about other people.

Bion reflects, though, that the objection may be correct, in the sense that, in the context, the adjective "wet" does not seem to be a way of expressing anything negative directed against another person (i.e. in the transference, against him) but conveys the state the patient would be in if he allowed himself to dream – actually, a very painful state of non-dreaming. Still, soon after this, he returns to a suspicious way of listening, linking the state of being "wet" to hatred and envy, such as the patient associated "with urinary attacks on an object" (309). In short, the idea that it is the patient who makes destructive attacks against the object (the analyst) resurfaces. Bion tells the patient that he is afraid to sleep because for him it would have been "as the oozing away of his mind itself" (309) – in other words, feeling wet. Indeed, expressed in this way, the interpretation no longer has a certain flavour of judgement.

However, this is simply the other side of the coin of the "attack", in other words, its consequence. Bion's line of thought becomes clearer when he adds that further associations convinced him that the patient was minutely breaking up all his "good interpretations" and that these became like "mental urine which then seeped uncontrollably away" (309). Clearly, he connects "urine" with "wet". At this point, Bion feels like telling the patient that for him to sleep meant falling into a state of "unconsciousness" or "mindlessness". The patient seems to respond positively and says that he now feels "dry". We have the impression of witnessing a dialogue between the deaf. Bion seems intent on following his agenda and adopts the usual antagonistic style of conducting the analysis. Basically, he interprets to the patient that there are things he cannot afford to see, while at the same time forcing him to see these things. Then, when the patient objects, he concludes it is because of envy.

In the third of the five vignettes in AL, interpretation, related in some way to the feeling of exclusion the patient experiences after the weekend break, centres on sexual intercourse between two people.

Nothing is more classic than the concept of the "primary scene". The patient, Bion observes, reacts *"as if he had received a violent blow"* (309, emphasis added). He surmises that the "shock" is the patient's answer to interpretation but soon sets this idea aside and describes it as coming from within, or more precisely as a "kind of a stabbing attack" (309).

Like Oedipus, the patient blinds himself in order to avoid facing up to a reality that frightens him. In this way, Bion calls himself out of this event, or rather he sees himself as only very tangentially involved. This is quite surprising. From the inside or from the outside here would make no difference – as if we could ever distinguish whether something comes completely from the inside or the outside. While remaining within a Kleinian framework, Bion's explanation is unprecedented in two ways. First, it is previously unheard of; second, from what *he* has seen, he deduces that the patient, who told him "he could not see what he saw", "*felt* he was 'seeing' an invisible object", or was experiencing an IVH. As I said before, an odd concept.[7] The experience of *déjà vu* comes to mind. The subject has the vague sensation of reliving a past scene but without being able to remember it. The experience is remembered in the feeling but no longer has a sensory vividness. It has become elusive or "invisible".

Curiously enough, having made this challenging assertion, Bion omits to give an explanation, or rather delays giving it ("I shall give my reasons later for supposing that in this and the previous example similar mechanisms were at work"; 309). So, he makes the reader live the same experience he is describing: a kind of invisible hallucination of a theoretical concept. At the other extreme, the exceptional clarity of the image of the stabbing attack is striking. Ultimately, in our view, he is illustrating how the patient "stabbed" his interpretation of sexual intercourse as the symbolic matrix of any link connecting two objects together.

I repeat, Bion himself rejects any *direct* responsibility. The "culprit" is the patient's envy. One of the strengths of the article lies in the illustration of the connection between the unwillingness of the object (as being only a "dutiful response"; 295) to take charge of the child's anguish and the hyperbolic growth of the anguish. Bion, however, sees this only as the historical cause of the development of excessive envy in the patient. Yet, from a different angle, it is Bion, like the analyst who "stabbed" the patient, who is the one who escapes responsibility; or, rather, from a "field" point of view, that is, considering that any fact of the analysis may be thought of as unconsciously co-determined, we could say that as they are both scared and aggressive or that their emotional linking is one in which they are actually "stabbing" each other.

As we saw, Bion thinks that the patient does not accept any of the good things he gives him. On careful reading, however, the text allows a different view. What may seem "good" to the analyst is not necessarily also good for the patient. The catastrophic outcome could be due not to the patient's envy but to lack of at-one-ment. On another level, we might also speculate that the analyst himself is "envious" of the possibility of accuracy possessed by natural sciences. This might prompt him to adopt a certain attitude and to tell the patient "at any cost" what he believes to be the truth (Civitarese 2021a) as a way of stimulating transformations in minus K (through *Knowledge*) over transformations in O (through experience).

In the fourth vignette, Bion again calls attention to how things can be "isolated" (separated, fragmented or split up) – in this case, a few observations made by the patient, which resonate with the "disjointed remarks" and the "very pronounced stammer" of the previous examples – so that they are no longer "significant". In the essay entitled "On Hallucination" (1958b, 342), Bion had already clarified that he uses "dissociation" to indicate a "more benign" division or separation into parts that can be recomposed, and "splitting" to indicate the malignant case where fragments are so minute that this possibility is excluded.

At some point, the patient speaks of a girl who seemed sympathetic. If we read this communication in terms of transference or of field, it would seem to indicate that the emotional "weather" of the session is taking a turn for the better. However, there immediately follows a "stabbing attack" as in the other vignette, at which point the patient sees a "blue haze" (a visual datum) in the room. Later the mist clears, yet the patient admits to feeling depressed. Bion thinks that there has been an oscillation from the schizo-paranoid to the depressive position, takes a positive view of the insight, and tells the patient that he had felt understood. Then he adds, as he does regularly, that the patient is capable only of destroying this pleasant experience. Bion says that when he pointed out to him the body movement corresponding to the "stabbing", the patient ignored him. For Bion, this meant that the patient had split the experience of feeling understood by the analyst and had then converted it in an image (presumably a horrible one) and ejected it in the form of "particles of sexual abuse" (309). Except that, in his own story, to our eyes, once again *Bion* is the one who seems to destroy it, not the patient. It is the analyst who says that for the patient, the word "blue" was associated with a "vituperative sexual conversation" (309).

The rhetorical power of the vignette is remarkable. On the one hand, Bion weaves us a brilliant and evocative narrative; on the other, he seems to need reassurance about the excellence and effectiveness of his work. We note expressions such as *understanding*, *understood* (three times), *correct* (twice), and *approximated closely* – the latter two both referring to interpretation. In the commentary to his article a few years later in *Second Thoughts*, Bion admits that his mistake may have been to resort to causalistic explanations in order to find his own peace of mind ("The discovery of a 'cause' relates more to the peace of mind of the discoverer than to the object of his research"; 1967, 163). The insight is important for understanding why, according to him, the analyst should listen without memory, desire, and understanding. This enigmatic and much misunderstood formula simply means that the analyst should be aware, as Bion says, of the "fallacious nature of reasoning based on the idea of 'causes'" (1967, 163).

In this regard, there is another pearl in AL. Bion complains of the criticism that was often levelled at him that by placing "too much stress ... on the transference to the exclusion of a proper elucidation of early memories" (1967, 104) he would neglect historical truth. Nothing new under the sun. It is surprising to note that this is the same criticism that is monotonously, and in a sense idly applied to Bionian field theory. However, even in the commentary, Bion still places the responsibility for the attack on linking on the patient's active stimulation of the analyst's memory and desire. Such an induction has precisely the effect of preventing the analyst from keeping himself in a situation of doubt. Let us keep in mind that, for Bion, the medium for a relationship of mutual growth is precisely "tolerated doubt" (1962b, 92).

The fifth vignette begins with the image of a patient again uttering some apparently *disconnected* sentences. We could see these as signals of the emotional climate of the session (as in the case of the "understanding girl" or the "blue haze"; 310). Bion, for his part, seems to read them as the patient's attempt to maintain some faint contact with reality and thus to contain what he feels is the fear of a psychic collapse ("he feared a breakdown"; 309). The patient comments that Bion has not understood him – and frankly he has every reason to do so. To put it in Bion's own words, the patient is really behaving with him as his "best colleague" (1980). In response, Bion interprets that the patient must see the analyst as a bad object and for this reason is unwilling to accept what he gives him. He also recalls that since the last session he has had the impression that the patient was thinking that the analyst was busy shielding himself from his projective identifications.

Showing a fine feeling for irony, the patient responds that there are "two probability clouds" (309) in the room. The two terms in the expression seem to reinforce each other – as if to say, to put it in the language of physics, that one cannot know what position the atom (i.e. metaphorically, each one of them) occupies on a certain trajectory (relation). Bion interprets "probability" as the patient's painful speculation about the *real* qualities of the object: whether the wickedness is real or only projected. Nevertheless, one of his comments points us towards an alternative reading: "*Whether my refusal to understand was a reality or hallucination* was important only because it determined what painful experiences were to be expected next" (309, emphasis added). Of course, as Bion himself conjectures, one possible way of seeing this is as an actual refusal/incapacity to accept the patient's anxiety transmitted via projective identifications.

A quick note. The whole article evinces two striking features: on the one hand, the frequent use of weather-related lexis ("probability clouds", "it was hot", the "blue haze" ...); on the other, the use of time-related vocabulary: the patient's stammering spreads out his speech "over a period of as much as a minute and a half" (308); talk that "occupied thirty minutes" (309); the idea of a sleepless vigil suggesting the image of frozen time, not marked by the usual sleep-wake rhythms; the mention of the "week-end break"; the lightning-fast temporality embodied in the "blows" of a knife or a dagger; the "isolated" observations in the "first twenty minutes of the session"; the instantaneousness and violence of the destructive attacks on links; the sudden, almost audible acoustic interruption caused by the noise made by a "piece of iron" falling on the floor.

We have now reached the sixth and last clinical vignette. The patient *obscurely* announces "that a piece of iron had fallen on the

75

floor" (309). Then, he shows the usual *convulsive movements*, as if he were being attacked and physically hurt from within. Bion suggests that the patient cannot get in touch with the analyst because he is afraid of what is happening inside him. The patient confirms that he feels he is being murdered. Again, Bion interprets his envy, which, he says, manifests itself in the act of taking the pair inside himself in order to kill their creativity and make them just a "dead piece of iron" and a "dead floor". At this point, the patient becomes "very anxious" (which is not surprising). Bion interprets that the patient is unable to go on because he feels "either dead, or alive" (310). In essence, once again Bion makes the patient aware of how he always destroys everything good that touches him and above all everything good that the analyst offers him.

We understand that if Bion acts in this way it is because he thinks that treatment means making the patient as aware as possible of his condition. From today's perspective of our general and shared greater sensitivity to the concept of the analyst's subjectivity, evidenced by the great expansion of the relational paradigm in psychoanalysis, it is easy for us to see the flaws in this way of working. There seems to be insufficient room for reflection on the role played by the analyst's unconscious participation in the analytic process. In this context, Bion's clarification, at several points in *Second Thoughts*, that he is dealing with the patient's personality and not with the role of the environment ("There is the environment, which I shall not discuss at this time"; 1957, 266), takes on a symptomatic value. Now, "not dealing with the environment" could be viewed as the mark of a certain Kleinian style of interpretation. The part played by the environment is in fact relegated to an archaeology of the psychic constitution of the subject. This concentration on the archaic, the originary, and the primitive ends up inevitably prevailing over the role of the environment (basically, the analyst) in the here and now, to the point where it seems to dissolve almost completely, except as a trigger for almost automatic responses.

It must be said, however, that apart from this kind of "deafness", Bion is accomplished at communicating the particular climate of madness that pervades these sessions. He shows courage in engaging with patients who are very seriously ill, as well as a great sense of dedication to them. Of course, we must not forget that everything should be read from a historical perspective. Actually, as can be said of Freud, Bion himself is among those who have enabled us to see the limits of his predecessors and his own.

Invisible-Visual Hallucinations

So, to ask the question once again: *what does IVH mean?* English usage dictates that the key adjective ("invisible") is put before the noun it refers to "visual hallucinations". The emphasis falls on the fact that these *visual* hallucinations – not tactile or acoustic, for example[8] – are *invisible*. The question is: to whom are they "invisible"? Visual hallucinations are only visible to the person who is experiencing them. An external observer could only intuit their presence. But why should Bion stress such an obvious fact? It would not even make sense if the intended meaning was that the analyst does not realize that the patient is hallucinating, since in this case Bion notices ("sees") that the patient *is* hallucinating. So, if he does stress that these visual hallucinations are not visible, we have to think that it is because their *invisibility* regards the subject himself who is having them.

But how does one see (hallucinate) something one is *not* seeing? A possible answer to this question is that the patient is having a kind of pseudo-hallucination. It appears to be a hallucination but lacks the vivid sensory component that usually accompanies such an event. Nonetheless, it remains illusory for what concerns its other components, since by definition hallucination involves perceiving an object that is not there to be perceived. In this case, the *experience* (actually, only the residual fragments of a non-experience, or what the non-psychotic parts of the personality are witnessing) would only be *like* hallucinating. As usual, there would be no *real* object to perceive, not even an illusory object according to the meaning we normally give to this adjective – that is, something springing from the phantasmagoria of the inner world. If in "normal" hallucination the object to be perceived externally is not there, but *is* there only as the projection of an unconscious representation that retains all its sensory vividness, here even this possibility seems to be missing. In the case of IVH, logically speaking, it can only be a non-perceiving of an object, i.e. *neither* an external object in the absence of a (real) object to be perceived, *nor* an internal unconscious object displayed as a phantasy. We are left with the sole hypothesis that a radical split between hallucinated image and affect takes place in which only the latter, imbued with an extraordinarily persecutory quality, is *felt* as a kind of implosion from within, a dramatic feeling that something has failed without knowing what it is.[9]

What remains there – to draw on the terminology introduced by Bion in *Transformations* (1965, 79) – is not a *no-breast* or *no-thing* (the trace of an object that is absent), but only "nameless dread". There is only a *minus-object* or a *nothing* (*noughtness*). The patient shows the attitude of someone who seems absorbed in a vision or is having some sort of seizure. Suffering the collapse of psychic space, he feels that he is being sucked into a void of undifferentiation. If we understand it as static, the notion of IVH is contradictory (an imageless image). To make it more intelligible, we need to see it as an indication of a process that takes place in two stages: (a) a terrifying hallucinatory image is created, triggered by a frightening stimulus and (b) it becomes "invisible" as it is *instantly* shattered and evacuated – it is as if it had *never appeared* to the subject.

A visual hallucination is generated – for example, the hallucination of being sexually attacked by someone – but the sight is so daunting that the image is erased by a lightning-quick process of fragmentation: as if something depicted on an A4 sheet of paper were shredded into a thousand pieces and then scattered in the air by a gust of wind. Bion's approach is to use the image of urine. The pieces of IVH drip away like "mental urine". Because urine is in a liquid state, the molecules cannot be seen with the naked eye when they disperse, and in any case, they flow over each other and lose their original shape. With this mental urine, the same ability to represent, a kind of "gluing" the liquid molecules to each other, also "drips away".

Bion seems to have taken the image from the speech of a patient he reports on in his essay on the theory of schizophrenia. This patient complained that very bad tears came from his ears, sweat from the holes in his skin, and that urine came "from the hole that was left in a person when his penis had been torn out" (1954, 116). His discourse was made of "a completely chaotic series of words and noises" (1954, 116). Bion interprets to the patient that this "flow of destroyed language" (1954, 116) was the consequence of the attacks perpetrated by a bad and hostile object inside. It was tearing apart their "verbal intercourse" in the same way the patient felt that in the past, he had torn apart the verbal and sexual intercourse between the parents. Outside of AL, the only other mention of IVH can be found in *Cogitations*. Bion (1992) speaks of it as the extreme point that the (self-)evacuatory process of the psyche can reach. First come transformations into "pictorial images" (1992, 79). Then, through "splitting attacks on the superego, common sense" (1992, 31) or "splitting attacks on the depressive position" (1992, 102), these images are fragmented "into very small pieces", which remain "undigested" and not suitable for coalescing into larger aggregates. As they have not been made "fit for storage" and are therefore not "memories proper" (1992, 102), they are ejected "by the eyes to a great distance", giving rise to "bizarre, hallucinatory objects" (1992, 79).

The patient's capacity to form visual images is thus impeded. As a result, he is no longer able to memorize the experience or use it either "in unconscious waking thought, or in dream-thought" (136). Here, Bion uses remarkable images: the toothed psyche, or the typewriter that works backwards, absorbs sounds-words, crushes them and reduces them into images of letters of the alphabet, and then evacuates them through the eyes. All these descriptions fit in well with his earlier clinical observations of disconnected speech patterns, stuttering, and convulsive body movements.

If we are to reach a deeper understanding of IVH, we need to do more than read AL. All the essays in *Second Thoughts* seem to refer to the same patients and the same clinical fragments and also to develop the same theoretical points. For example, Bion also mentions in other essays of the book the same body movements in the patient he describes in AL, and which for an external observer represent the only "visible" aspect of IVH. For instance: "convulsive jerks" (1957, 272), "a sudden convulsion" (while the patient exclaims "Brilliant interpretation. O God!"; 1957, 273), "a shudder of his head and shoulders which is so slight and so rapid that I might suppose myself mistaken" (1958b, 341), "jerky convulsive movements which were confined mostly to the upper part of his body. Each syllable that I uttered seemed to be felt by him as a stabbing thrust from me" (1958b, 343), "convulsive twitchings of his chest" (1958b, 343), a "muscular action" which in fact is an "actual murderous assault" (1958b, 348), etc. As is often the case, Bion is guided here by a concept of Freud's, precisely, by his description of "motor activity, before the establishment of the reality principle, as not directed to alteration of the environment but to an unburdening of 'the mental apparatus of accretions of stimuli'" (1958b, 346).

A further point this essay makes that is worth mentioning is the idea that intrinsic to projective identification is the psychotic individual's unconscious conviction that they can use sense organs as "two-way" (1958b, 349) channels or as if they were long arms that could grasp and store or violently throw away certain psychic contents – and also parts of the personality and the "capacity for judgement" itself (1958b, 347). Bion also states that seeing the senses as capable of expelling psychic content in this way makes it easier to diagnose hallucinatory processes than it is with traditional semiotics.

The picture he paints is quite graphic. In describing "an ideo-motor activity" (1958b, 348), Bion strives to keep to the concept of the proto-mental system (1961, 102) and not to separate out the psychic from the corporeal. The thrill or convulsive movements in the body are, as it were, ways of enabling the violent expulsion to be visualized. It is only after the expulsion and the shaping of bizarre objects that the *true* visual hallucination (and not only "invisible", since it was immediately aborted) would begin. IVH would then be nothing but the first stage of the process, or, more precisely, the second sub-step of the first stage, i.e. the dreadful sensation of fading into *nothingness* produced by the bleeding of the self that follows the destruction of hallucination. This is the precise instant in which the "mental urine" is felt to flow away and the subject feels that they are falling into a "void and formless infinite" (Milton, cited in Bion 1965, 151).

Bion's vignette, however, is open to another reading. Rather than thinking that an initial hallucination forms and then explodes, the description urges us more to think of the influx of sensory impressions that the patient is unable to transform ("dread of imminent annihilation;" 1975, 266) and that leave him in "a state that is neither life nor death" (1957, 266). IVH then comes to resemble more what results from an explosion of proto-sensoriality that sweeps away the first barrier represented by the image and fragments it as soon as it forms or has already done so during the process of forming it. Drones armed with missiles destroy the dream screen of negative hallucinations (see below), the "canvas" that normally "supports" the representation, and not so much a representation rendered on the canvas. The image would be invisible in the sense of not yet visible.

By analogy, let us imagine seeing the various features that make up the Gestalt image of a face, but arranged in a confusing way. We would see each individual element but not the face. Now, by itself, the concept of splitting does not contain all these references to the nature and role of image in thinking. It does not give us a glimpse of the dramatic tension that at some point arises between the drive to represent and the drive to destroy.

Therefore, our understanding is that the adjective "invisible" is not in any banal sense synonymous with "unconscious" – what then would be the difference from any other pictogram of waking dream thought? – but instead translates the effect of psychic trauma: *invisible* as *unable* to be made visible. It is also "unconsciously" invisible. The point of calling it IVH would be to underline the *impediment* (or early failure) to moulding an image. So, the question becomes: is the destruction of the image that normally acts as a link (actually the indivisible conglomerate of image, emotion and concept) the "direct" traumatic effect of the emotional tsunami, as it would be if one were actually stabbed, or is it a barrier that opposes it?

Bion's description offers no easy answer. Essentially, he seems to lean towards the second hypothesis. He talks about splitting and projective identification and points out that the patient uses the tiny fragments resulting from the destruction of the image to attack the analyst – directing, as it were, a stream of "mental urine" at him. But maybe it is both. If I deflect the blade of a hypothetical aggressor with my arm, the gesture has a defensive meaning. However, indirectly I force myself to suffer a trauma, albeit a less dangerous one. Or if I am forced to look at the sun, I see its image but I burn my retina. *IVH involves the simultaneous destruction of both the content and the container, both the canvas and the capacity to paint.* It is like vomiting. You vomit not only food but also the electrolytes that are needed for the proper functioning of the digestive system.

As I understand Bion's teaching, and, as it were, updating it, IVH is the wound produced by the trauma, while the formation of bizarre objects is defence in the proper sense of the word. The hallucinatory neo-proliferation, like a kind of keloid that hinders the functionality of wounded skin, does, however, restore shape to experience, albeit at the very limits of consensuality. It symbolically expresses a request and demands a response from the other. At the same time, above all, it secures the subject a new safety distance from the object and installs a filter against future "aggressions".

This theoretical perspective is more congruent with a reading that is not strictly Kleinian of what happens between Bion and his patient. From the point of view of object relations theory, we would be entitled to think that the analyst has inflicted a wound on the patient by means of interpretation. In radically intersubjective or field terms, we would read the narrative of the session as reflecting an unconscious (symmetrical) emotional functioning of a couple or small group in which "each is attacking the other" – although role assignment dictates then that the analyst should consciously take charge of it.

Bizarre Objects

Bion characterizes the non-psychotic part of the personality as the one that uses repression as the main defence and is capable of projection and introjection. Instead, the psychotic part is capable only of projective identification. When he comes to say that there is also a normal projective identification, he somehow puts aside the mechanism of repression, and the difference between the normal and the pathological part of the personality comes to lie only in the balance or imbalance between projective and introjective identification. Pathological projective identification is the sum of massive projections and a failure to introject. The material it makes available to the non-psychotic part of the personality is confused. Thought and therefore the ability to stay in contact with reality are affected.

The "particles of ego" (or, perhaps better, of proto- or bodily ego) of personality (1957, 268) are discharged outside with violence ("sadistic splitting eviscerating attacks"; 1957, 268), and what true hallucinatory activity shows at this point is that, in order to repair the cruel splitting that has occurred in the ego, they are glued to concrete objects, covering them completely. In the end they "swallow them up" – but also, as Bion writes, it is as if they have inserted themselves into them. Such strange agglomerates arise from the rather unsuccessful attempt to bring together internal and external perceptions and abstract meaning.

Bion's description of how the "mental urine" ends up in concrete objects to form bizarre objects is inspiring. It emphasizes the fact that at the origin of the process, there was a certain "concreteness" of the object-as-other, or rather their unavailability to take on the projective identifications of the subject, *before* the IVH was produced. So the bizarre object, even when it concerns not a person but a concrete object, is not really a material object but the symbolization of an object-as-other incapable of reverie.

Then, What Happens?

After a massive activity of projective identification, the personality is dramatically impoverished. The risk, if the process continued, would be that of losing the ability to represent altogether. So, to try to restore the capacity to bind, it needs to take back some of the fragments of ego scattered around and encysted both in concrete objects and in people. But this can only happen through a process of *reverse projective identification*. It goes without saying that the reabsorbed fragments are loaded with anger for having been expelled before. They continue to possess characteristics peculiar to the bizarre object, i.e. they are incapable of binding together in any meaningful way. Thus, it is not a matter of true introjection, assimilation, reunion, or integration. It is a reintrojection that itself has the character of a violent attack. It would be like swallowing pieces of plastic or metal (as some schizophrenics do), which therefore cannot be part of a new synthesis. What is introjected remains as a foreign body.

That is why, when the fragments are piled up, the only way they can bind together is still only by compression – as would be the case for a number of Lego bricks held together in a container but which, lacking real connecting studs, could only give rise to shapeless conglomerates. Having already expelled it, the capacity to link remains in a degraded form: "it can compress but cannot connect, it can fuse but cannot articulate" (1957, 270). At this point, reverse projective identification is like gorging oneself, as a way of controlling the void one feels inside but then ending up vomiting again.

The so-called bizarre object forms something, an internal object (of course, it was *always* internal as part of an omnipotent phantasy) that is not structured. Instead, it is a mass that in turn presses on the personality and somehow holds it together, encapsulating it in "extremely painful tactile, auditory, and visual hallucinations" (1957, 275); ultimately, in a sort of orthopaedic cast or envelope, or like staunching a haemorrhagic wound with a piece of cloth as opposed to surgical suturing. In a sense, bizarre objects, as it were, exact their revenge for the imprisonment to which they have been subjected. As Bion writes, "The object, angered at being engulfed, swells up, so to speak, and suffuses and controls the piece of personality that engulfs it" (1957, 268). In this way, it makes the particle of personality similar to itself, a *thing*. It is still a way of uniting but one that generates relationships without emotional resonance and therefore devoid of life. We see this clearly in the six vignettes of AL. In the psychotic person, this regressive process goes so far as to destroy the links between letters, syllables, and words. In the neurotic individual, it is limited to preserving logical or merely cognitive links at the expense of affective ones. The neurotic individual has their own way of thinking in a concrete way, but without losing the symbolic links of abstract type. Halfway between the two are psychotic patients who look neurotic but function using massive transformations in hallucinosis (Bion 1965).

We see how Bion brilliantly draws on his mythopoeic capacity to portray the knife-edge struggle between the construction and the destruction of linking. His description of the formation of the bizarre object is stunning in showing how the subject defends themself from pain by dehumanizing themself, i.e. through a kind of partial fusion with the world of matter. The subject is no longer able to make real introjections: *this is where the real block of thinking is produced*. They cannot partially break down the alterity (the *non-me*) that they have taken inside in order to recompose it with the *me*. The object of the introjection, which for this reason is a pseudo-introjection, remains *unchanged*. In fact, the similarity-based exchange mechanism that generally makes metaphor and symbolization possible is locked down. Only symbolic equations (Segal 1957) are possible. Compared with the simple hole in the fabric of meaning, these symbolizations are, yes, pseudo-symbolizations, i.e. equations, but as their name implies, they still retain something related to the area of the symbolic.

In other words, compared with IVH (the tear in the canvas or pure beta-elements), bizarre objects are a kind of beta-screen, a way station to actual symbolization, beta-elements that are not isolated but organized at some rudimentary level. Let us not forget that "the capacity for non-verbal communication" depends on beta-elements: "they are essential to the functioning of projective identification" (Bion 1992, 181–183). Bion advances the hypothesis that "dream-work-α operates on β-elements and not directly on sense data" (1992, 183). This means that "knowledge" is based on the creation of both alpha- and beta-elements. In the first case, it is based on visual-rational thinking, in the second on non-verbal communication (from a metapsychological point of view, on projective identification). Logically, one should postulate a beta-function as responsible for transforming sense data into beta-elements.

Unlike beta-elements, which in isolation do not have the capacity to bind together – as I said, like Lego bricks without studs – the beta-screen has a confused coherence of its own. Although it represents "a rigid traumatic organization" (Brown 2005, 400; see also Bronstein 2015), it has a peculiar "capacity for evoking emotions in the analyst; ... [they] are less related to his need for psycho-analytic interpretation than to his need to produce an emotional involvement" (Bion 1962b, 24). Thus, in the formation of bizarre objects, we see not a simple regression of the contact barrier to the state of dispersed beta-elements, but to beta-elements that preserve a "tincture of the personality adhering to them" (1962b, 25) and are the result of the stripping away of meaning to which the alpha-elements have been subjected.

Bizarre objects are hybrid formations in which hallucination is encysted in objects concretely existing in space or, vice versa, in which it incorporates fragments of reality. Persecution is not as severe as it was during the phase when the catastrophe was still active, and it is *bearable* yet still very intense. The subject attempts to put back together the fragments of the broken mirror, to restore a basic function of representation or hallucinatory capacity. They live in a reality akin to a civilization that has been through a catastrophe. Some remains are intact, others have been pulverized, as in a post-apocalyptic scenario – for example, McCarthy's *The* Road (2006). Micro-communities of human beings try to survive but in a state of extreme regression. As in any of such dystopian fictions, the essential question is that posed by the child in the novel, who, after losing his father, asks the stranger he meets along the road if he can *trust* him.

As Bion has made permeable the caesura between the psychotic and non-psychotic parts of the personality and between normal and pathological projective identification, from the perspective of a theory of symbolization, bizarre objects can also be seen as expressions of both pathology and normality. In "Development of Schizophrenic Thought", the 1956 essay reprinted as the third chapter of *Second Thoughts*, Bion explains that particles of ego (apparatus of consciousness) fragmented, expelled, and encompassed or encompassing external objects are "prototypes of ideas-later to become words" (40), and also that the compressed core of expelled and subsequently reintroduced bits of ego, although not suitable for verbal thought, is nevertheless appropriate for musical language ("is more appropriate to music"; 43), i.e. non-verbal communication.

After all, the relationship between sign and designated, symbol and symbolized, word and thing *is* bizarre. Bizarreness stays in the lack of a notion of truth based on metaphysical correspondence between words and things. And the only way that remains to the human subject in order not to sink into the abyss of the absence of meaning is the network of sociality. In short, we discover that McCarthy's novel is an allegory of life. The apocalypse is always already here. The difference between symbolic equation and true symbolization depends on the ability to introject, and this is based on mutual trust.

Schizophrenic Dreaming

Now that we are somewhat more familiar with the concepts of IVH and bizarre object, if we want to further deepen our understanding of it, we must take a longer look at an analogy Bion himself draws between IVH and schizophrenic dreaming. Once the clinical part is complete, Bion finds himself facing the difficult task of explaining what he means by IVH as an event in the analytic session. His way of going about it is to talk about dreams, or rather, about a form of pathological oneiric activity. He says that the examples he gives throw light on schizophrenic dreaming. But it is in fact the other way round. What he should have said is that schizophrenic dreaming throws light on the examples he gives here. In my experience, reading this paragraph was the moment I finally got a sense of what Bion means by the concept of IVH. Let us also consider that describing the same phenomenon in dreaming and in waking, Bion reaffirms his ground-breaking principle of substantial equivalence between dreaming and thinking.

First, he points out the element common to the various vignettes he has just recounted – which, as he states at the beginning, refer indistinctly to two different patients. At all events, there is destruction of meaning which is identified with the "link" (the link *is* the

meaning) and which emerges symptomatically in stuttering, disso-
ciated speech, and insomnia that prevents dreaming. Indeed, since
it is impossible not to dream, the psychotic's insomnia as a "symptom" the patient complains about is merely a way of referring to
the particular *quality* of schizophrenic dreaming – which is not true
dreaming ("insomnia", then, as a metaphor of a given metapsychological functioning), just as stuttering is not the same as speaking
intelligibly.

What is going on? For a long time, these patients have not had (or
rather, have not reported) dreams. When they do report dreams, for
them these dreams stand in relation to the non-dreams of the previous period – dreams that are not told but only "deduced" by the
analyst – in the same way that faeces, which are like solids and have
a certain form, stand in relation to urine, which is liquid and has no
form. Indeed, we are again faced with the problem of describing
something that is not there, that is "a phenomenon analogous to the
invisible-visual hallucination" (310). Not the *same* phenomenon, but
an "analogous" phenomenon.

Bion uses schizophrenic dreaming as a model of AL or
IVH. He speculates that "the dream that is not there" or the
"dream-made-of-urine" is made up of visual hallucinations that are
invisible to the subject who is dreaming; and that, on the other hand,
the dream that can finally be told or the "dream-made-of-faeces"
springs from the experience of having actually dreamt "visual objects". We understand that in the latter case, dreams retain a concrete quality – as long as the subject renders it almost insignificant,
they are not too frightened by the object – whereas in the former it
is as if seeing and destroying ("liquidating" what is seen) were one
and the same act. So it is not that untold dreams have no form or visibility at all. They do, but their material is "so minutely fragmented
as to be devoid of any visible component" (310). It is like IVH is: a
mush of images.

Imagine seeing a wax-smeared tablet on which the ancient Ro-
mans wrote, or a snowman. When exposed to heat, these objects
would lose their shape. We would no longer see anything but accu-
mulations of liquids (a "continuum of minute, invisible fragments";
310). The quality of being "invisible" thus logically refers to the loss
of any meaningful *form*. Or imagine enlarging a digital image until
you see the pixels of which it is composed. You would no longer see
the figure. It is true that we could also picture a fragmentation that,

without having to assume any magical disappearance of matter, is so minute that it is no longer perceptible, as happens, for example, with water that turns into steam.

With IVH the subject may have won a battle but the war continues; or rather, Bion sees it as a war. Yet surely, it could also be the search for contact and a container. The attack itself is perceived by the patient as uncontrollable – just like sleep, which would set off a similarly uncontrollable flow of projective identification – as something that is also an attack against themself; and by the end of the process, they find themself mindless. By attacking the object, they attack themself, since "themself" is their *capacity* for linking with the object.

To the patient, interpretation is equivalent to seeing "the state of mind of the coupling parents" ("the sexual pair" or "the parental couple", "The couple engaged in a creative act" and "felt to be sharing an enviable, emotional experience"; 310–311). The patient's fear is twofold. On one side, they are afraid of destroying the object upon whom they depend if their projective identifications are to be accepted while still maintaining a state of equilibrium; on the other, they are afraid of what arouses the envy that might easily rob them of their reason, that is, that very availability interpreted as greed, and the equilibrium of the object interpreted as a sign of indifference. It is obvious, then, that the attack betrays the presence of the feeling of envy that it is supposed to prevent. It is therefore directed both at the feeling of envy and at the awareness of missing something essential for life that it entails.

Basically, in AL, Bion still uses the concept of linking within the framework of a one-person psychology. He does not yet make it the notion of a common or third unconscious where, for example, the assumption is that there is something, an object, that patient *and* analyst together cannot bear to see. Bion always interprets one way. He sees the patient as the aggressor who systematically attacks the analyst's creativity or capacity to understand; as the one who makes the relationship sterile. Although the environment may have a contributory role to play, underlying everything is the innate factor ("inborn disposition of the infant", "inborn characteristics" or "primary aggression and envy"; 312–313). In doing so, Bion imposes an epistemological-cognitive interpretive grid that is pre-established. To some extent, this scales down his intuition regarding the role of emotion and affect.

This said, Bion brilliantly equates link, meaning (awareness, consciousness), (true) dreaming, and emotion. Even if he does not yet take this intuition to its extreme consequences, he will do so more and more in later essays when he will insist on the concept of O as the basic assumption or unconscious bond of the analytic couple or group of two (Civitarese 2021b). In AL, his discourse already goes beyond the teachings of Klein for the very reason that the concept of linking anticipates that of field,[10] as will be seen in the developments of his thought promoted by Madeleine and Willy Baranger (2008 [1961–1962]) and the other authors who advanced the theory of the analytic field. Linking is inherently dialectical; it generates a dynamic field. Focusing on *linking* between A and B (as *human* beings) paves the way to stop considering A *or* B separately. What connects them is *common* to them. Inevitably, A is seen as made also by non-A or B, and B by non-B or A.

Moreover, we should realize that here Bion is already relying on his redefinition of the unconscious and dreaming, a fact that paves the way to radical changes. The psychotic patient is incapable of dreaming either asleep or awake because they are unable to form genuine (i.e. meaningful) dream-like images and are therefore incapable of waking up the same way one would wake up from a dream or a reverie. It is important to emphasize this connection between the significance of the images of dreams or reveries to the possibility of waking up. The hallmark of any "true" dream is this possibility. Waking up does not depend on something extrinsic to the dream itself but rather on the quality of the work of meaning-creation it carries out. For the same reason, hallucinations in true dreams (those that are followed by an awakening) are not pathological hallucinations but mostly adequate perceptions of the inner landscape of the psyche.

By analogy, under normal conditions and when they are awake, a person is capable of "falling asleep" in response to the irrelevant stimuli that may also reach them, that is to say, they select them, and are capable of *dreaming* or "digesting" sense-data and raw emotional experience. Instead, the psychotic individual is incapable (or at least largely incapable) of performing this same function. For them, many of the stimuli they receive are nothing other than exploding mines that interrupt the channels of communication represented by images.

Usually, we think of dreams as a succession of incongruous, absurd, disconnected images. But this is not the case. We need only reflect on how dreams (like poetry) activate a powerful hermeneutic function in each and every one of us. This is the sign that, in a more or less obscure way, we feel that *there is* meaning in dreams (or reveries). So, dreams made up of IVHs are non-dreams or minus-dreams (–Ds), dreams that do not call for any interpretative function. It is as if we already knew that they represent nothing other than the destruction of meaning, the attack on linking. According to Bion, for these patients, sleep and insomnia were equally unacceptable.

Negative Hallucinations

But could IVH be a negative hallucination? Speaking of hypnosis, Freud (1890) gives the example of the hypnotic injunction *not* to see someone and calls it a negative hallucination. The subject who has been given the order treats a given person in the room "as 'air'". Freud therefore considers negative hallucination a functional phenomenon, which can also be produced experimentally. Elsewhere he notes that negative hallucinations predominate over positive ones, but he does not develop the issue. However, the annotation may have led some to see negative hallucination in general as a precondition for positive hallucination and representational activity.

For example, Green (1997, 1081) speaks of it in terms of "framing structure" and likens it to the transparent sheet that, in Freud's (1925) description of the Mystic Writing-Pad, erases traces – but actually preserves them more deeply – to allow new writings. In negative hallucination, the subject negates the image, makes it disappear, but the image remains and could be retrieved. All that would be needed is to remove the veil that conceals it (after all, it would be a kind of "mild" or physiological repression). This individual does not see an object they should see, but there is no destruction. Consequently, negative hallucination is mainly conceptualized as what furnishes the screen upon which *positive* hallucination can then be projected.

IVH, on the other hand, is like breaking down a painstakingly completed puzzle, destroying the individual pieces and throwing them away. The image (or better yet, the canvas upon which it is depicted) is fragmented, and with it the function of synthesis that corresponds to it. Unlike in negative hallucinations, where the picture cannot be seen because it has been covered with a cloth or because the light has been turned off, in IVH, the image is *no longer* there. Either it could not be formed or it has vanished and left only

90

a void. The experience that the IVH concept tries to capture on an intuitive level is much more similar to the non-experience of "fear of breakdown" as described by Winnicott (1974 [1963]). It produces a trauma that has far-reaching consequences but can never be "lived" or experienced by the individual who suffered from it. If Bion calls this hallucination "invisible", it means that the explosion of the image, and not its mere negativization, corresponds precisely to the description of the attack on linking. My hypothesis, then, is that IVH is not equivalent to negative hallucination – in which a representation would be hidden but would continue to exist and exert its effects – but rather to real "holes" in the psyche, like ulcers in a digestive canal affected by rectocolitis. *If anything, IVH is the destruction of negative hallucination.*

The very terminology used by Bion excludes the possibility that IVH may retain a paradoxical integrity, by either subtraction or disappearance. He clearly speaks of it as "destructive attacks" and "destruction" of the link (the word "attack" recurs 40 times, and "destructive" or "destroy" 23 times). As always in his writings, the war metaphor leaves little doubt as to its interpretation: in this case, the fate of IVH is total annihilation. What strikes us as surprising is the equation *destruction of bond = destruction of hallucinatory image.* But if the image is identified with the link, this means that it normally performs the positive psychic function of binding together separate objects. The perceptual image, in the proper or hallucinatory sense of the word, always expresses a linking function to the extent that it is *sense* and *meaning*, two domains of the human being that are by definition intersubjective. Conversely, there is no word that does not always correspond at least to the signifier provided by its sound and visual body. No word is disincarnate. Image "binds" together both on the pre–reflexive plane of instincts and embodied simulation (Gallese 2005), and when matched with words. *Image is only awake in concept.* In other words, it is concept that awakens the image from the sleep of our animality and makes it a *human* dream/thought.

Dream Screen

Another concept to relate to IVH and negative hallucination is that of "dream screen", as Lewin (1946, 420) calls it: "the surface on to which a dream appears to be projected. It is the blank background, present in the dream though not necessarily seen". Reinterpreting

Lewin, we understand the dream screen as a level of sensation-based bodily integration; the original institution of bonds of an already symbolic (social) nature, as even the shaping of a semiotic space for the infant always already implies cultural inclusions and exclusions; the first form of transindividual subjectivity as living corporeity; the intersubjective and *forgotten* ground that acts as a transcendental scheme for the activities of the conscious ego; "the latent at the heart of perception" (Romanyshyn 1977, 218); that which precedes knowledge given by reflective thinking.

This layer of embodied personal identity that is anonymously received by the infant, but is then always and continuously produced, constitutes the canvas on which the subject can paint with the colours of senses now working in a coordinated way – as "common sense", i.e. with "some 'sense' that is common to more than one sense" (Bion 1965, 10). From this angle, the dream screen is more or less an equivalent of negative hallucination.

Fear of Breakdown and Primitive Agony

We have no way of knowing, but it is possible to speculate that Bion's expression "he feared a breakdown" in AL (309) served as the inspiration for Winnicott's famous essay "Fear of Breakdown", which was published in 1974 (even though, according to the editor of *Psycho-Analytic Explorations,* it might have been written in 1963). As an aside, in his article, Winnicott makes the same remark as Bion makes in "On Arrogance" (1958a) about the risk of treating psychotic patients as if they were neurotic – except that they get worse.

In this famous essay, Winnicott describes a dramatic fracture of the mother-child bond. This produces a kind of "primitive agony" ("the unthinkable") and then leads to the structuring of psychotic defences. The subject could not frame ("dream") the event within his life experience. All that remains is the fear of a psychic collapse that in reality has *already* happened. At the same time, there is the feeling that something might have happened but did not – a psychological state of "excitement", but one detached from any representation. For Winnicott, the traumatic nature of the breakdown of linking, its environmental origin, is clear. The same can be said of Bion with regard to the historical origin of the attack on linking, but not so with regard to what happens in the here and now of the session.

"Disintegration", which Winnicott describes as the psychotic organization that defends the child from the terror of losing the bond with the mother, corresponds in Bion to the formation of bizarre objects. Although threatening, the hallucinatory world of bizarre objects is still "a world", the reconstruction of a version of it that is deficient but in its own way complete. After all, the "experience" of bizarre objects is not only the consequence of the attack on links but also a true reflection or echo of them. I mean that, in a way, it "symbolizes" or retains the character of an activity of fragmentation, as it manages to preserve the sensoriality that IVH evacuates. Even if precariously and with several side effects, a space-time dimension is generated that exerts pressure on the psyche and in this way keeps it together "from the outside".

Winnicott recognizes the game of transference-countertransference as the occasion that permits the analyst's technical errors to finally fill in the gap in the psyche that is primitive agony, provided they only occur "in doses that are not excessive" (1974, 105). In the protected space of therapy, the patient can finally make sense of the experience of breakdown by reliving it in a non-traumatic reiteration. It is not that the memory of the crisis is not somewhere; but it stays only in the body – in Bion's terms, as an agglomeration of beta elements unconnected to any image. For Winnicott, "memory" is a word that is worth using only if it refers to something that has a meaning. He goes so far as to say that a patient can even commit suicide in an attempt to finally make sense of his lived unlived psychic collapse. For others, though, it is a matter of experiencing emptiness; not something traumatic that has left its (negative) mark, but something that should have happened and did not.

Compared with Winnicott, who refers to primitive agony, just as Bion does when he points out that psychotic patients have suffered from a "primitive catastrophe" (1958a, 145) or from fear of dying, in the latter attention gradually slips into the present of the session. In Winnicott, the occasional technical error of the analyst reactivates the ancient failure of the "facilitating environment" (1974, 105). In Bion and even more so in the post-Bionian theory of the analytic field, without this possibility being ignored, however, the emphasis is on "fear of breakdown" as a *model* of *any* attack on linking that may come about – in extreme cases even without it being necessarily already present in the patient's history.

Similarly to primitive agony, IVH is a trauma that has been suffered but not really experienced: sensoriality that has not found the "inert material" (Bion 1961, 125) that could cushion its violence is discharged into the body as a way of engaging in more effective research. *And it is (partially) successful.* Bion observes the patient's convulsive movement and sees an image of a stab wound from within. In this way, his reverie helps him come to the rescue and he tries to repair a damaged capacity for thinking.

Hints for a General Theory of Representation

From our inquiry on IVH, we see that it is a process that has a negative quality. As such, the concept of IVH can help us to "see" not only what happens when the subject loses the ability to represent, but also the negative side that is present in any ("positive") act of representation. In a tentative model of a general theory of representation, the "invisibility" of hallucination would correspond to the infinitesimal fraction of time in which a solution of continuity is produced in the psyche-soma, or in the intersubjective tissue of the personality that is the source of the creation of meaning, that is, primarily in its affective constituent. Then, as it were "around the sixth hour" – as in Kafka's (1919, 10) short story *In the Penal Colony* – some sense begins to be organized from the wounds themselves in the guise of bizarre objects. Another (partially) useful analogy might be with the blind spot on the retina, corresponding to the emergence of the optic nerve, which is necessary for the unfolding of the sensory fibres. In other words, in psychoanalytic terms, at the origin of *any* representation, there would be a minimal experience of "breakdown" or IVH. Whatever the response of the subject to staunch the bleeding that has occurred, there would always remain an element that cannot be assimilated or fully reintegrated.

We then could conceive of "normal" invisible hallucinations that infiltrate perception, at a physiological level, as simply the very beginning of representations that are formed in response to the stimuli that promote differentiation of the psyche. We might speculate that underlying *any* urge to represent there is always some kind of lack or micro-trauma stemming from the "real". IVH would be the hidden side not only of *visible*-visual hallucination that ignites hallucination activity, but also of representation itself at its *degree zero*.

94

If things were not so, we would not talk about "the violence of interpretation" in the way Aulagnier (1975) does. After all, it is in the nature of *any* trace that is etched on the wax tablet of memory, as Freud (1925) describes in his paper about the Mystic Writing-Pad. The inscription leaves a trace on the smooth surface of the wax. There is no way for a trace to be engraved in the memory without a certain violence. It produces a "cut" in the psychic skin – but a cut which is also a cut as the term is used in film direction. *The trauma may be limited to the layer of wax needed to transform the inscription into sense and significance ("in doses that are not excessive"), or it may be so violent as to break the tablet itself.* What is at issue here is not the violence of language per se – you can be a "subject" only to the extent that you subject yourself to a system of norms – but rather its *measure*.

We thus obtain an image that links the relative violence of the impression and its effect: whether a representation or a pathological IVH will arise. In the end, "physiological" IVH may be the marking of the trace that does not shatter the support of the representation or shatters it to only a minimal and useful extent – like immunization by vaccination, or like the black frames in a film that rhythmically separate the impressed frames. That is why it turns into images and normal projective identification. IVH's "blindness" becomes a model for vision or intuition. The different fate of normal versus pathological IVH is that, for the subject, this alienation of the self by what is other than the self is tolerable – or rather, made so by sociality.

With these notes, I hope to contribute to make the reading of one of the classic texts of psychoanalysis even more interesting and rich. More specifically, my hope is to reintegrate the concept of IVH into the lexicon of metapsychology. Because of the penumbra of associations, as Bion likes to say, that the term carries, IVH allows us to broaden our conception of the process of splitting, as originally described by Klein (1946), that is at the beginning of pathological and normal projective identification.

The concept of IVH can have an enormous theoretical value. Thanks to Bion's very detailed account of splitting and the possibility we have of reading it from new points of view, we become aware of its inherently intersubjective and functional nature. This insight allows us to visualize the risks and benefits of *at-one-ment* or linking that takes place on the primarily and intercorporeal level of the relationship which, following Lewin, I have evoked here with the concept of "dream screen". Additionally, it helps us to better understand Green's (1993) brilliant concept of the work of the negative. In fact, IVH suggests that at the basis of *any* perception there is always some minimal "primitive agony". As odd as it may seem to us, there is no linking and therefore no object that is not tinged with some touch of "bizarreness". At the levels of both language and affect, the connection itself *is* bizarre, always weirdly making *one* of two different terms or entities, while at the same time maintaining their respective differences.

Notes

* Translated by the current author, revised by I. Harvey.

1 This paper is the last in a series in which I reread some of Bion's most important contributions; see Civitarese 2008, 2013a, 2013b, 2017b, 2019a, 2019b, 2019c, 2021a, 2021b, 2021c, 2021d.

2 References to single pages, with no indication of the year, are to this article.

3 http://www.pep-web.org/statistics.php?mode=cite&sort=all (accessed 16 April 2021).

4 On AL, see the collective volume edited by Bronstein and O'Shaughnessy 2017.

5 For reasons of space, it is not possible here to explain the basic principles of the post-Bionian field theory. Right from its name, it is clear that it does not sterilely oppose Bion, but rather it draws on and expands upon his thought. For an easy introduction to this model, see Civitarese and Ferro, 2018; and Civitarese, G. (2022). *On Arrogance: A Psychoanalytic Essay*. London: Routledge, 2024.

6 See Bion (1962, 669): "From the emotional experience the infant abstracts certain elements".

7 Once again, the inspiration may have come from the aesthetics of the sublime (Civitarese 2014), as I suggest in the epigraph.

8 Actually, all the senses are involved in the transformation of beta-elements into alpha-elements. If we say that alpha-elements are for the most part images, it is because human anatomy and physiology assign the sense of sight a much more important role than the other senses. Besides, for a subject, an alpha-element – as suggestively indicated by the very letter chosen by Bion to designate it, not just any letter but part of the word "alphabet" – could never be independent of language.

9 See Klein (1946, 103): "The various ways of splitting the ego and internal objects result in the feeling that the ego is in bits. This feeling amounts to a state of disintegration".

10 See Bion (1967, 146): "There is a *field* of emotional force in which the individuals seem to lose their boundaries as individuals and become 'areas' around and through which emotions play at will. Psycho-analyst and patient cannot exempt themselves from the emotional *field*. ... That state of mind is easier to understand if it is regarded as the state of mind of a group rather than of an individual but transcending the boundaries we usually regard as proper to groups or individuals".

THE CONCEPT OF TIME IN BION'S "A THEORY OF THINKING"[1]

Bion's paper "The Psycho-analytic Study of Thinking", published in 1962 (Bion 1962a) and reprinted as "A Theory of Thinking" in *Second Thoughts* in 1967,[2] includes an original notion of time and its genesis. This aspect has to my knowledge never been discussed, other than tangentially, in the psychoanalytic literature. The text centres on the distinction between a *conception* and a *thought*, one of which arises from an experience of satisfaction and the other from an experience of frustration in the infant. These two elements must be understood not as isolated segments of a succession, but as bound together in a dialectical relationship, in which each term simultaneously negates and reaffirms the other. This matrix gives rise to an initial pre-reflective order of time, which takes on the full status of subjective time – in the sense both of time as duration and as its abstract representation – only when it is incorporated in the symbolic order by way of the function of language. The meeting of a preconception of the breast with the mere alternation of the breast's absence and presence cannot generate a concept of time unless a name is given to the experience at a certain point. It is only with effect from this essential conjuncture that the dialectic of conception and thought organizes the *horizontal* transition between the two opposing affective states of pleasure and unpleasure and the *vertical* transition from the concrete to the symbolic. In this way, the subject structures his[3] existence temporally in terms of past, present, and future, and later on the basis of "consensual", measurable

DOI: 10.4324/9781003625247-4

time – which is nothing less than a concept drawn from the indistinct flow of lived time. Compared with speculative thought, psychoanalysis has the advantage of basing its theory on the empirical foundation of clinical practice, in which various degrees of destruction of time are observed. To describe the formation of thoughts and the intimate connection between them and the birth of the sense of time, in "A Theory of Thinking", Bion adopts an innovative model of the primary mother-infant relationship that differs from Freud's, by which he overturns some of the traditional assumptions of psychoanalysis about the unconscious, dreams, and affects. He also resorts to an idiosyncratic form of language. It is unsurprising that the text may in some respects be hard to understand for readers unfamiliar with the postulates of its author's new theory and his writing style. However, a discussion of these postulates is beyond the scope of this article, as is even a brief review of the psychoanalytic and the non-psychoanalytic literature on the concept of time[4] – which for Husserl (1928) is the most important and the most difficult of all problems in phenomenology. For this reason, I shall now present a detailed and precise critical reading of Bion's text in order to reveal a theory of the origin of time contained within it.

Marginal Notes on Freud

"A Theory of Thinking" explicitly presents itself as a rereading of "Formulations on the Two Principles of Mental Functioning" (Freud 1911; Civitarese 2016b). Freud's paper, which amounts to just 14 pages on the Psychoanalytic Electronic Publishing database, compared with five for Bion (style is also an element of the challenge here), addresses the problem of reality testing – Janet's *fonction du réel*. The protagonist of his narration is a "psychical apparatus" already capable of thinking or wishing ("whatever was thought of [wished for])" (Freud 1911, 219) and of achieving satisfaction in hallucination ("just as still happens to-day with our dream-thoughts every night") (Freud 1911, 219). It was "only the non-occurrence of the expected satisfaction, the disappointment [*Enttäuschung*] experienced, that led to the abandonment of this attempt at satisfaction" (Freud 1911, 219), and induced the subject to turn, precisely, to reality. The subject of the action is described in atomistic terms: "The psychical apparatus [elsewhere he uses the word 'faculty'] had

99

to decide to form a conception of the real circumstances in the external world and to endeavour to make a real alteration in them" (Freud 1911, 219). In this way, the *reality principle* is established, in step with the gradual extension by consciousness, understood by analogy with the senses as an organ for the perception of psychic qualities, of its receptivity to sense impressions, and with the gradual development of the functions of attention, observation, and judgement.

However, Freud realizes that his description of the process of development of the capacity to think is unrealistic and therefore qualifies his argument, but only in a footnote. Here, he concedes that his account is only a "fiction" (*Fiktion*) and states that this artifice corresponds to the situation of the infant "provided one includes with it the care it receives from its mother" (Freud 1911, n4). That is the point: overcoming this fiction and *actually* including the mother in the theory of becoming-a-subject, with the concomitant semiotic dimension that inevitably connotes the beginning of the process – that is the mission to which the whole of post-Freudian psychoanalysis has dedicated itself. But why does Freud compel himself to adopt this fiction? Is it a case of theoretical repression? And if so, on the basis of his own definition of this psychic mechanism, what agency would underlie it? Could it be – given the spirit of the times – the unavoidable principle of a naturalistic approach to the study of the psyche?

Freud's interpretation of the infant's conquest of the reality principle is indeed based on the postulate of "a psychical system shut off from the stimuli of the external world" (1911, 219), for the key image in the text is "a bird's egg with its food supply enclosed in its shell; for it, the care provided by its mother is limited to the provision of warmth" (1911, 219), or of the child confined within the bubble of primal autoerotism. Freud's approach is essentially far removed from the prevailing present-day view, grounded in infant observation, attachment theory, child psychoanalysis, the neurosciences, and so on, that a newborn is already capable of in-depth interaction with its mother (Civitarese 2016a).

"Formulations on the Two Principles of Mental Functioning" also attracted the attention of Winnicott. He offers a clear critique of certain aspects of it in "The Theory of the Parent-Infant Relationship" (1960), published in the *International Journal of Psychoanalysis*, discussed in 1961 at the same 22nd International Psychoanalytical Congress held in Edinburgh where Bion read "A Theory of Thinking" and finally included in *The Maturational Processes and the Facilitating Environment* (1965). In his view, Freud disregards infancy as such and, while acknowledging the role of maternal care, sets it aside. In particular, Winnicott addresses the famous footnote 5, in which Freud mentions child development and comments that "Freud's words here are inadequate and misleading in certain respects, if taken to refer to the earliest stage" (1965, 587). As if that did not suffice, he too provides a footnote, also numbered 5 (!), and moreover backdated to 1940, which contains the phrase for which he is best known throughout the world: "There is no such thing as an infant" (1965, n4).

For Freud, the coming of the reality principle is based on a two-fold frustration. The first frustration gives rise to a *regressive* impulse and the second to a *progressive* one. An infant that fails to find a breast initially retreats to hallucinatory satisfaction. Then, discovering that this solution is illusory, he autonomously forces himself to cathect reality. However, there is something unconvincing in Freud's thesis. How could the infant possibly turn *by himself* to reality after having experienced the futility of hallucinatory gratification – and especially if reality remains frustrating?

It is admittedly the case that, besides footnote 5, there are at least two other passages on the process leading to acceptance of the reality principle in which Freud waters down his solipsistic vision. The first is his statement that the infant's motor discharge gradually becomes a means of communicating his internal states to others ("it learns to employ these manifestations of discharge intentionally as methods of expressing its feelings;" Freud 1911, 219n4) – a note that in fact anticipates the concept of projective identification. The second is his mention of the role played by the "offer of love as a reward from the educators" (1911, 224) in psychic growth. Even so, the central problem remains unresolved. In "A Theory of Thinking", Bion seeks a solution. As O'Shaughnessy writes (1981, 184):

Bion's hypotheses disagree with theories which view thinking as merely the emergence of maturation or as an autonomous ego function. According to him, K is hard-won by the infant ego from emotional experiences with a nurturing object, functioning normally on the reality principle.

Kant and Thoughts Without a Thinker

Aware of the extent of his recourse to speculative thought, Bion feels the need, at the beginning of "A Theory of Thinking", to specify the distinctive features of his theoretical system – namely, a practical aim and the necessity of measuring the system against "empirically verifiable data" (1962a, 306) – the only point that recurs with a difference of emphasis in the 1967 commentary contained in *Second Thoughts*. This statement calls to mind the phrase *Qui s'excuse, s'accuse*, because the issue of thinking – of what makes us human – is after all the cornerstone of *any* speculative theoretics. Why is Bion now so concerned to draw attention to the differences? Could the reason be that, as an enthusiastic connoisseur of philosophy, he realizes that he is rewriting one of its key chapters? And that he is therefore afraid of being accused of "contaminating" the pure gold of psychoanalysis with extraneous theoretical elements and of distancing himself from the empirical field, for instance in asserting that "philosophers have concerned themselves with the same subject-matter" (1962a, 306)? Alternatively, might he fear being seen as an amateur philosopher?

It is indeed the case that philosophy immediately takes centre stage in "A Theory of Thinking".[5] In outlining his own ideas, Bion takes inspiration from Kant and makes the theory of knowledge coincide with the theory of becoming-a-subject. Following the example of the German philosopher, Bion proceeds from an inquiry into the object to an inquiry into the subject and to the latter's possibilities of knowing reality. This is what we mean in referring to the transition from a psychoanalysis that investigates repressed contents to one that seeks to develop the psychic container. This is not a spurious distinction as some hold, because it establishes a hierarchy between the two different approaches to treatment. For Bion, the contained is true only if it finds a space in the other in which it can be accepted. As usual in his arguments, he takes advantage of his familiarity with the particularities of psychotic thought, even if he then also extends his vision to a general understanding of the nature of thought. That, in my view, is what enables him to develop a modern theory of *temporality*.[6]

Bion in fact immediately leaps ahead of Kant, in wondering whether it is the psychic function of thinking that gives rise to thoughts or whether it is thoughts that impel the function of thinking to emerge. In other words, is Kant's transcendentalism a property of the individual (the subject) and not derived from experience, or does it originate from belonging to the community (the "inter-subject") and depend on experience? Which comes first, the individual or the group; the drive or the meaning – that is, what Grotstein (2004) calls the "truth drive" and Bion himself the "emotional drive" (1963, 75)? Bion counterintuitively chooses the latter ("scandalous") option, in asserting that it is thoughts that take priority in order for a function of thinking to be organized. Common sense suggests the contrary. Just as spiders secrete the silken threads, they use to make their webs, so we take it for granted that we are individuals who "produce" thoughts. On reflection, however, it becomes clear that this is not the case. Let us see why.

Bion subdivides the actual process of thinking into the two consecutive stages of the formation of thoughts and the function of thinking, each of which may become a locus for the development of pathology. In the former, thoughts are synthesized, while in the latter, these thoughts "ask" to be thought (managed, correlated, systematized), and in this way initiate the development of the apparatus for thinking thoughts. That is the "official" explanation of the concept of "thoughts without a thinker". From the perspective of thinking, an (individual) thought is a semi-finished product. However, where do these thoughts that are waiting to be thought come from and what is their nature?

Depending on how "well-cooked" they are, thoughts belonging to the first phase of the overall process of thinking can be classified as: (a) ideas, preconceptions (also defined as an "analogue … of Kant's concept of 'empty thoughts';" 111), a priori knowledge, inborn expectations, waiting states predisposed to receive stimuli from a limited range of phenomena; (b) conceptions or thoughts; and (c) "finally concepts" – where the adverb expresses, precisely, the idea that in terms of development concepts come *after* thoughts: it is only after having "thought"/perceived many trees that one arrives at the concept of a tree and proceeds from the particular to the universal.

An idea or preconception becomes a conception or a thought (these here still being seen as equivalents) when mated with a realization, in the sense of the reality data that best correspond to it. In other words, it originates from an experience of satisfaction. However, Bion does subsequently distinguish between a conception and a thought. He explains that, while a conception results from the sum of a preconception and its *positive* realization, a thought is the outcome of the sum of a preconception and its *non*-realization – that is, its *negative* realization. *I contend that this key distinction is the founding act of Bion's theory of temporality.*

Note that Bion's first example of the triggering of this process concerns the formation not of just any conception but of the conception of a breast. This is not an accidental choice because it possesses the obvious theoretical significance of immediately introducing the mother-infant relationship as the model with the greatest heuristic value for investigating the origin and development of the psyche. Nothing of the kind is to be found in Freud, whereas the influence of Klein is here manifest. Bion writes:

> ... the preconception (the inborn expectation of a breast, the a priori knowledge of a breast, the "empty thought") when the infant is brought into contact with the breast itself, mates with awareness of the realization and is synchronous with the development of a conception [but not a thought!].
>
> (111)

A thought, on the other hand, forms only in the event of a *negative* realization of the breast – that is, if an inborn preconception meets with a *frustration*. It is important to note that in this case, the infant is not confronted with an absolute void. Put simply, he fails to find the breast he is seeking, but his mind retains the memory trace of the breast. Here again, Bion is seen to emphasize the *emotional* quality of the infant's proto-experience of an increase in tension and disappointment which "appears to be painful" (1962b, 48) – again, "a breast that is 'not there' and by not being there gives it painful feelings" (1962b, 57) – but not the mere perception of the breast's absence.

Hence, the meanings of a conception and a thought are as follows. The former signifies awareness (which is in reality pre-reflective, at least pending the development of a fully established subjectivity) of a certain experience of satisfaction; the latter signifies awareness of the lack of this experience. However, even this does not yet suffice for having a *concept* of it. In the sequence outlined above, a thought admittedly tends towards a concept and ends up *between* a conception and an actual concept. Yet, it is only the addition of a *name* to a thought – i.e. to the experience of non-realization – that can lead to a concept. Bion explains that "concepts are named and therefore fixed conceptions or thoughts" (111). The key word here is "fixed", which implies that the act of naming has to do with a process of subtraction of individual features from the infinite number of concrete entities to which they refer. The deeper significance perhaps lies concealed in the double meaning of the word "fix", as both fastening and repairing. But who is repairing what? Who supplies the name to reassemble the scattered fragments of the vessel of the psyche? Who can be the agent that "cooks" the name so as to form the experience? It can only be the *O/other*, or, put differently, the *other* as agent of caring and spokesperson of the *Other* as the unconscious, culture, and sociality. Again, might the slash not stand for the invariant, the third element that binds the subject to the group? So before the name is added – as when the mother, in the wooden-reel game, interprets the sounds produced by the infant as *fort* and *da* (Civitarese 2018) – a conception and a thought are nothing but primitive forms of awareness, resulting from the mere capacity, already present at birth, to register the effect of external and internal stimuli.

Whereas the realization represented by the event of the breast's presentation of itself to the infant's inborn preconception of it draws our attention to the fundamental role of the relationship with the mother, what brings it to this point is the entire element of sociality (the divine, O, the spirit, language, the unconscious-as-infinite, etc.), which takes the stage because the name (language) by definition cannot but be a community-based fact. It follows from all these clues that, from the very beginning of his paper, Bion is assuming a radically social conception of the origin of the mind. Thoughts without a thinker are therefore possible because relationship – i.e. sociality – *precedes* the coming of the subject. The "divine" or "sacred" aspect of language is embodied again and again in a new individual, whom it enables to become a subject. If this were not so, no newborn would ever be induced to think his own thoughts. Thoughts without a thinker can thus be understood, not merely in Kantian terms as the sequencing of pre-thoughts (conceptions and thoughts), but also in terms of the pressure exerted by society on the infant to become a new member of the circle of the symbolic. In this way, the two vertices – active and passive – of subjectivity are outlined:

105

being spoken by language, because the infant is "subjected" to it; and speaking language in the sense of expressing himself or *meaning*; that is, the unconscious and the conscious, respectively.

Once formed, these "thoughts" act as preconceptions (*ideas*) for new and richer experiences of satisfaction or lack of satisfaction or of the gradual fading of the memory trace of satisfaction (second- or *n*th-level *thoughts*). As they progressively forfeit quanta of their sensory character owing to the natural weakening of the strength of the mnemic impression, the individual representations are transmuted into each other and "melt together" in a process of mutual metaphorization that ultimately leads to identification of the essence that joins them all together – namely, their *concept*. The forgoing of a series of particular determinations then opens the way to the universal, to what is (more or less) the same for everyone and thus links everyone in a bond of sociality.

In terms of the establishment of the reality principle, the advantage is obvious. The subject gradually has at his disposal more abstract, or as it were "sublimated" (Civitarese 2016a), representations that are more all-embracing – quasi-concepts, psychic containers, forms capable of receiving new experiences and of partially tracing them back to the bedrock of the known, and schemata that allow for more singularities. The compass of the concept enables the individual to take his place on the common ground of sociality so as to get his bearings in the world. He succeeds in communicating with others and can approach the infinite without excessive anxiety. The concept extends the "commonsense", understood in Bion's terms as "common to the senses" – that is, the coordinated and consensual functioning of the senses acquired by an infant by virtue of the integrating role of the object, or common sense as judgement common to more than one person.

The Destruction of Time

As always in psychoanalysis, the test bench for theoretical hypotheses is pathology. In this case, what matters most are the events that may occur in the absence of the capacity to tolerate frustration. Bion introduces the subject with a reference to Freud:

> This initiates the state, described by Freud in his "Two principles of mental functioning", in which dominance by the reality

principle is synchronous with the development of an ability to think and so to bridge the gulf of frustration between the moment when a want is felt and the moment when action appropriate to satisfying the want culminates in its satisfaction.

(112)

Now in the scene described by Freud, it is not at all evident that the essential transition is from the thought back to the conception. Freud writes not that the infant turns to reality because he is caught up in the agreeable rhythm of a relationship, but that he does so because he is discouraged by remaining in a state of frustration.

In signifying his agreement with Freud, Bion goes beyond him by supplying an amended version of his thesis. While the infant admittedly seeks the object – and in this seeking the future-directed tendency characteristic of temporality can be glimpsed – it is equally true that much will depend on the object's receptivity and its capacity to allow itself to be found. What remains of the mating of the preconception with the negative realization of the breast, Bion writes, is experienced as a no-breast, or "absent" breast inside. *The next step depends on the infant's capacity for frustration*: in particular it depends on whether the decision is to evade frustration or to modify it. ... The result [in the absence of the capacity to tolerate frustration] is a significant departure from the events that Freud describes as characteristic of thought in the phase of dominance of the reality principle (111–112, my emphasis).

Now the *departure* (reading between the lines, before it was the "gap") could be understood as an allusion to the departure-as-interval of the necessary wait before the experience of a fresh state of concrete satisfaction; as the difference from the *normal* process of thought (according to Freud's conception, which Bion still seems implicitly to accept – i.e. turning to reality merely as a result of the pressure of frustration); or, lastly, as what distinguishes *his* explanation of events from Freud's.

I would emphasize the third reading. This is first because, as we have seen, Bion is *already* using the mother-newborn model and the concepts of "breast" and "no-breast" in a way not paralleled in Freud's "fiction" (Green 1998); and second because he then immediately introduces the Kleinian concept of projective identification. This is, as it were, a lens not included in his predecessor's toolbox. Bion instead resorts to the concept of projective identification in order to understand how an infant who experiences a frustration can communicate with his mother, and how, if the mother responds with her capacity for reverie, this mutual understanding constitutes the first thought. This thought will have not only a positively sensory quality on the infant's part, but also a cognitive quality as seen from the perspective of the mother. However, the decisive step taken by Bion is to regard the dimension of the couple-as-*system* as the origin of properties that are more than the sum of its individual components. Invoking an impressive resemblance between an infant and an adult patient, Bion then even more forcefully reaffirms the model of the mother–infant relationship as that which takes priority in psychoanalysis, and then broaches the subject of hallucination.

What Freud connotes negatively as a hallucinatory experience instead takes on, in "A Theory of Thinking", the positive status of the germ of an image, the memory trace of the experience of satisfaction, the "no-breast" (not *noughtness!*), the hallucinatory aspect of representation – and indeed already of perception. For the infant, this is the equivalent, as described by Winnicott, of the omnipotent illusion of "creating" the breast. Bion completely disregards the state of hallucinatory satisfaction postulated in Freud's description of the establishment of the reality principle. This is not surprising because Bion's aim is, precisely, to conceive theories of the unconscious, dreams, and affects that differ from Freud's. Of the various manifestations of the spectrum of dreaming, Bion stresses the creative (*transformative*) aspect rather than that of *distortion* or removal of sense. Hence, the hallucinatory is not in itself regressive but becomes so only when it borders on non-consensuality. The ultimate court of appeal is always the explicit and implicit judgement of the community. Like the moment of waking compared with a dream, the hallucinatory is merely a phase in the process of "dreaming" the emotion so as to assign a meaning to it. The transition outlined by Freud in terms of a dichotomic conception of conscious and unconscious as two separate systems is subsumed by Bion in the "continuistic" definition of the α-function and the un/conscious.

Another important difference is that Freud never refers to the capacity to tolerate frustration, but only, much more generally, to "predisposing factors" (Marcelli 1986, translated). Bion explains that frustration has three possible vicissitudes: (a) the sensation of no-breast – i.e. an internal and *tolerable* sensation of hunger – is transformed into a thought, or, to be more specific, let us say a time-related sensation or time-related thought; (b) an internal and *intolerable* sensation of no-breast induces the infant to *modify* the frustration (this shows that the aim of thought is action); or, lastly, (c) an intolerable internal sensation of no-breast impels the *evacuation* of this state or its evasion.

To return for a moment to Freud's schema, in strictly logical terms, *more* frustration ought to induce the infant to embrace the reality principle (i.e. to *think*), and not to evacuate the thought, which is now identified with a bad, "concrete" object to be expelled by projective identification. For Bion writes that what "should be a thought, a product of the juxtaposition of pre-conception and negative realization, becomes a bad object, indistinguishable from a thing-in-itself, fit only for evacuation" (112). Instead of the development of thought, what grows to excess is the apparatus for projective identification. At this point, the good breast and the bad breast become equivalent.

In terms of a theory of the origin of time, the sequence of events described here by Bion is impressive. He manifestly still has in mind Kant's transcendentalism, because, according to his theory, the flight from frustration, which here means the impossibility of tolerating or modifying it, gives rise to *the destruction of what for Kant are the a priori forms of sensible intuition – namely, space and time.* Yet in constructing a model of what makes it impossible to experience things, Bion conversely also develops a theory of the *origin* of these forms. For Kant, these are not derived from experience – that is why he calls them transcendental – but this is precisely the point on which Bion's psychoanalysis can help to cast light, while also benefiting speculative thought itself. After all, he demonstrates, on the one hand, their non-aprioristic nature and, on the other, their perfect coincidence with subjectivity itself.

By way of projective identification, Bion holds, an infant seeks to eliminate the internal bad breast. To be released from the persecution with which he feels afflicted, he rids himself of the internal breast as the space of proto-subjectivity that is both private and common. Since everything takes place in highly *concrete* terms, this entails halting the development of the apparatus for thinking thoughts. In other words, the establishment of a state of terror prevents the virtualization of the experience of gratification that accompanies the transition from perception-sensation to mnemic or imaginative representation. The infant feels that his only possibility of not dying is to remain *stuck* to the object – that is, to identify adhesively with it. As in a painting by Salvador Dalí, time liquefies and space collapses.

Fascinatingly, while the process is described as connoted by an essential negativity – blocking of the development of thought, concrete thought, and evacuation instead of transformation – what is actually occurring on the theoretical level is a change from a psychologistic to an intersubjective vertex, which can only be seen as a step forward. The use of projective identification to get rid of the internal bad breast increasingly appears as a way, by antonomasia, of *communicating* with the mother non-verbally and of trying to think *with* her. As if by accident, projective identification gradually forfeits its negative connotation and takes on a more "positive" aspect – that is, as a physiological and no longer exclusively pathological mechanism. What is now paramount is no longer the infant's inevitably limited capacity to cope with frustration, *but instead the degree of receptivity denoted by the object's response.* The infant could now be said to arrive at a fork in the road where he has to choose between the path of evasion or that of modification of the frustration. However, before this choice is considered in wholly intersubjective (couple-related) terms, the scene could instead be described as if the two options were evasion or frustration, one of which must be chosen *not by the individual but by the mother-child or analyst-patient couple.* Hence, the importance assumed by the concept of the analyst's receptivity in psychoanalysis with regard to the factors involved in the treatment (Civitarese 2015, 2016c).

The infant's dilemma is therefore whether to change reality or to take flight from it. The deciding factor is quantitative and is essentially a measure of the quality of the object's capacity for reverie. If the degree of intolerance of frustration is less malignant than that resulting in the complete destruction of time and space, a state of omnipotence, with concomitant omniscience, is established. The psychotic part of the personality predominates and the capacity to distinguish between truth and falsehood is lost. Albeit less catastrophically than in the case of evacuation, the individual fails to take account of reality – as when one has a toothache and everything else becomes a mere blur – and suffers from a chronic lack of truth, truth for Bion nevertheless representing food for the mind. What takes root is an annoyingly reason-based and pseudo-moralistic kind of thought totally disconnected from the living world of the emotions. The outcome is an unconscious urge, as a rule destined to fail, to correct in others what is experienced in the sufferer as a painful lack of hospitality.

If the degree of intolerance of frustration is more malignant, on the other hand, the flight from reality is a more intense and dramatic process and takes the form of "destructive attacks" (113) on the consciousness of the data of reality. That is what happens when *non-thoughts* or *concrete thoughts* are produced instead of thoughts, and are then "evacuated at high speed as missiles *to annihilate space*" (113, my emphasis). On the basis of Bion's earlier definition, *non-thoughts or concrete thoughts are to be understood as "thoughts" derived from problems arising when the infant encounters negative realizations.* In reading this passage, one is reminded that Bion always has in mind Kant and his concepts of space and time. Let us now consider the word "attacks". It ineluctably carries us towards a traditional conception of the unconscious and the idea that a destructive, narcissistic part of the mind is active in everyone. It does not take account of the possibility that failures by the couple system to translate experience might be responsible.

Whereas in Freud's model repression as the elimination of a disturbing stimulus concerns a specific content, Bion here states that what is "eliminated" – i.e. sabotaged – is the *function*[7] of consciousness itself. The intolerance of frustration dismantles the psychic entity that serves for the toleration of frustration. However, if space and time are annihilated, the subject lacks any reality data (facts) to saturate the preconception (or the corresponding idea) and can neither experience reality nor learn from experience.

The intolerance of frustration results in an inability to know not only external but also internal reality (the self), for a newborn can develop "a rudimentary and fragile reality sense" (114) only if projective identification functions normally in the relationship with the mother. This is because it is she who "manipulates" his personality and renders it capable of tolerating frustration to a greater or lesser degree. In other words, she registers the infant's experience in a meaningful space-time that is simultaneously personal and impersonal. To explain how he came to postulate that intolerance of *pain* can ultimately destroy space and time, Bion here inserts the vignette of a patient who complains of constantly wasting time. The tragic situation reminds him of how, in *Alice's Adventures in Wonderland,* time comes to a halt at the Mad Hatter's tea party, *where it is always four o'clock*.[8] What further need could there be to confirm the utterly central role of the concept of time in "A Theory of Thinking"?

The imperceptible transition in Bion's text from the breast-as-a-character to the mother-as-a-character may be noted, thus immediately suggesting a further extension to the environment-as-a-character and society-as-a-character. The mother, Bion explains, must be "well-balanced" and the projective identification "realistic" and not excessive. Here again, however, one observes the factor which – given the manifest asymmetry of the levels of psychic maturation of the couple's members – governs the newborn's capacity to tolerate frustration. It can only be a matter of the mother's ability to accept his anxiety and to return it to him in a version he can assimilate. As Winnicott (1949) puts it, she must be able to present the world to him in small doses (but also to show herself to be capable of "failing" a little at a time). Only in this way can she allay the newborn's fear of dying. If, on the other hand, the mother does not succeed in this process of psychic digestion, she gives rise in the infant to violent reintrojection of the projective identifications and to the installation in his psyche of a greedy object that is unable to contain anxiety. Evidently, if a person is unable to tolerate frustration adequately, this means that there has not been (or is not) an external or internal container to give a name to the most disturbing emotions.

When an infant feels that his projective identifications have not been accepted, Bion writes, "the infant is reduced to continue projective identification carried out with increasing force and frequency. The increased force seems to *denude the projection of its penumbra of meaning*" (115, my emphasis). The activity of non-verbal intermediation of the meaning of the emotional experience is as it were reset to zero, *so that the possibility of establishing time is also lost*. Bion goes on: "Reintrojection is affected with similar force and frequency" (115). Deficient development of the faculty of thinking may result, among other problems, in *failure or deficiency of development of consciousness*, which, in agreement with Freud, he sees as the "sense-organ for the perception of psychic qualities" (115). This can rightly be seen as Bion's response to the criticism levelled at Kant by many authors for failing to take into account the origin of a priori forms of experience. However, it could also be seen as supplementing Heidegger's conception of temporality, which, centring on a description of the ontological structure of being, likewise does not address the issue of genesis (Sandowsky 2004).

112

The intolerance of frustration, or, in other words, of doubt as the element favouring expansion of the psychic container (Bion 1962b), destroys space and time. Conversely, it must be considered that tolerance of frustration (the complex interpsychic and intrapsychic experience subsumed in the formula) is the factor that establishes the forms of time and space. In the absence of normal projective identifications – i.e. of the balanced organization of this deep affective form of mother-infant communication – consciousness does not develop, because the infant cannot internalize the α-function.

This concept, as put forward in "A Theory of Thinking", without much ado marks the consummation of Bion's final separation from Freud. This emerges with greater clarity and in more detail from our text's twin, *Learning from Experience* (Bion 1962b). Here, he explains clearly why he thinks it is now appropriate to go beyond Freud. The starting point is again "Formulations on the Two Principles of Mental Functioning" (Freud 1911). Bion writes:

> For personalities that seem to be incapable of true dreaming, the border-line psychotic and psychotic parts of the personality, *the theory of consciousness as the sense-organ of psychic quality is not satisfactory; by the standards of clinical practice contradictions become apparent which are resolved if the problems are approached with a different theory.*
> (Bion 1962b, 54, my emphasis)

Bion here means that "the wondrous, onward-marching destiny"[9] of consciousness as the organ for the perception of psychic qualities cannot be realized in the way that Freud describes it – that is, without the involvement of the object – so that his description remains tenable only for a newborn's rudimentary consciousness.

Bion's new theory instead holds that it is the α-function that generates the contact barrier. Hence, conscious and unconscious are produced continuously, but "do function as if they were binocular [and] therefore capable of correlation and self-regard" (Bion 1962b, 54). At any rate, he goes on:

> This theory is weak in the need to postulate two systems at the point where, in my theory of an alpha-function, an emotional experience is transformed into alpha-elements, to make dream thought, unconscious waking thinking and storage in the mind (memory) possible.
> (Bion 1962b, 54)

So there are not *two* systems, even if interdependent, but a variously interlinked single system that is constantly in operation – a conception to which, after all, Freud was drawing nearer in his second topography, in locating the roots of the ego in the id. A "monocular" vision – exclusively conscious or exclusively unconscious – would, Bion asserts, be false and partial. The distinction will be better understood if it is recalled that a dream comprises the sum of dreaming and waking, the latter being conceived as the *displacement* of attention, rendered possible by language, towards a restriction of the field of consciousness (Vygotsky and Luria 1934). "Binocular vision" means that conscious and unconscious are like the two surfaces of a Möbius strip, in which a single surface turns back on itself but without any discontinuity. It is this concept that makes it possible, in an analytic session, to listen to *any* reference to concrete facts of past or current reality as something dreamed by patient and analyst together.

Consciousness understood not in the normal sense of the word but in accordance with Freud's definition would give rise, in the absence of an α-function, to β-elements that could not be converted into α-elements – that is, elements endowed with meaning. This would be a consciousness conceived as a function for recording stimuli, and not a true consciousness of self in the accepted sense of the term. However, that is exactly the *rudimentary* consciousness of a newborn, who, in order to achieve consciousness of self, needs there to be a mother to supply a "complement to its primitive consciousness" (Civitarese 2011, 278). Bion stresses that he accepts Freud's definition of consciousness only with reference to the very beginning of the phase of life preceding an infant's entry into the social field. Full consciousness is present only on condition of deeming it a property of the system represented by the mother-infant dyad.

The image is fascinating. Just as the lovers' embrace in Plato's *Symposium* reconstitutes the lost primal unity, so the newborn and the mother form a unity in which both conscious and unconscious are *already* present. The subject comes into being precisely *out of* and *within* relationality. This is expressed not in the mere satisfaction of the instinctual impulse, but in the *meaning* – the same "initial meaning" which, as shown above, is lost when the object cannot accept the infant's manifestations of pain. From this perspective, if we say that all sensations are conscious, we mean that they all lack meaning (they are only "conceptions"), at least until they are rendered unconscious – in Hegel's (1807) terms, human, divine, or infinite. Rendering un/conscious is equivalent to immersing perceptions in the field of human meanings. This enables Bion to specify that at birth, exchanges via normal projective identification take place "between the rudimentary consciousness and maternal reverie" (1962a, 309).

The Un/Conscious and Binocular Vision

The final part of TT describes the apparatus for thinking thoughts, or for linking thoughts together; as thoughts, Bion here includes "conceptions, thoughts, dream thoughts, alpha-elements and beta-elements" (117) – yes, even beta-elements! Bion imagines this apparatus as made up of four sectors: (a) thinking ("associated with modification and evasion"); (b) projective identification ("associated with evasion by evacuation"); (c) omniscience (the source of moralistic attitudes): and (d) communication.

As the mating of a preconception with a frustration, any thought is the expression of a problem awaiting the finding of a solution. It is a thought awaiting a thinker. The apparatus for thinking thoughts, which therefore comes into play in the second phase of thinking considered as a whole, behaves similarly to the α-function in its first phase. Just as the latter is required to bridge "the gap between sense-data [β-elements] and appreciation of sense-data [α-elements]" (113), so the former must process thoughts so as to prepare them for translation into actions.

To facilitate understanding of this processing of thoughts with a view to action, an idea of *time* is again invoked: "bridging the *gap* between cognizance and appreciation of lack and action [i.e. the *moment* of action] designed to modify the lack" (117, my emphasis). By "translation" of a thought into action, Bion means "publication, communication, and commonsense" (117). This statement suggests the meaning of column 6 of Bion's grid. It is not action in itself that should be contrasted with a thought, which moreover is itself a form of action (an "experimental kind of acting;" Freud 1911, 221), but a thought that is not included under the heading of "commonsense".

Publication of conceptions and thoughts concerns translation "in language, or its counterpart in signs" (118). In the same way as one is speaking to others even when conducting a dialogue with oneself, so sense impressions are translated into verbal form. Man, Bion reminds us, is a political animal, and must therefore always engage with the *necessary* conflict between socialism and narcissism, which, when it becomes explicit, entails the possibility that emotional problems will arise.

Hence, the issue of communication enables him to re-emphasize the social nature of human subjectivity. The first form of communication is realistic projective identification. Although Bion uses the phrase "in its origins" (108), it can in our view also be referred to the basic, or less abstract, level of communication. The development of "the social capacity of the individual" (119), he notes, has never received serious attention. An emotional problem of communication is something that often provokes persecutory reactions, which, moreover, can frequently be mitigated only by recourse to abstraction. Communication is obviously a function whose purpose is to correlate groups of sense data with each other. "If the conjoined data harmonize, a sense of truth is experienced" (119). Otherwise, the result is "a mental state of debility in the patient as if starvation of truth was somehow analogous to alimentary starvation" (119).

The conclusion of the paper is extraordinary in that it bases the theory of truth as food for the mind on affectivity. In this way, Bion in fact reformulates the problem addressed by Freud concerning the establishment of the reality principle: "a sense of truth is experienced" – i.e. a fact reveals itself in the guise of "[unmistakable] reality" – only if it arises from a "common emotional view" (119). It is not only the conscious but also the unconscious, or rather the binocular vision that both permit (the un/conscious as a single system), that gives us the sense of what is true and real. However, this truth is intrinsically contradictory – that is, it contains mutually irreconcilable perspectives. If the concept of truth is held to include a principle, not of reduction as in science, but of *expansion* of the meaning of existence, then truth is being apprehended from a number of different perspectives at one and the same time.

Emotions are psychic qualities – i.e. "perceptions" – that concern not external time and space, the sphere in which we accommodate objects we think we can observe objectively, but instead internal time and space. However, like external perceptions, their internal counterparts also give us a sense of truth when mutually consistent. Bion uses the classical example of the working through of emotional ambivalence towards the object. What then comes into being is a correlation between many different aspects of the object which are known by way of a multiplicity of experiences that are in themselves divergent. Yet, Bion has previously explained that this experience of

116

consciousness, of succeeding in the perception of psychic qualities, is bound up with the existence of a good relationship with the breast. Hence, *both* the possibility of a perceptual experience in which the senses function harmoniously, *and* an "internal" perceptual experience in which consciousness functions consistently, are based on the degree of consensual truth achieved in the primary relationship with the object, and furthermore that relationship itself forms part of the wider sphere of sociality.

A Dialectical Relationship

Let us now consider the concept of time in greater depth. For this purpose, the crucial issue to be addressed, as previously indicated, is the relationship between a *conception* and a *thought*. If considered purely in terms of a succession of psychic elements that are isolated and, while of opposite sign, homogeneous, the distinction between the two modes of encounter with the object which it denotes is unhelpful. The important point here is that, even where consciousness of self is present, the sense of time (which is a "feeling") could not arise from a mere juxtaposition of punctiform events and their purely intellectual apprehension. What would then be the origin of the essential aspects of the experience of *duration* and the *directionality* of time? To explain their appearance, it must instead be postulated that a conception is *alive* in a thought and that a thought is *alive* in a conception.

When it is stated generically that symbolic thought arises from the capacity to tolerate frustration, the essential nature of this dialectic is lost, as if the source of a thought could lie in mating with a mere void or lack – the "gap" – rather than, as seems obvious, in the controlled interplay of figure and ground, of satisfaction and frustration. How could a thought ever come into being out of mere frustration unless that frustrations were identified with the gradual fading of an experience of concrete satisfaction (a presentation) from sensory plenitude into the pallid form of a psychic trace (a multisense pictogram or representation), and hence, *under the pressure of a need and subsequently of an un/conscious wish*, also of the imaginative anticipation of a fresh experience of satisfaction? If this were not preceded by the *conception* of a breast – the star (*sidus*) from which the *de-sire*[10] is a measure of the distance – and if it were not preserved as *both* a mnemic impression *and* a "hallucinatory" anticipated vision of the future, the mating of a preconception of the breast with the

117

mere absence of the breast could not possibly generate a *thought*. The frustration stemming from the no-breast experience must instead be imagined as the gradual virtualization of the experience of the breast, like the progressive thinning of an elastic band that is stretched to hold the extremes of past and present together.

Logically, however, whereas in normal circumstances a modicum of realization persists in a *thought*, an element of negative realization is always embedded in a *conception*. What one is led to imagine as a diachronic relationship of succession between discontinuous and antithetical segments is in fact also a synchronic relationship – i.e. one of simultaneity. The qualities of harmony (of superimposition and concordance of "emotional" sounds or unison) and melody (the sounds' duration and their accentuation – high in a presentation and low in a representation) of the encounter with the object transform a simple succession into a rhythm. The present will then appear to us as the controlled interweaving of both implicit and explicit memories of past and future, a friendly mating of phantasies of what has been with what may (it is hoped) be once again.

In a word, the stuff of time, which, then, is the same as that of the psyche, can logically only be made up of *dialectical* relationships based primarily on the physical capacity to retain memory traces of positive and negative realizations. In a dialectical relationship, opposite terms join together to form dynamic unities that furnish the rational and real essence of things. The bond of metonymic/metaphorical *contact* connects two or more elements in such a way that, since they are in tension or of opposite sign, they negate and affirm each other. An automatic process of comparison of multidimensional traces takes place on a number of levels and identifies similarities and differences. However, this mutual influencing is conditional upon the existence of a relationship of *proximity* between the elements involved. In the absence of this relationship of proximity, which for Bion turns them into a "constant conjunction"[11] (110), the dynamic situation of mutual co-involvement is loosened to the point of complete dissolution. In other words, the matrix of the sense of existing comes into being at the moment when a set of synchronic groupings made up of the quantitative and qualitative aspects of the relationship are arranged along a diachronic axis and therefore become meaningful.

However, how can this meaningfulness be explained in greater depth? It could be thought of as the factor that orients lived time towards the future, as *expectation*. The direction of the arrow of time can then be seen as dictated *avant-coup*[12] by *anticipation*, as permitted by the order of time, of the end of the "melody". Winnicott (1958 [1975], 184) puts it as follows: "It is for this reason fundamentally that form in music is so important. Through form, the end is in sight from the beginning". Hence the advantage of a relative pre-dictability of things, which equips us better to deal with what may happen to us. The number of possible surprises is reduced, and the course of events is accommodated within a horizon of expectations and therefore of sense. Now is this *having-barely-in-sight* (an indistinct or distant kind of sight, as if fleeting – i.e. more of a sighting or presaging) not a synonym of no-breast? The "meaning" cannot but lie in the seeking of the object (pleasure), or rather, on a more *primal* level, in the avoidance of pain (unpleasure). Note that both expressions include the negative element of an absence that persists in presence and vice versa. The equation for the dialectic of *breast* ↔ *no-breast* can thus be rewritten as *breast* ↔ *(no* → *breast)*. The arrow between the parentheses (the sum of a minus sign [–] and a sign of direction [>]) is what most strongly suggests – more cannot be presumed – that the origin of "intentionality" as defined by philosophy (consciousness always being consciousness of an object) is the *direction* of time.

Not even the most authoritative philosophical theories succeed in giving a convincing account of why we experience time as a flow in the direction of the future.[13] This is because they are inevitably unbalanced towards abstract representation and fail to take account of affects. It can be postulated that the flow corresponds to *affective tension* and that, notwithstanding conscious experience, it is not so much a *directing-oneself-towards* or a *going-close-to*, or even a *being-attracted*, as a *distancing-oneself-from*, or a *being-driven*. As Freud writes (1915, 139, my emphasis), the object arises out of hate, and the narcissistic ego effects a "*primordial repudiation* of the external world with its outpouring of stimuli". What is thus repudiated if not pain? Our commonsense perception of time as a kind of metaphysical space in which we move reflects a profound intuition. The container that comprises time, which *supplies* time, is the object as a container for anxiety in Bion's sense – the agent that performs the "specific action" of repressing that anxiety (Freud 1950, 297).

If this is considered to be an acceptable interpretation of what Bion calls thought, it will also be acceptable to hold that thought is made up not only of a lack (in that case it would be only the "no", without the second half of the undivided expression "no-breast" – i.e. without the "-breast" that in itself stands for the memory/conception of satisfaction), but also, in the state of privation, of an appearance of presence that steers the wish. The "no" or crossed-out no-breast ("no-bre**X**ast") would then be what Bion calls *noughtness*, the state of nameless terror in which an infant experiences an absolute void of meaning, without even the memory or the concept of the thing. When reduced to a mere "no" or noughtness, the no-breast (a virtual breast) can no longer be the retina that intercepts the vibrations of light from the multiplicity of memory traces of the breast (a concrete breast) as condensed by memory. It can no longer function as their resonance chamber or "reverberation" space (Birksted-Breen 2009). However, what is the sense of time if not the experience of echoing – as when a sound impinges on an obstacle or reflection point – the perception in memory, and then, ad infinitum, of the memory in a (new) perception? There would not be an echo without the *no*, in the absurd situation of an infant who never separates from the breast, but nor would it exist if the obstacle were infinitely far away. *Yet, it must always be borne in mind that what moves Echo is her unsatisfied love for Narcissus.*

The characteristics of the arrow of time mentioned earlier (*minus* and *towards*) must now be supplemented with a third element, that of *intensity*, as expressed earlier from a different vertex in the concept of "proximity". As stated, conception and thought – the experience of satisfaction and the experience of frustration – cannot be separated. The former runs into the latter and the latter is revived in the former. The two terms are connected by a relationship of mutual inclusion, which is why we call it dialectical. Neither would make sense if isolated from the other. However, at the birth of the psyche, someone would in that case be required to regulate the distance between them. Only in this way, if the intensity falls within the tolerable range, can the two forms of experience persist in this relationship, so that – to return to our earlier metaphor – the elastic band that links them neither snaps nor collapses (two examples of time coming to a halt). The concept of differing intensities thus suggests why time sometimes seems to pass extremely slowly but on other occasions at an accelerated pace.

A seeming aporia must now be addressed. Bion's argument clearly illustrates one point: what renders the alternation of breast and no-breast (more precisely, of the terms derived from these – namely, conception and thought) dialectical and not a mere succession of mutually unrelated experiential data is the factor of *time* that lies concealed in the concept of the toleration of frustration. However, the hypothesis underlying this paper is that the opposite is also the case – that is, that time as the sense of existing is the *product* of the rhythms of presentation of breast and no-breast. How is this to be resolved?

Distinguishing between phylogenesis and ontogenesis would usually clarify such a problem. In terms of the former, what comes first are the intervals that allow the human species *for the first time* gradually to acquire language and subsequently, in the relevant order, primal temporality, lived time, and its abstract representation as linear time. From an ontogenetic perspective, the sense and concept of time are lacking in an infant, but because they are *already present in the object*, he is immersed immediately at birth in a matrix able to supply interaction with the dynamic structuration necessary for establishing the order of time. Logically, therefore, an infant acquires the concept of time from the experience of the primary relationship. What the mother in effect gifts to her child *is* time. In this way, she weaves the (bodily, semiotic, implicit, or procedural) warp of meaning into which the threads of concepts will subsequently be incorporated. It is therefore true that in a sense time can indeed be said to give rise to time. However, that is not tautologous because the subjects of the giver and the receiver are different.

Let us now be more explicit on this point – that is, the role of the *name* (of language) as a means of access to the symbolic level. A logical assumption is that from a genetic perspective, it is the rhythms of care that lay down the primal structure of time in an infant. At first, there is rather a pre-sentiment of time, while a true consciousness of time (of self, of existing) comes into being only later, when the *name* is added to the dialectic of realization/non-realization. At this point, the triangulation of the *conception*, *thought*, and *name* that affords access to the symbolic level can be said to have been internalized.

Kant attributes transcendence to time and space as a priori forms of sensible intuition, and from a different point of view, Heidegger ascribes transcendence to primal temporality. Could this transcendence be translated by means of psychoanalytic concepts in terms of an actual knowledge, but one that is *schematic* or *procedural* – that is,

121

of the body? Or as what Merleau-Ponty (1945) sees as an embodied form of temporality? After all, we know *how* (a *mode* of being) to ride a bicycle but would be hard put to it to describe riding a bicycle as a *thing* (an intrinsic content). This might help to resolve Saint Augustine's (1961) familiar paradox concerning time: that it is something that is well known, but only until we enquire into what it actually is. In that case, however, it would certainly not be transcendent in the Kantian sense, because it would have to be deemed not already given but instead learned.

The Order of Time

In order, if possible, to gain an even clearer impression of how time comes into being, and in particular how it becomes *lived time*, let us now consider Bion's model of the mother who constantly "hooks" herself onto the infant in the moment of at-one-ment. At-one-ment is a state of being a complete unity that corresponds to a conception – that is, the experience of concrete satisfaction; what is needed here is in fact a fractal model of what we call "experience", or in other words of an object in which the same structure is repeated recursively on different scales. This enables the mother to construct the *links* between breast and no-breast which, in a seesawing play of repetition and variation, allow the infant to formulate thoughts and subsequently to link them together in the "second-degree" thoughts represented by dream thoughts and waking thoughts.

At-one-ment is derived from "atonement", or sacrifice and reconciliation with the Divinity. It is therefore in itself already pregnant with meaning, partly because it suggests a sinusoidal curve with upward and downward undulations (expiation and guilt). However, by dividing the word up with hyphens, Bion is also playing with the signifier. The unity of the word is fragmented into the evocative "trinity" of *at*, *one*, and *-ment*. This can be seen as the coincidence of the three moments of conception, the act of naming, and thought with the three modes of experiencing time – future, present, and past, as differing from measurable/linear time – which Bergson weaves into the concept of "duration" (Massey 2015) and Heidegger (1927b) into that of the three "ek-static openings" of "originary temporality".[14]

After all, "at", from Latin *ad-*, is an expression of location or movement towards; "one" suggests *unity*, *oneness*, or *sameness*, O;

while "-ment" comes from -*mentum*, a suffix which, when appended to word roots, indicates the result of an action. The *at* in the sense of "towards" expresses the *future*-oriented direction, so that it is *thought* – i.e. frustration – which we have learned to see as never absolute, supplied by the absence of the object. The -*ment* corresponds to positive realization or the experience of gratification, or *conception* or the *past*. However, let us now take a closer look at the *one*. *It could be said to express the present*, because, between an "after" (*at*) that comes first in the word and a "before" (-*ment*) that comes afterwards, it denotes the synthesis of being-one with the object and thereby with the wider network of sociality. In other words, a schema can be imagined in which time (*consciousness*) emerges in the void/negativity of frustration (*thought*) into which the subject avoids plunging because it is anchored to the gratification (*conception*) by the intersubjective *present* of the *concept* (i.e. essentially by the ego).[15] As stated, the position of the -*ment* (the completed action) at the end of the word is significant, first because it suggests the importance of the *end* in assigning meaning to everything that comes before it (and to the whole of existence) and vice versa, and second because, by reversing the ingenuous order of the arrow of time, it comes *after* the future alluded to by the *at*-.

At the heart of the compound word, "one" tellingly expresses the concept of unison as a proto-concept – that is to say, it is first and foremost *emotional/affective* (!)– and the first kindling of consciousness of self, as well as of the "indeterminate One" of the sacred seen as the foundation, value, or absolute essence of human life. Hence, the central syllable of the word essentially references both the process of mutual mother-infant recognition, which can initially only be non-verbal or semiotic in nature, and that of identification of the dyad with the "divine" aspect of language and the community. This is a key point. In order to arrive at the establishment of temporality and its derivatives, an indispensable factor is that which brings about the attribution of a name to a thing, as described by Bion in "A Theory of Thinking". Put differently, *from the infant's perspective*, once the dialectic of breast and no-breast (or conception and thought) has arisen thanks to the object – this dialectic can be deemed to be the "implicit"/primal matrix of time – the third stage, that of naming things, or of the *concept*, is essential in order for lived time to be arrived at.

Although this issue is barely touched upon in Bion's short paper, it is absolutely vital. The grafting of temporality onto an infant's body, which is the prelude to the opening up of the world of life, takes place, Bion writes, when the object "fixes" *conceptions* and *thoughts* – i.e. when it gives a name to the infinite experiences of presentation and representation that are already linked together in a bond of mutual affirmation/negation, thus providing the infant with access to the concept. Only then, once consciousness of self has been established *intersubjectively*, can he begin to be – that is, to have consciousness of time as an experience or presence to himself. There is no other way of initiating an infant's sense of self and of the flowing of time. Animals, it may be conjectured, do not have time.

We experience the present subjectively as *the only thing that exists* if it is the case that conception and thought are nothing but traces of past and future respectively. We are of course conscious of past and future, but only *in* the present. We project backwards and forwards, but always *from* the present. It must at the same time be acknowledged that logically the present, consisting as it does of the sum of something that is no longer and something that is not yet – i.e. of two nothings (*no-things*) – does *not* itself exist. At least, it cannot exist as a given of nature among other givens. Hence, the *now* afforded by the dialectical relationship of elements that immediately negate and simultaneously affirm each other must be thought of as a paradoxical locus. However, what might its nature as both existing and not existing consist in?

Here is a hypothesis. The present (the Cartesian experience of the *cogito*, the unquestionability of being in the here and now) is the awareness afforded by the *name* (concept, language, O/other), achieved by way of moments of at-one-ment, of the differential play of psychic traces which, although, as we have seen, they are identical in both internal/structural/psychological and external/"material"/neurological terms, nevertheless differ in subjective content and direction. It is the consciousness of the functional split between perception and representational activities – on the level of memory and imagination respectively – to which Bion's concepts of conception and thought can be traced back. The *now* exists because it is the concept of self that results from the abstraction of their infinite registrations in memory. However, returning as we must to the *name*, we cannot fail to attribute to it too the nature of a *process* and are bound to note the coincidence of its structure with that of temporality. For when we speak of a name, concept, or abstraction, we are referring to the dialectic of recognition and intersubjectivity.

Hence, the present shares the paradoxical nature of the psyche and of language. Could it possibly be said that a word exists other than in a relationship of identity with and difference from all other words – words that affirm it by negating it and negate it by affirming it? This point being clearly understood, it appears obvious that the relationship between thing and no-thing, between change[16] (or movement) inherent in the real and its intuition in the subject as time and space, is no different from the equally paradoxical relationship between any name and the thing it denotes – for instance, the word "cat" and the animal "cat". It is in the nature of linguistic signs that they do *not* exist if taken individually but exist only if seen as elements of the *system* of language. To use a formula, the *tending-towards* or *distancing-from* of the arrow in "no → breast" can be revealed in the clarity of consciousness as *now* only by virtue of the *between* (individuals) of language, whose nature is radically intersubjective. It would be ingenuous to see the *now* as pure presence and to trace it back to perception and its difference from memory. On the one hand, perception itself is steeped in representations,[17] while on the other, being conscious, it is at all events a phenomenon of *intermediacy*. The present does not exist because it can find a home for itself only in the virtual space of intersubjectivity and language.

The name is therefore indispensable. If the breast is always a "psycho-somatic breast" (Bion 1962b, 34) (or rather, I would say, a somato-psychic one) – that is, an agent that initially supplies an infant with a "schematic" (bodily, semiotic) meaning and later with a more properly psychic (conceptual, linguistic) meaning – then in the absence of this second component, that of consciousness of self, temporality will still be incomplete. What is lacking is the ego (-*one*-) that notices its effects and refers to itself the feeling of being *pulled* in opposing directions owing to the simultaneous presence of contrasting (affective) tensions towards the past (-*ment*) and the future (*at*-). The subject feels alive when the summation of these forces is directed towards the future, when the avoidance of pain coexists with "faith" in the possibility of finding the object again.

In conclusion, even if the origin of time will always necessarily be an enigma, I hope to have adequately supported the thesis that a sophisticated and up-to-date conception of temporality is contained in the concepts, presented in "A Theory of Thinking", of the *breast, no-breast, at-one-ment, conception, thought, name,* and *projective identification*. Bion achieves the highly creditable result of conceiving a *psychoanalytic* theory of time – in other words, one based on the subtle empirical knowledge that only our discipline can claim for itself – of the innumerable facets of the infant's primary relationship with the object, and of the various expressions of mental suffering. It is moreover a theory consistent with the deepest and most evocative productions of contemporary philosophy on the subject. It is indeed not abstractly based on a consciousness-related approach, because it attributes the origin of time to the facticity of an infant's existence, which is in itself intersubjective in nature, and on his "being-in-the-world", although that world can only be conceived of as substantially confined to the relationship with the breast and the object.

I see our discussion solely as a preliminary to a more extensive consideration. However, if asked to summarize its conclusions in a formula, I would say that the primal *structure* of time is supplied not by a succession of discontinuous elements disposed as if along a line of infinite length, even if in ordinary parlance this is one of the derived forms of lived time. It stems instead from the movement of an indivisible totality apprehended *intersubjectively* in the consciousness of self. Space-time (or time-space) cannot be thought of as a property or entity of the physical world, as *absolute* time, existing in and for itself without regard for what makes us human. It is more reasonable to see it as a form – determined by history and mediated by language, like subjectivity itself, with which it in fact coincides – of *human* apprehension of the world. In a "nutshell", perhaps long, long ago – to paraphrase Ian McEwan – time (the *now*) was begotten, and is over and over again begotten, by *pain*.

Notes

1 Translated by Philip Slotkin MA Cantab.
2 All quotes indicated only by the page number refer to this version.
3 [Translator's note: For convenience, the masculine form is used for both sexes throughout this translation.]
4 Here I can mention only a few of the contributions on this subject, and in particular those which, in contrast to Kant and to Freud's essentially "neo-Kantian" vision – neo-Kantian in the sense of monadic and "physiologistic", because intrinsic to consciousness – centre on the non-aprioristic nature of time, i.e. the view that it is already given and precedes experience): Sabbadini (1989), Priel (1997), Butler (1999), Noel-Smith (2002), Birksted-Breen (2009).

5 As to the value of a dialogue with philosophy, see Bergson (2002, xix f.): "Without denying to psychology, any more than to metaphysics, the right to make itself into an independent science, we believe that each of these two sciences should set problems to the other and can, in a measure, help it to solve them".

6 In the jargon of Heidegger (1927b), which I borrow while adapting it to my own context, this term denotes the *primal* structure of time (*Zeitlichkeit*), from which there stem both the sense of lived time (*Zeit*) and the abstract representation of linear, measurable time.

7 The essential significance of the concept of a function is that it compels one to consider the pair of terms it connects rather than each term individually.

8 I thank L. Zanni for letting me know that here Bion misquotes from L. Carroll's novel, as the Hatter says: "It's always six o'clock now" (2003, 64).

9 [Translator's note: Suggested rendering of a line from a poem by Giacomo Leopardi (1798–1837).]

10 In the Romance languages, the notion of a wish is rendered by a word cognate with English "desire" (e.g. Italian *desiderio*).

11 The term occurs for the first time in "A Theory of Thinking".

12 [Translator's note: That is, as the opposite of *après-coup*, or of Freud's *Nachträglichkeit*.]

13 However, see Heidegger's concept of *Bewandtnis*, for which a possible Italian translation is *appagatività*, or the potential quality of giving satisfaction. [Translator's note: The term is often rendered in English by "involvement".]

14 Heidegger uses the concept of ecstatic time (*ékstasis*, from ἐξίστημι, meaning to put outside or to go out of oneself) to emphasize primal time's nature as non-presence or non-substance, but instead as essentially off-centred. The quality of meaningfulness afforded by the possibility of temporalizing experience stems from the fact of being a subject always *outside itself*, of ex-tending oneself from the past into the future and vice versa. Opening a window onto the world signifies running the risk of leaning out into the void of *nothingness* and alienation from the Other.

15 In order for time not to be out of joint, as Hamlet complains, these three actors must deliver their hidden lines in harmony with each other. Time falls ill if one of the three takes over the entire stage.

16 It may be postulated that, in objective terms – i.e. external to the subject's experience – the ultimate origin of this unceasing movement can only be the conception proposed by physics of the matter of the universe and the principle of entropy (Rovelli 2017). Subjectively, however, what the hypothesis of this primal "movement" suggests

(Bergson [1896] describes it as "vibrations"), although understood in a more general sense as *change*, is that it would be difficult to conceive of time other than within a concept of space.

17 Cf. Bergson (1896, 25): "However brief we suppose any perception to be, it always occupies a certain duration, and involves consequently an effort of memory which prolongs one into another a plurality of moments".

5

INTUITION AND *WE-NESS* IN BION AND POST-BIONIAN FIELD THEORY[1]

The person who uses a word like "intuition" … has to take the risk of somebody saying, "What do you mean by intuition?"
(W. R. Bion, "Penetrating Silence")

In this article, I discuss the concept of intuition in Bion as a specific psychoanalytic concept and as a principal one in his thought. As he himself writes: "Intuition is a term which I can use for purposes of mental observation" (Bion 1990, 39). Second, I try to demonstrate that coherent and radical adoption of the *we-ness* vertex (a concept that I introduce as being both explanatory and integrative of the concept of the analytic field) expands the possibility of the analyst intuiting the "facts" of the analysis – and I immediately remind the reader that, for Bion, emotional experience ("feeling") is the thing that comes closest to what we could call a "fact" in analysis (Bion 1987 [1976] [1987 [1976], 234).

A Misunderstanding of Theory

The decision to clarify for myself finally what Bion means by intuition was a revelation (and apologies to all those for whom what I am about to say is already obvious). First of all, I discovered that it is the concept he uses more frequently than any other in his writings, perhaps with the sole exception of "unconscious" and "function"; and then, that for him the only thing that matters in analysis

DOI: 10.4324/9781003625247-5

is the intuition in the session of the emotional climate that is present at a given moment; and lastly, that for Bion, although he worked to the Kleinian model, placing so much emphasis on intuition represents a way to move beyond that model. And not only the Kleinian, Bion uses the concept of intuition as a lever to differentiate himself from all the psychoanalysis that aims at reconstructing the past and bringing to light the nexuses of cause and effect between traumatic events and the transference.

In order to assert this principle, he writes ironically that potatoes cannot be sung (Bion 1965). It is as if analysts who aim at reconstructing the history of the patient's traumas suffered from the illusion that they were singing potatoes (not the word but the thing), i.e. identifying something (the traumatic event) which belongs to the category of neither a memory in the form of a representation nor a memory expressible in words; or else, when they do indeed evoke representations and these can be recounted, they remain split off from affect.

Like it or not, for Bion, there is nothing to be done about the past. He also stresses that what is distant in time and space inevitably withdraws from the deep (affective) apprehension that can only be achieved through corporeality (or rather, intercorporeality) and the proximal senses in the here and now. Only what is before the eyes of both parties can be known. Thus, he uses the term "intuition" to indicate this unique possibility of grasping what is present and shared on the unconscious level of communication. Unlike perceiving, intuiting entails both a functional blindness to everything that would hinder phenomenological experience and the "visionariness" of emotional perception. For Bion, intuiting has the same reliability that perceiving has in the basic sciences – and not the kind that "intuiting" would have in those sciences, in the current everyday meaning of the term.

If Bion bases everything on intuition, it is because potatoes are for planting, digging up, cooking, and eating. The type of emotional truth that nourishes psychic growth[2] can only emerge from the encounter of analyst and patient. Only in the flesh-and-blood encounter of the actors in the analytic scene can emotional events become "intuitable" or "sense-able" (Bion 1965, 115), i.e. capable of "hallucination", "the moment an evolution takes place" (Bion 1967, 160).

I could justify my not having grasped the true weight of this concept in Bion sooner by saying that it does not appear in either the Freudian or Kleinian dictionaries of psychoanalysis. In the Bionian dictionaries, López Corvo (2002) devotes only a few lines to it;

Meltzer (1978), despite being one of the first to revive and expand Bion's thought, says nothing;

Ferro and Grotstein have never discussed it as a concept in its own right. Even in *The W. R. Bion Tradition* (Levine and Civitarese 2016), a multi-authored volume featuring the most authoritative Bion scholars, there are only a few references here and there. I myself mentioned it in connection with the role played in Bion by the aesthetic of the sublime and the immaterial dimension of the elements of psychoanalysis (Civitarese 2014, 2016a), and recently in a paper on Bion's concepts of point and line (Civitarese and Berrini 2022a, 2022b), but overall still in a fairly generic manner.

We might think that some of these authors have expressed what intuition means in Bion by addressing related concepts; reverie, for example, or insight. However, the word "intuition" brings with it resonances of its own that cannot be completely substituted by other terms. In the end, the topic of intuition is singularly ungraspable. In fact, almost nobody treats it as a genuine tool to be used in clinical work or is able to endow it with precise attributes. A partial exception may be the contribution of several authors gathered into a recent volume edited by Grimalt (2022). Closest, however, to the perspective I am trying to illustrate here is that of Ogden (2015), but again with obvious differences. I do not have space here to discuss the literature but, as far as I know, none of the authors I have mentioned frames intuition in Bion in relation to post-Bionian analytic field theory[3] (Civitarese 2023a, 2023b, 2024).

The misapprehension to be cleared up straight away, one that has partly been my own, is that Bion does not use the term "intuition" as anyone else might use it. For him, it is a psychoanalytic concept. Obviously, it is not as if I did not already know that Bion puts emotion at the centre of psychoanalysis, and hence the necessity of intuiting it. However, I had not realized "affectively", passing through the experience of an active learning, the extent to which he does so, and how radically. If, as I have found myself thinking many times, the characteristic of genius is to be extreme in drawing out the consequences of their intuitions, this is surely one of those cases.

In the re-reading to which I have committed myself, the concept of intuition has little by little become for me a species of selected fact (indeed, an intuition in itself), one that more clearly and coherently connects elements of Bion's psychoanalytic theory with each other and his theory with post-Bionian field theory (FT). I had not even gained that kind of awareness from the reading of certain excellent essays on the subject (for example, Levine 2022; Aguayo 2019; Bergstein 2022).

In my case, I believe the decisive factor was the, as it were, "sceptical" decision to do as St Thomas did, i.e. to examine one by one all the occurrences of the term intuition in Bion's *Complete Works* which the careful editorial work of Chris Mawson (2014) has made available to us. This is why, in order to catch the nuances of an elusive concept, I am quoting, more than I do in other cases, the exact expressions used by Bion. Only after doing this, getting to grips with my own unease at not grasping the concept, have I surrendered, although with satisfaction, to the evidence of my previous misunderstanding. Thanks to a term I had earlier viewed with a certain irritation caused by the unscientific halo of vagueness that often surrounds it, but which I now read correctly, I was able to insert a series of disparate concepts into a more ordered picture. I have finally convinced myself that the concept of intuition plays an essential role in Bion's thought.

Bion's Intuition

The concept of intuition recurs a great many times in Bion, a good deal more than other key terms. For example, a cursory search of the *Complete Works* gives 216 occurrences of "intuition", 122 of "alpha function", 38 of "reverie", 26 of "negative capability" (NC), 20 of *at-one-ment*, 2 of "unison", etc. This first indication makes us speculate that for him the concept of intuition takes on an entirely distinctive theoretical meaning. Let's say straight away what intuition is *not*. It is not the untrained attitude of spontaneity that allows one the freedom to think and say whatever one likes in the presumption of having an immediate and direct knowledge of reality. For Bion, on the contrary, intuiting is an ability acquired with study and experience, to the extent that if the analyst did not demonstrate the capacity to use it, he or she could be required to go back into analysis:

> It is possible that the test of sensuous deprivation involved in eschewing memory and desire will bring to light a need for analysis that exists because the analytic experience has not been sufficient, or … analysts may have to accept that advances in insight have

to be matched by further analysis. Such a contingency imposes revision of training and maintenance of capacity for a psycho-analytic career.

(1970, 67)

The problem to be immediately addressed is how to differentiate in-tuition from insight and from "imaginative conjecture". As far as in-sight is concerned, from an etymological viewpoint the term overlaps perfectly with that of intuition. In some languages, the same word is used to translate them. And yet there are differences that are high-lighted in the way Bion uses them. *Insight* evokes more easily than *intuition* a "capacity for judgement" (1967, 81; "insight and judge-ment", 89) based on the theories of psychoanalysis ("psychoanalytical insight"; Bion 1965, 8). Insight can grow over time, as we see from expressions such as "increased insight" (1961, 118), society "has not achieved sufficient insight" and "growth of insight" (1961, 14), "pro-mote a therapeutic development of insight" (1961, 159), "advances in insight" (1970, 67), etc. Moreover, *insight* may represent the content of an interpretation that is accepted or rejected by the patient.

Bion sometimes uses the term *insight* as a synonym not only of "awareness" but also of something more penetrating than the mere abstract knowledge of something. In this sense, it may be ordinary or inspired. It is also the case that Bion uses *insight* in a discursive context where it would be wholly interchangeable with the meaning usually given to *intuition*. Mawson (2014, 120) well conveys the difference be-tween insight and intuition when he talks about a "shift from insight to becoming real". And perhaps he is evoking the hoped-for transi-tion from a form of mere knowledge (K) to a form of knowledge that passes through experience (O).[4] As Rugi (2022) observes, insight may precede intuition, but it is not the same as intuition.

The concept of imaginative conjecture, however, which Bion sometimes calls "wild thought", "guess" or "pictorial image" (Bion 1980), is distinguished from rational conjecture. In fact, the former seems to correspond more to intuition and the latter more to insight because of their imaginative and rational element, respectively. By contrast, regarding the conjectural element – and therefore "judge-ment" based on precise indicators, even if these are not conclusive – I would tend to attribute it exclusively to insight.

It may happen that an imaginative conjecture evolves into a rational conjecture, which in turn may become something that can be confirmed scientifically. When this concept appears, Bion most often accompanies it with hypotheses about embryonic and foetal life, and this seems to be his way of trying to backdate the beginnings of psychic life even further than Melanie Klein had done. It can be seen how in the expression imaginative conjecture the meaning conveyed by the first term of "conjecture" prevails, i.e. according to the dictionary, "supposition" or "judgement".

In the Mirror of Husserl

The concept of intuition has a long history in philosophy, and Bion draws on it directly. Indeed, he refers explicitly to Kant, but quite clearly reveals other influences. It would, for example, be of the greatest interest to know if he ever read Husserl. Bion hardly ever quotes his sources and we do not know if and how he came into contact with Husserl's thought, but the similarities are striking, in particular those between their respective concepts of intuition and *eidetic intuition*, and between negative capability/faith (NC/F) and *epoché*.

Especially in the case of Husserl, recalling these more or less chance convergences is not mere historical curiosity or a theoretical suggestion awaiting further elaboration. On the contrary, it serves our purpose to define as clearly and distinctly as possible what Bion means by intuition. In this way, we remove the concept from the aura of vagueness and mystification that sometimes surrounds it – what Lacan (1966, 210) would call the "vacuous buzzword of intuitionist and even phenomenological psychology". Indeed, even the accusations of mysticism that will be directed at Bion are the same as those suffered by Husserl:

> Husserl claims that, besides seeing particular things and events in sensuous perception, we can *see* essences through a non-sensuous intuition that is founded on sensuous perception and is analogous with it. Husserl occasionally calls this "ideation". *Husserl's critics ... claimed that Husserl was invoking a mystical vision* but Husserl denied it was in any way mysterious although he did think *eidetic insight requires trained attention.*
> (Moran and Cohen 2012, 91, emphasis added)

It is astonishing to note that if we changed the names, the passage could refer to Bion and his concept of intuition.

134

Husserl is interested in highlighting the transcendental – i.e. not directly accessible to consciousness – structure of subjectivity and hence the background elements that render experience possible. To this end, as far back as 1905, he introduces for the first time a new way of doing research, which he publishes a few years later in *Ideas* (1913). The method is set out in three stages.

First, the observer *suspends* the naive natural attitude of placing themself in front of some object, puts in brackets everything they already know about it, and regards it with eyes as unencumbered as possible by prejudices, beliefs, ideas, etc. Husserl christens this way of freeing oneself from the already known "epoché", "phenomenological reduction", or "transcendental phenomenological reduction". Looking at an object *as if* for the first time is something entirely counterintuitive but reveals itself to be a powerful device for identifying characteristics, and indeed specifically those that are *necessary*, which could otherwise pass unobserved.

The second step is "eidetic or imaginative free variation" or "phantasy variation" (Moran and Cohen 2012, 92). The observer strives to grasp the essence of the object under examination by putting their faculty of imagination to work. If in their mind they imagine an object according to various resemblances and from different visual angles, adding and eliminating certain attributes, in the end, they succeed in selecting those that are *essential*, the components that cannot be absolutely excluded. For example, in the concept of tree, we could not fail to include roots, trunk, branches, and leaves.

The third and final move, made possible by the exercise of the imagination, is eidetic intuition proper. Husserl uses both the word *eidetisch*, "eidetic", which derives from the Greek εἰδητικός, in turn derived from εἴδησις "knowledge", from the root εἰδ- "to see",[5] and *Wesensschau, or Wesenserschauung,* i.e. "eidetic seeing" or "sight (*Schau*) of the essence (*Wesen*)". As we see, both the terms that compose the expression "eidetic intuition" refer etymologically to "visibility" or "seeing". In the term *Wesensschau*, the repetition of two words that both refer to seeing could appear pleonastic, but, in fact, it possesses theoretical value and is equivalent to the sense intended by Valéry (Magrelli 2002) in coining the expression "to see oneself see oneself": when grasping the invariants of experience, not only the object is in play, as could be seen from a naively realistic perspective, but so too is the *relationship* between the intentionality of the subject and the observed object.

Naturally, what I have briefly described is also the coming to birth of one of the most brilliant and influential philosophical currents of the past century. We glimpse the similarities between Husserl's method of the phenomenological epoché and his "twin" Freud's (Aenishanslin 2019) method of freely floating attention. But even more surprising and cogent are the similarities with Bion's concepts of NC/F (Civitarese 2019b) and intuition. To list the main ones: (a) intuiting the essence of a phenomenon, even if not exclusively, is a seeing with the eyes of the imagination; (b) intuition needs to be practised; (c) the practice consists in actively performing the transformations of phenomena (that which shows itself); (d) in order to intuit, it is first necessary to activate a radical suspension of all that is not essential to the object of observation; (e) the key feature of the suspension of judgement, writes Husserl – but the same holds for Bion – is "to effect an "alteration of attitude" (*Einstellungänderung)*" (Moran and Cohen 2012, 110); and (f) is the active method of intuiting the object's essential qualities which is actually something we always do without realizing it.

In the mirror of Husserl, Bion's concept of intuition acquires clearer and less mysterious outlines. In fact, we can comfortably conclude that *the phenomenological epoché is to eidetic intuition according to Husserl as the principle of NC/F is to intuition according to Bion*. It goes without saying that, from this perspective, the fact that Husserl is interested in highlighting the formal essences of the object and Bion the emotional-affective ones is of no consequence. In the same way, the Bionian precept by which the analyst must listen without memory and desire becomes clear as a simple abandonment of the habitual naively realistic or natural view of things.

Another clarification to be made immediately concerns the theoretical postulates that lie upstream of Bion's definition of intuition; to mention only the essential ones: the rejection of the dichotomy between primary and secondary processes; the new conception of the unconscious as a psychoanalytic function of the personality; the idea that dreaming is a digestive activity of the psyche that is carried out not only when we are asleep but also when awake; the definition of emotion as a relational truth that nurtures psychic growth[6]; and the adoption of the mother-infant relationship as a model of the analytic process, etc. If we do not take account of these premises, the intuition we are talking about in relation to Bion is "the wrong one".

Definitory Hypothesis of Intuition

To use his own terminology, intuition is a definitory hypothesis (the name) that Bion gives to a constant conjunction, i.e. to a series of elements that recur together in a given context.[7] In the case in question, the hypothetic aspect of the definitory hypothesis is even more accentuated than usual. On several occasions, Bion claims that he does not know what intuition is and that the analyst can only understand it by using it:

> All he can say is, "If you hear me use it often enough, I hope you may get a rough idea of what I am talking about." The pattern will emerge in which it would seem to be appropriate to say, "Ah, that's what he means by intuition".
>
> (Bion 1976, 42)

Not only is the object of intuition elusive but, as is generally said, intuition itself is obscure. The elements that compose it are heterogenous and have their origin in disparate domains. I will make a provisional list of these now and immediately afterwards give an individual description of each in turn. Meanwhile, I will point out that in three of the five cases (c, d, e), we find ourselves in the domain of a rhetoric of blindness and sight. The elements are (a) the meaning of the term in ordinary language; (b) the meaning that the term acquires in Bion's thought as an instrument of technique; (c) Freud's definition of consciousness as a "sense organ for the perception of the psychic qualities"; (d) the letter to Lou Andreas Salomé of 25 May 1916 in which Freud (1961) confesses that when he does not understand something he resolves the problem by striking it with a beam of darkness; and (e) the inspiration drawn from Kant's transcendental analysis.

Intuition in Ordinary Language

Intuiting means "looking inside". In the Latin *intueri*, there is also the idea, as in the French *garder*, of both "looking" and "protecting" (Ernout and Meillet 1985, 706). So, I wonder if the verb "intuit" might also connote the idea of penetrating into a domain that is especially protected and hidden. Certainly, in the common understanding of the verb, it is not a looking or seeing with the senses, and indeed in philosophy, the expression "sensible intuition" is synonymous with perception. Instead, it denotes an extrasensory capacity for seeing, so to speak, not in the sense of the paranormal but simply of not being conveyed by the senses.

Indeed, Bion writes that emotions cannot be seen with the senses but only with the "senses" that perceive the objects of the internal world – in this case, therefore, it is no longer properly speaking a matter of senses but of an imaginative faculty with a passive inflection. The oneiric and mental views of an object lack the lively sensory qualities that by contrast characterize perception in the strict sense.

Nevertheless, it would be a mistake to think that intuition can really do without the senses – and this applies even to categorical intuition, i.e. intuition lacking some or all of the elements of sensoriality. Not directly but indirectly, and in a manner that is distracted and attentive at the same time, intuition can only be based on data gathered by the senses. "Indirectly" means, however, that these data are obtained from interiority. It is along a different route from that of perception that the subject comes to make the data into a synthesis.

For our purposes, the definition of intuition that we read in dictionaries, for example as a synonym of "a supposition or hunch or suspicion" (Bion, 1977, 54), may be misleading. The risk is that we presume to know what Bion means by intuition. So, because intuition is an ability we all recognize, we could think all that is required in everyday life is a "normal" capacity for intuition, even if we are prepared to acknowledge that we do not all have it to the same degree. Instead, although the meaning of intuition in ordinary language *plays a part in it* and can in turn be illuminated by it, this is not the definition of intuition according to Bion. Just as Freud rightly mistrusts the concept of insight as vague and irrational (Rugi 2022), so Bion, even though he gets mistaken for a mystic, carefully avoids relying on a conception of intuition that is pre-technical.

Intuition as an Instrument of Technique

Grotstein (2007, original emphasis, 15) observes that "Bion, the intuitionist, was almost obsessive about achieving *precision* in his ideas". So the intuition he talks about is a "psychoanalytic" intuition that must be "accurate". We deduce this from expressions like "psychoanalytically developed intuitions" (Bion 1961, 165), "the intuitions developed by present-day psycho-analytic training" (1961, 142), and "psycho-analytically augmented intuition" (1990, 40). The analyst must undertake "practice, analogous to the musician's scales and exercises, to sharpen and develop intuition" (1963, 73) and "to follow the advice I am giving is a difficult discipline" (1970, 56). Engaging in "the psycho-analytical game may develop the analyst's intuition (as a musician's exercises facilitate an actual musical creation though not themselves being more than scales and other manual exercises"; 1965, 130).[8] Bion also invents an instrument for doing these exercises and "training" himself in psychoanalytic intuition: the Grid.

This is an important aspect because it allows us to refute the idea of Bion as a mystic. I often read reflections on the limits of technique. However, it also needs to be said that technique is not the enemy of spontaneity but its best ally. Only a refined technique has the privilege of access to spontaneity. Spontaneity is not the same thing as a simplistic and pre-technical spontaneism but the opposite. If this were not so, Bion would not accompany the concept of intuition with the handmaid represented every time by the recall to exercises, to discipline, to the "psychoanalytic game" of the Grid, etc. The desire to give up technique can be just as harmful as using one that is stereotyped and distancing. But technique must be integrated by unconscious memory. Estranged from itself, it can then be elevated to another level.

Technique goes wrong when it is still visible, when it is insufficiently mastered and thus imposes itself on the subject's conscious attention. When instead it is unconscious and, so to speak, "automatic", technique can operate with speed and precision, and in an atmosphere of confidence. For this reason, even a disciplined way of using intuition may appear irrational because we do not see the various transitions entailed in the process: neither the logical steps nor the effects of the lightning-fast work of integration between various forms of memory (both procedural and declarative), of sensitivity (external and internal), and of knowledge (categorical, affective, and corporeal).

One way of making intuition more and more unconscious is to do *conscious* exercises, which is to some extent contradictory, in avoiding memory, desire, and understanding. What I mean by this is that if the analyst trains herself to de-concretize the analytic story as if it were nothing but an infinite metaphor of the field's emotional transformations, she has a way of internalizing this ability, i.e. of rendering it steadily more unconscious. As Bion writes: "the psycho-analyst should exercise his intuition in such a way that it is not damaged by the intrusion of memory, desire and understanding" (1992, 315). In this case, repetition has an integrating and emancipating function, creating both explicit and implicit "concepts" of things that little by little require less and less deliberate attention. The attention becomes incorporated by the concept itself, by its readiness to be recalled and used at the right moment. The more the capacity for intuition grows, the more conscious space is left for catching the differences between various situations.

According to Bion, we are always dreaming, and "dreaming" means unconscious thought (Ogden 2010). So it follows from this that we are always striving to "intuit" the truth of what is happening inside and around us. The component of "Faith" (F) in NC, the mental state of receptivity induced by it, arises from having had so many experiences of our capacity for intuition, and as a consequence, it facilitates our ability to give ourselves up to it.

To sum up, renouncing technique in order to cultivate an instinctive, rapid, reliable mode of thought requires *more* study of technique, not less. Clearly, the negativity of NC/F is not in fact negative at all (Fusini 2015). Presuming to learn the principles of a new model of psychoanalysis in a rush causes an immediate *disturbance by excess of attention*, in other words, a deficit of attention. The paradox is that the more attention exercises we do – for example, as I will suggest later, in adopting the vertex of "we-ness" – the more we can hope to rely on intuition, i.e. on the unconscious comprehension that can do without focused attention.

Sense Organ for the Perception of Psychic Qualities and Psychic Growth

As the senses are deputed to perceive concrete objects that are located outside the individual in a spatial and temporal dimension, so – writes Freud – we can think of consciousness as "the "sense organ" of psychic reality" (quoted in Bion 1967, 164). Intuition as oneiric or imaginative "perception" is for the domain of the mind or thought what sight and the other senses are for concrete objects. Psychic qualities are depression, anxiety, fear, "disturbances, perturbations, turbulences that are violent, invisible, insensible" (Bion 1975, 61), jealousy, shame, possessiveness, etc. They cannot be seen,

140

touched, sniffed, tasted, but by analogy can be seen, sniffed, touched, tasted with the intuition.

Between perception and intuition, the two radar systems that provide the psyche with data, one that must probe the external world, the other the internal world, there are some differences which favour the latter, including its great versatility. Whereas concrete objects are perceived by a variety of senses, psychic qualities – or rather, "sense impressions" (although that is not literally what they are) – of emotional experience are all perceived by a single "sense": intuition, of course. But from another vertex, it is not single, given that it presents itself in different guises.

Why is it important to have a sense organ like intuition, one that is obscure in the same way as the objects it must detect? Because if it is missing or does not function well, the subject is not aware of their emotional experience, and this means deprivation of truth, the essential factor that nurtures psychic growth. In order to understand this point, it is essential to bear in mind that Bion has an intersubjective and pragmatic conception of truth as an agreement within a community – it matters little whether it be the plurality within one subject or in a group of two or more individuals – even though it could never be based solely on an explicit agreement.

A Beam of Intense Darkness

In a passage from a letter sent to a fascinating woman, a genius and a dear pupil, herself destined to become famous, Freud writes that when he does not understand something he needs to illuminate it with a beam of darkness. We are in 1916, but Freud has already developed the concepts of the fundamental rule and uniformly suspended attention between 1892 and 1898 (Le Guen 2008), while Husserl teaches the concept of epoché in his university courses of 1906–1907. With the fundamental rule Freud explains his own phenomenological working method. We can see the essence of things more clearly if we eliminate all the noise of the already known: in other words, the limitations of logical thought.

In Freud, the simple practical rule expressed in a private letter is embodied in the conjoined concepts of free association and uniformly suspended attention. Out of the same rule, but reformulated as NC/F, Bion makes one of the architraves of his theory of technique. Reasoning is logical and linear: the aim of treatment is to increase the patient's capacity for making use of their own emotional experience as an embodied form of knowledge; in order to increase this capacity, the analyst must know how to see better, i.e. be in a position to deputize for the patient's insufficiently developed or temporarily overburdened function. Therefore, the analyst must develop to the maximum the capacity for "night vision"; in order to develop this capacity and more clearly see the feeble signals that reflect what is happening, analysts must exert themselves to eliminate every source of light pollution from the field of observation.

The sources of light pollution are the *voluntary* memories, desires, and understanding. But prior to these, they are also the data that we receive from the senses. The senses give sensory impressions that promote *logical thought*, not intuitive thought. Intuitive thought is not made of sensory impressions but impressions of another order: sensations and feelings that have not been rationally and critically screened; ideas not based on abstract reasoning, which are equally indefinite with respect to their origin and to the form they assume, and not without the subject being unaware of their nature.

Let's use a metaphor here. Bion would say that if you want to be a Michelin-starred chef, you must obtain high-quality ingredients. The flavours should never be the tired, standardized ones of the food industry. The problem of preparing and cooking the dishes only arises afterwards. For the subject, "understanding" means depending on being able to provide oneself with data in the form of images. Cultivating intuition is learning to recognize the most genuine ingredients, which are then prepared and cooked by concepts and plated in the forms of discursive thought.

It is easy to see how the technique that enables us to exercise intuition coincides with the principle of NC/F. Among all Bion's theoretical formulations, this is perhaps the best known and most misunderstood. If I had to explain it in a few words, I would say it is about making *unconscious* memory, desire, and understanding work. Nothing could be further from the common-sense definition of intuition, precisely because, on the basis of common sense, analysts for the most part disregard Bion's militaristic injunction to forget the past and concentrate only on the present. The criticism that is still most often directed at the theory of the analytic field, which is the only theory that picks up and radically rewrites this instruction of Bion's, is that it neglects the patient's history. It is exactly the same criticism against which Bion vigorously defends himself in certain passages of his writings.

For my part, however, I have to say that only by concerning myself with the notion of intuition at a deep level and finding a sense of relief and gratitude (for psychoanalysis, for Freud and Bion, and for my own efforts to make it live for me) have I come to appreciate the enormous significance of the concept of NC/F. Anyone who thinks about NC/F without keeping in mind the other wing of Bion's theory – that it is a technique for seeing in the dark, and that what the analyst *must* see ("one has to 'intuit'"; Bion 1990, 127) is the unconscious emotional experience of the moment – will have difficulty grasping its profound meaning.

To say it is a matter of not letting oneself be blinded by nexuses of cause and effect that have nothing to do with what is before the eyes of the analyst and the patient, a matter of privileging involuntary memory, of resisting empathism, of avoiding the flat application of grids and pre-constituted reading, is correct. But these formulations still seem a bit generic to me. Something is missing. If, with Bion, we let ourselves be persuaded about the meaning with which emotional experience is endowed in promoting psychic growth, *it becomes self-evident that concerning oneself with anything else is merely a distraction and a waste of time.*

After all, Bion's concentration on the evolution of what he calls the O of the session – as he explains, the "absolute essence … this central feature of every situation that the psycho-analyst has to meet" (1970, 89) – is merely a magnification of Freud's concept of transference neurosis and a refinement of Melanie Klein's idea by which interpretation must be directed at the anxiety emerging in the here and now. They are both concepts that lead us to take the analyst's subjectivity increasingly into account. The novelty is not in the way Bion works as an analyst, which is Kleinian when all is said and done, but in the emphasis, he places on the meaning of emotional experience and the absolute necessity of intuiting it. If we combine this with the redefinition of projective identification as a non-verbal mode of communication, we see that his theorizing inevitably starts to characterize itself little by little as increasingly intersubjective, although it never becomes entirely so.

So, it is taken for granted that "psychoanalytic "observation" is concerned neither with what has happened nor with what is going to happen, but with what *is* happening. Furthermore, "it is not concerned with sense impressions or objects of sense" (Bion 1992, 288). How could we ever concern ourselves in any way but abstractly with an emotion that is not present but only remembered? By contrast, the analyst can get into contact with the present emotion – as the only emotion they really can get into contact with – if they see it as something shared, something with which they can be at one. Freud's concept of the enemy who cannot be destroyed "*in absentia* or *in effigie*" (1912, 108) – i.e. by making use of memories in the form of mere representations – becomes in Bion the absolute centrality conferred on emotion in theory and in clinical work.

So, what is missing is the active part: i.e. imagining that when they operate with NC/F the analyst is like the soldier who carries out a dangerous mission in total darkness. The instruments they make use of for night vision only work if they avoid turning on sources of light. *We can identify these instruments in the ability to use reverie or other manifestations of dream-thought in the technically correct manner.* By reverie I mean waking fantasies, sensations, emotions, actions *by which analysts allow themselves to be visited and surprised.* Abstract contents, ideas, can also have the quality of reverie if they arise as in a dream. What matters is the spontaneity and immediacy with which they present themselves.

To sum up, the concept of NC/F acquires pregnancy only if seen as preparatory to intuition, not in a general sense but, as Bion defines it in an absolutely idiosyncratic manner, linked to a series of other concepts. The *active* part of intuition lies in the inhibition of memory, desire, and understanding. This means putting oneself in a situation of "sensuous deprivation" (Bion 1970, 67), which can also be troubling and difficult to maintain.

In practice, the analyst's aim becomes that of observing the elements of psychic reality. All the rest is of absolutely secondary importance. Bion writes like someone who has discovered a new domain and behaves accordingly. What guides him is his theory of thinking, which is no longer Freud's. For Bion, it would be entirely incongruous to hold onto concepts that no longer correspond to the new way of seeing psychic development: definitely, for example, no longer in terms of a psychology of the isolated subject.

The Freud of the letter to Lou Salomé and Captain Bion meet in Horatio Nelson, the latter two being characters in the phantasmagorical *A Memoir of the Future*. The episode evoked is the famous one from the Battle of Trafalgar when the admiral put the telescope to his blind eye in order to pretend that he could not see the incontrovertibly greater size of the enemy fleet. The analyst, says Bion to himself, must do something like this. Indeed, he asks rhetorically:

> When we are seeing our patients tomorrow would it be a good thing to know as much as possible about psycho-analysis, to have as brilliant an illumination as possible to bring to bear on the facts which we shall come across in tomorrow's session? Or would it be better to blind ourselves artificially so that the dark should be so pervasive that any very faint object will show up – like the expression about looking for a black cat in a dark cellar without any light?
>
> (Bion 1990, 104–105)

The gesture also expresses a certain arrogance, as Bion himself admits: "A most dangerous thing to do! It is arrogant, and in some ways, you have to be a bit of a fool to ignore everything that you have been told and imagine that you would know better" (Bion 1990, 223–224). The association that comes immediately afterwards is equally interesting: "But even in our own childhood our parents were sometimes wrong; they knew much more than we did about how to bring up children, but sometimes, when we were being really naughty, we may also have been quite right – no credit to us" (Bion 1990, 224), because "naughty" could refer to his own attitude to other analysts who think differently. What I mean is that Bion knows how his way of being and doing could make others see him as "arrogant" and "naughty".

Nevertheless, like Nelson, Bion believes that he (and any analyst) must courageously accept the risks inherent in maintaining theses that are unorthodox and consequently may turn out to be disturbing for some people. So Bion refers to the image of "turning a blind eye", but together with another eye "with good enough sight", not only to the technique that leads to intuition but also to the debate within the psychoanalytic institution and the visceral (theological) disputes that characterize it. In any case, if he thinks he is being arrogant because of how he conceives intuition, it means he is certainly not proposing an ordinary definition of it, as would be the case if it were a definition that posed no problem.

Blind Intuitions and Empty Concepts

In order to develop his thinking about intuition, Bion (1987 [1976], 234) begins with a famous quotation from Kant. It is found in the *Critique of Pure Reason* and says "intuitions without concepts are blind, concepts without intuitions are empty". As usual, although Bion often mentions Kant and quotes this sentence in particular, he makes no claim to be a faithful interpreter of the philosopher's thought. What matters is the inspiration he draws from it to develop his own thought. What intrigues him is this distinction between intuitions and concepts and their mutually interdependent relationship. But why does this sentence impress him so much?

One reason could be that it resonates with clinical experience. Kant's sentence anticipates the theory of psyche/soma splitting caused by the fear of the object as the origin of every kind of psychic suffering. Certain patients are all uncontrolled emotionality, in the common sense of the term, and lack the capacity for abstract thought; others are all logic and rationality but lack the vital sap of intuitions in the sense of emotions, affects, and corporeality. Infants, writes Bion, "must be marvellous Kleinians because they know all about what it *feels* like, but they have no concepts, they cannot write any of these great books – their concepts are blind" (Bion 1980, 40). The jocular comment gives us a better understanding of what Bion means by intuition than many explanations in a more abstract vein. The infant *feels* but has no instruments for reading what happens to it. In fact, infants are not only Kleinians but also Kantians since they marvellously demonstrate what Kant means when he talks about *blind* intuitions, those lacking concepts. *It is like saying intuition is what is felt but one does not yet know what it is.*

Later on, adds Bion, the opposite can easily be the case:

> they have forgotten what it is like to feel terrified; they pick up these words but the words are empty – "I'm terrified". You have to notice that it is an empty phrase, it is a concept; it is only verbal; the intuition is missing.

> (Bion 1980, 40)

There is a residue of concepts like empty shells but no longer with emotions (intuitions). And he goes on, "If we can draw attention to this fact then possibly the *concept* of terror and the *feeling* could be

146

married" (Bion 1980, original emphasis, 40). Here is the point: the analyst is the marriage broker who brings together intuitions and concepts, and the priest who celebrates their wedding:

> The task confronting the analyst is to bring intuition and reason to bear on an emotional experience between two people (of whom he is one) in such a way that not only he but also the analysand gains an understanding of the analysand's response to that emotional situation, and does so through an appreciation of the evidence to which the analyst is drawing attention in the course of his interpretations.
>
> (Bion 1992, 46)

We could speculate that the quotation from Kant gave him the model for beta elements, the sense impressions still waiting to be endowed with concepts.

Kant's sentence, which Bion cites many times, means that we can only experience what we can grasp with our senses, i.e. objects situated in space and time. In other words, without concepts, there can be neither thought nor self-consciousness. Here, Kant is referring to sensible intuitions, i.e. perceptions. But we also "perceive" emotions, or rather we do *not* perceive them but are affected by them. We can only call them emotions once we have fused them with concepts, otherwise we are in the situation, recalled above, of the infant (or animal) that *feels* but does not *know*. What are we to do?

Becoming Clairvoyant or Intuition *vs.* Reverie

We have differentiated intuition from insight but, in order to progress further, we must now distinguish it from reverie, which I regard as an exemplar of all the manifestations of the oneiric. To this end, we can take as our starting point a significant passage from *Transformations* where Bion gives a splendid definition of intuition: "intuition itself is a *function* of $\pm \underleftarrow{\uparrow}$" (Bion 1965, 110, emphasis added), i.e. of the sign he calls "in search of existence" (107). Bion uses this formula to indicate the positive emotional valence of a state of openness, expectancy, and creative availability, which allows the subject to come into contact with the not-known. Accepting the suggestion that intuition is a *function*, let us then say that reverie represents one of its *factors*[9]

Another passage we can surely draw upon is the one where Bion (1962b, 36) calls reverie "a factor of the mother's alpha function", the highly important function through which she expresses her love for the baby. Widening this definition to embrace other, overlapping concepts of Bion's, we can say that besides the maternal *capacity for reverie* (which is not the same thing as reverie, but something broader, like "psychic digestion"), in Bion's theory "intuiting" is what is done by the alpha function as a more general concept, by the unconscious as a psychoanalytic function of the personality, by the container-contained relationship, by the function of being "in search of existence" (Civitarese 2021a), etc. The list includes some of the concepts invented by Bion to describe the mysterious passage from sensations and raw emotions predominantly to images as constitutive of visual thought.

In this regard, the term *intuition* is the concept that sums them all up, *the concept of these concepts*. All those listed are *functions of transformation* whose final product is the interweaving of sense and meaning. The *factors* of the general function of intuition, which, I repeat, make themselves manifest in the various modes mentioned above, are instead the single elements that can stimulate or inhibit it, but do not in themselves coincide with the function. A painter knows how to paint (function) but it may happen that the quality of the light in the room (factor) does or does not give him the conditions in which to fulfil his task. An analyst knows how to be receptive to the discourse of the unconscious (as a function of the personality) but, depending on the circumstances, the permeability – which can be variable – to reveries of various kinds and to other manifestations of what we call the oneiric spectrum – i.e. the capacity for insight (according to the definition I specified at the start) – may increase or reduce the analyst's capacity. In other words, I repeat, *the difference between reverie, insight and intuition is that the first two are factors of the third, which is instead conceived as a function.*

But, more precisely, what does this function called intuition consist in? *For Bion*, I would say, in achieving "intuitive deductions" about the unconscious emotions that pervade the analytic field. What is indicated by the expression "intuitive deduction" – which is a species of oxymoron, like boiling ice or "affective idea" or "conceptual affect" – is that intuition must also be intellectual and the intelligence of things must also be affective, i.e. integrated. From this, requirement derives the need to include in the definition of intuition a marked character of sensoriality, an element that characterizes the various forms in which intuition presents itself – essentially via the manifestations of the oneiric spectrum. Dreams, hallucinoses, reveries, oneiric flashes, etc. are the *sensible, i.e. visible, counterparts* of the *invisible* psychic qualities represented by the emotions.

In themselves, emotions are affections of the body which are born out of the subject's interaction with the environment. By their nature, they are not directly accessible to the senses. We feel them but cannot objectify them. Feeling an emotion is not perceiving an emotion. It is more like eating chocolate. The taste cannot be "said". Jealousy, anxiety, anger, etc., apart from their possible expressive correlatives, are like eating chocolate or riding a bicycle. Indeed, when we say "jealousy", "anxiety", etc., we are giving a name to something that in itself is ungraspable – like wanting to say the taste of chocolate. Nothing will ever replace the direct experience. All the more so if we are talking about *unconscious* emotions. Put another way, their object exists but withdraws. It could not show itself even if it wanted to; *that is not in its nature*. It is like our saying "I see what you mean". We don't really see anything and yet we still say "we see". What we see does not belong to the category of words or to the matter of concrete objects.

The analyst is someone who is able to make themself visionary or clairvoyant – which is essentially what Keats and Rimbaud say. The analyst is familiar with the world of hallucinosis and dreams. Emotion is not sensory but it is *sense-able, i.e.* it can be grasped thanks to the mediation of waking-dream-thought. If we closely link intuition and the oneiric, intuition is literally equivalent to seeing inside, but in the sense that images may *really* be perceived as intersemiotic translations of present proto-emotional experiences.

We can see where the theoretical and technical-practical aspect stands in this. *Theoretical*: the psyche is engaged all the time in digesting raw sensoriality and does so by generating pictograms that are predominantly visual because of the pre-eminence that this sense has in man, but also olfactory, kinaesthetic, tactile, gustatory, etc.[10] *Technical-practical*: unlike what we tend to do in everyday life, the analyst is "trained" to create the presuppositions for seeing this cinema of the mind and, like the artist, knows how to cultivate the art of shock as a technique for revitalizing experience (Benjamin 1955).

We do not perceive the thing-in-itself of emotions, or emotions as things in themselves, but we "perceive" them in the form of their

149

various hallucinatory derivatives – hallucinatory precisely because they do not correspond directly to the nature of emotions, which is that they cannot be formulated (said, thought) or depicted any more than can the ability to ski or play a good backhand in tennis. So *intuition* refers to the derived or indirect visibility of the emotions, which are themselves affections of corporeality.

The Analyst's Real World and Intuitive Deduction

The human capacity for making up images is a natural and innate fact, but one which every infant needs to have re-inscribed in the category of the symbolic. Let's call emotions transformed proto-emotions and proto-sensations now rendered visible in pictograms.

The problem Bion sets himself is that these emotions are sometimes intense and evident, so the translation takes place without hindrances, while sometimes they are "faint and … obscure" (Bion 1990, 105). *But then it is all the more important that they can be intercepted in time, before they become uncontainable.* Bion has not the slightest doubt that emotions are the reality that concerns psychoanalysis: "These are the psychoanalyst's real world" (Bion 1992, 381). In order to explain the revolutionary potency of the way he gives centrality back to emotion, Meltzer (1984) goes so far as to say that Freud does not have a real theory of the affects because he sees them as a mode of discharging psychic energy and not as a mode of generating meaning.

The idea is that the "sensory impressions" associated with psychic qualities – and impressions from outside too – are transformed into pictograms. The equivalents of external perceptions are the internal perceptions we call hallucinations. *The ability to intuit emotions is equivalent to the ability to hallucinate (but also in sensory modes other than sight). The conceptualization of the intuition of psychic qualities happens in hallucination.* Whether this is true hallucination, hallucinosis, or the normal hallucination of dream and reverie is only a function of consensuality and does not concern the *nature* of the process.

For Bion, an overactive use of memory obstructs intuition. It is like deceiving oneself into thinking there is something to be found in a set of drawers without realizing that in fact they are empty. Voluntary memory, which also means paying too much attention to external reality, prompts the illusion of being able to see something with the senses that is not within the category of the visible – like imagining one can perceive ultrasound or see ultraviolet rays. That which is within the category of the visible is only a derivative. Hence, memory, desire, and understanding cannot be eliminated but one can attempt to ensure that they interfere as little as possible with the intuition or "vision" of emotions.

Shared Unconscious Emotion in the Theory
of the Analytic Field

So far I have tried to argue that intuition is the one word that is more important for Bion than all the others because it designates the analyst's own capacity; what the analyst must be able to do: psychoanalysis itself as an art of intuition, a *capacity* for hallucinating or dreaming or imagining. Capacity for intuition means being able to set up the ideal conditions so that the natural human ability to create pictograms derived from raw sensoriality can both be intensified as a kind of augmented reality and "specialize" in grasping the facts of the analysis.

What I propose here is not merely a reading of the concept of intuition in Bion. Rather, my intention is to present FT as a device that can further increase our capacity for intuiting emotional experience, already "augmented" in intensity thanks to Bion's concepts of dreaming-as-thinking and NC/F, through the coherent and radical introduction of the sense of *we-ness* as a further factor of the function of intuition. My working hypothesis is that even if it is in some respects an illusion to think, we can disentangle the complex dialectic that is established between the thinking of an original author and the developments to which it gives rise – which will thus discover aspects never noticed before or will endorse others previously considered marginal, or even invent them claiming that they were there already – nevertheless, the differences between Bion's thought and FT are clearly identifiable.

Bion lays the foundations for a radically intersubjective theory, and we see this in retrospect from the vantage point of FT, but he does not yet erect the walls of the house. I have always thought that without FT, we would be left with a Bion as inspired as one could wish, but forever confined – as still happens in the panorama of contemporary psychoanalysis, and it's perfectly legitimate, for heaven's sake – in the Kleinian model and the paradigm of an ontological and metapsychological split between *I* and *you*. For Bion at work, and despite his highly original "openness to the O of the session", etc., intuition remains the analyst's intuition of the patient's emotional truth in the here and now. This is the main difference between the use of intuition in Bion and in FT.

I have been prompted to revisit the concept of intuition in order to clear up a problem that bothered me long before, i.e. what we can understand unconscious emotion and shared unconscious emotion to be in the session on the ontological and metapsychological levels. It is an aspect of theory that I have often found myself addressing in supervision and I have noticed that from the radically intersubjective viewpoint which is proper to FT, I struggle to explain it in a persuasive manner.

My thesis is that emotion can be unconscious for two reasons. First, it is not "seen" because it is extremely weak or embryonic, or because it is the object of a projective identification and therefore split off in the patient and evacuated into the analyst, or split off in the analyst and evacuated into the patient; and up to this point, we are in an *I/you* paradigm of two distinct and separate persons. Second, it is not "seen" because, although experienced in a clear manner or else abstractly acknowledged – i.e. deduced – it is considered as either belonging only to the patient or only to the analyst, *but is not considered, as would strictly be dictated by the principles of FT, as a shared emotion.*

The first point should not cause too many problems. That emotion is to be intuited specifically because it is unnoticed seems also to be Bion's opinion: "The emotion to which attention is drawn should be obvious to the analyst, but *unobserved* by the patient" (1963, 74, emphasis added). This stops a painful but unfelt emotion from becoming distressingly obvious to the patient: "Since the analyst's capacity for intuition should enable him to demonstrate an emotion before it has become *painfully* obvious it would help if our search for the elements of emotions was directed to making intuitive deductions easier" (74, original emphasis).

We think about the importance of intercepting hatred before it is transformed into turbulences that are destructive for the patient, the analyst and the analysis. We also understand the emphasis placed on what is unknown. The unconscious aspect of the emotional or proto-emotional realization that it is there to be intuited is re-included in the very definition and use of intuitions as, precisely, "intuitive deductions". There cannot be one term without the other.

The second point is not as obvious but is the focus of the question that this article is posing, a question with practical consequences for analytic technique, is: *is it legitimate to attribute also to the analyst an emotion that is experienced in a clear and distinct manner by the patient or deduced by the analytic conversation even when the analyst does not have the least awareness of it – and naturally vice versa?* The question is obviously rhetorical and, in my opinion, the answer can only be affirmative. The main technical consequence is that, by adopting the *we-perspective*, the viewpoint of *we-ness*, we are better able to challenge the tendency to restrict the analyst's degree of unconscious participation in determining the so-called facts of the analysis. The theoretical vertex of *we-ness* becomes *a further factor of the analyst's capacity for (or function) of intuition.*

Although this principle was already sketched out by Bion in various ways, it is only clarified effectively and efficaciously by FT, and often with hesitations and ambiguities even here.

Giuditta

I am listening to a case being presented at a group supervision. I am struggling to understand how old the patient is. My attention is drawn absent-mindedly to a sentence that begins the second section, "She has been separated for about 10 years". The word "separated" is underlined. In reality, it is as if I were reading only the second part, "about 10 years". So I think that Giuditta (the pseudonym she has been given by the analyst) is more or less ten years old. A little later, listening to the others, I realize I am mistaken. With some surprise, I go back to reread the passage and I see that the correct age was given in the first line, "twelve-year-old", and that ten years refers to the length of time the mother, who is seeking help for her daughter, has been separated from the father. However, I keep faith with my erroneous perception and wonder if, from another point of view, it might be absolutely correct. But then, what might it mean to say that Giuditta has been "separated for about 10 years"?

Intuitively, I think it could represent a way of telling me that it is as if a deep crack (separation, cut, caesura) had worked its way into her personality ten years ago. It is the fracture that Winnicott hypothesizes as being produced between the true and false self and that Bion believes may be the pathological way of surviving in a tyrannical regime of affects. A similar regime is set up when the object asks you rigidly to satisfy its expectations and not to deviate by a millimetre from this imperative.

The initial intuition, with a sense of wonder that is no less intense, was reiterated by other images of splitting: a pair of twins, one of them a graduate while the other had failed at almost everything in life; an early separation in the family history, not only from her mother who had handed her over to a nanny, but also from the nanny herself who died when Giuditta was seven; the gap between the girl's brilliant cognitive abilities and a serious difficulty getting in touch with her own emotions; the figure of the father, alternately impulsive and aggressive, then sometimes affectionate and sociable; lastly, Giuditta's own description of herself as being very close to her friends but also "naughty"; the entirely "anaffective" and fatuous justification that she gives one day for having left a farewell note in which she expressed the intention to harm herself because her mother had "gone shopping" and left her alone in the house.

What I would like to underline is that, for a fraction of a second, it is as if I were *visually* imagining her as cut in two with a sword like the protagonist of Calvino's famous story *The Cloven Viscount*. It is not by chance that, without thinking too much about it, the analyst renamed her Giuditta (Judith), as one who knew a lot about cuts suffered or inflicted. This intuition, which was nevertheless guided by the theoretical preconception of transformations in hallucinosis (Civitarese 2015), shows itself to be authentic for the very reason that it arrives unexpectedly and almost in spite of conscious, voluntary attention – like something being imposed from outside. What it offers is a chance to give sense to a series of elements that would otherwise remain mute. Furthermore, although an image or metaphor is less precise than an abstract formulation, it is nevertheless much richer and seems inexhaustible because of its constituent ambiguity: which we could reformulate as the relative inaccessibility of the semiotic to conceptual translation.

The advantage that the function of intuition has over the factors of mere intellectual comprehension or the simple appearance of a certain image is that it is integrated, that it conveys ideas but also emotions and affects. In the very act of "seeing" the split, I am already starting to close it with my intuition. So, differentiating *factor* from *function* helps us to understand that it is not merely a question of hallucinosis as an "error" or of a certain image in itself, but of a more complex process.

The subsequent passage towards the *we*, in a direction of greater integration, would then involve wondering if the split is *in the link* and therefore also in the person who is doing the observing (the therapist, the patient-analyst group of two, the supervision group). For example, it could be the case that in setting out Giuditta's problems, at some moments, the analyst, or rather the couple, is using too much memory or is resorting too much to causal explanations. It would be like reading, "we are telling ourselves that *we* are separated for ten years". The intuition would no longer refer only to the patient's life story or her intrapsychic organization, or even the analyst in isolation, but to the couple.

A Slip in Reading or a Hallucinosis?

S. says, "My parents live together and have done their best for me; they tried to make me lack as little as possible. Or rather, on the material level they made sure I didn't lack anything". The sentence "they tried to make me lack as little as possible" is written in an unusual way. Normally we would say, "they tried to make sure I lacked as little as possible". In fact, I absent-mindedly read, "they tried to make me lack as *much* as possible". My mistake opens up a wholly new and also disturbing perspective. That an unconscious micro-dream of the couple has in a flash made its way into the strange architecture of the sentence is confirmed by the fact that, straight afterwards, the patient uses the more fluent and correct form, "they made sure I didn't lack anything". Once again it is clear that not only reverie, but also hallucinosis can be a *factor of intuition.*

At this point, the analyst must wonder what he could do to get out of the shared feeling of being victims of this situation. From the viewpoint of *we-ness* it would be, "even though we do not know how and why it happened, it may be that we are (absurdly) trying to make ourselves lack as much as possible". What I mean is that, on the level of the manifest narrative text, the hallucinosis of which the analyst makes himself the spokesman – but seen as a dream of the field, or else dreamed unconsciously by the couple – suggests a situation of mutual incomprehension. Neither patient nor analyst feels recognized. Neither of the two experiences their emotional needs as satisfied.

The emotion or linking function that the analyst can deduce *consciously* from it, *and in this case as a separate subject*, is probably frustration and bitterness (more in H than in L) for both of them. It may be that, even before having an idea of the why it has arisen, what matters is that the analyst asks himself how to contain and transform the climate of negativity that has come over them and might go back seconds, minutes, weeks, months, etc. But the essential point I would like to emphasize here is that, *thanks to the vertex of we-ness, the analyst obtains information that he could not have had he persisted with a vertex where a subject-object antinomy held sway.* Instead, "we-ness" enables us to depose an ontology of the absolute subject and object.

The reason for the negativity in the air may well remain opaque. What matters more is that the analyst takes proper responsibility for what happens: precisely, not in looking for causes, but in the ability to map the emotional field in terms of "us". Taking responsibility certainly does not mean "accusing" the patient or oneself of anything, but simply taking charge of the situation and, if possible, assuming the task of fostering positive transformations. Since the analyst looks at the unconscious dimension of the field from the viewpoint of *we-ness*, she is, first of all, in a position to dismiss any attitude of suspicion since she *has "faith"* in the images that the *common* unconscious produces and thus at the same time gives confidence to himself and to the patient, who by definition, never having felt recognized in his life, lacks confidence. In the second place, seeing herself as one of the actors deeply involved in performing the drama of the analysis, the analyst brings the field of observation as close to herself as possible, is more vital in her reactions and, above all, is less easily led to split emotional and affective understanding from intellectual understanding. This translates into an increase of intimacy with immediate effect.

By this point, the importance of intuition as a specifically psychoanalytic concept should be clearer. In the Bionian analysis, patient and analyst are two busy bees constantly engaged in collecting and refining the honey of truth as the food of psychic growth. This is why we can say that intuition is central to Bion's concept of therapeutic action. The analyst has the task of intuiting the sense of what is happening, i.e. the colour of the present emotional experience, whether it is favourable to the setting up of new links (in L/*love*) or risks making destructive links (in H/*hate*). The prototype of any link is the link to the breast in the primary relationship. This is why there are always fantasies in play that express the emotional quality of contact with the object in the primary relationship.

When the analyst, but sometimes the patient – or better still, the group they are bringing to life – succeeds in intuiting the emotional truth of what is happening, the very act of intuiting is already by its nature carrying out the transformative function of detoxifying the air of negative elements since it generates sense and meaning, i.e. "existence". In this way, it fosters the psychic growth of the two–person group and of both its members.

So, from this viewpoint, interpretation guided by intuition is generally unexpressed, stays most of the time in the analyst's mind, and is indeed synonymous with receptiveness to the unconscious. It can sometimes be made verbally explicit to the patient or just expressed as an interjection or in a gesture but in any case, to use Bion's jargon, it is already in itself "evolution" or psychic maturation.

Indeed, what is produced is *ipso facto* an enlargement of mental space or the psychic function of containment and transformation of raw sensoriality. The mechanism intrinsic to this process consists in the tying of a new link or interpsychic "agreement", which obviously also corresponds to the creation of a new *intra*psychic link. After all, if it is true, as Nancy (1966, 1) says, that "we are meaning", every new link represents an act of "solidarity" that endows subjectivity with a *foundational* value.

In an image, two waves, distinguishable but not separable, forming part of the same liquid surface, meet and enter into resonance, generating a larger (more individualized) wave as a common part of the two original waves. They only partly become the same thing and indeed also continue to exist as single entities. In a similar way, the effect of integration which the reuniting of split-off and fragmented emotional experiences brings with it enables the couple – and simultaneously both of its members – to gain the feeling of being *real* and to feel the reality of what surrounds them.

For Bion, this special capacity for emotional attunement is also at the origin of psychic life, like the force of attraction which atoms of hydrogen and oxygen exercise over each other in order to fuse into the molecule of water. It is not abstract rationality that lies at the heart of thinking, but the more primal logic of emotion. And emotion is not something that is felt in solitude, nor even when one is alone, but is always the result of an encounter with the other and testimony to a fundamental co-being: an encounter that has already happened and was able to take place because it already subsisted in a common transcendental field that organizes the experience – Husserl's "we-community" (Zahavi 2017, 131). The two waves are, so to speak, part of the same sea but weaker, before becoming partially fused. Put another way, the subjectivity of the subject is like a glove that, turned inside out, shows itself to be composed of a dense fabric of intersubjective threads.

Rubiera

We are examining the text of a session in which E. tells the analyst that she no longer wants to live in the city, that she was born in Rubiera, a small village in Abruzzo which I immediately *visualize* against a background of snowy mountains. What is someone like her doing in Milan? As if pausing the work of supervision, I ask my colleague if by any chance she knows Dr R., an excellent analyst and dear friend who is also originally from Rubiera and still spends several weeks there in the summer – as indeed I do when I go back to the nearby town where I was born. The colleague says no (but I had written *"noi"* [we]) and I conclude that I will introduce them to each other at the earliest opportunity. The digression over, we return to the text. With surprise, I read for the first time what E. says straight afterwards:

Still, I've heard from a friend who lives there [Rubiera], she[11] used to work with me at P— and she's practically told me that she's bought a house with her brother, *and maybe she's also renting a room …* The problem is that I'm scared I won't cope, I'm scared that while I'm here [in the city] on my own I'll get horrible thoughts like the last time …

At this point, I cannot help thinking it's as if I had *intuited* – putting my own affectivity into play, that is to say, everything I feel when I think about my friend and Rubiera – what E. is starting to experience in the therapeutic relationship: a place where one can be, a safe "room", where horrible ideas don't come, a room where friendly people live.

It is also clear how I regard the function of supervision as a linking function or one of connection or integration. After all, my task is to help patient and analyst attain a situation of greater intimacy without feeling too much in danger, to bring together what still remains alien and for this reason causes fear. "The friend in Rubiera who may soon have a room to rent" is the character who signals an emotional function of the field both between patient and analyst and between analyst and supervisor.

And then the fact that the village is called Rubiera is extremely interesting. If we listen without memory and understanding – i.e. putting brackets around understanding based on the (naively) realistic view of things, and instead rely on aesthetic-oneiric understanding – the name of the village, which is now between inverted commas, not Rubiera but "Rubiera", evokes the paradoxicality inherent in any affective link. The safe room to be regained is perhaps the one that was violently taken (robbed – "rubata" in Italian) from her long ago. However, it is also the confidence which someone (from the perspective of we-ness, not only E. but symmetrically the analyst too) risks being robbed of again every time they risk entering into a new affective link.

As we see, although it was promoted by a banal association, the type of intuition that I experienced in recounting this vignette belongs above all in the visual-affective category. Other times, it may be an insistence on a single word that recurs in different but close contexts, like a leitmotif that makes it stand out. For example, in the same text, there is the evocation of a door being knocked off its hinges after a row with the parents, and again after one with a partner, and then a banal comment from the analyst like, "Sometimes it's as if a switch is thrown inside you and leads you to act ...".[12] There is an obvious nexus between *porta*-door-portal-caesura and a cause that leads (*porta*) to violent action. But it may that in her head the analyst hears "sometimes it's as if a switch is thrown inside *us* and leads *us* to act ..."

October 2024

This is the date at the top of the text of a session. But it's two years ahead. It is as if, passing through the analyst's hands, the couple were intuiting that they will still be there in the future, doing *therapy*. In the meantime, nothing terrible will happen, despite what they sometimes fear. Read from the viewpoint of we-ness, it could lead us to speculate that they are *both* very afraid of an unexpected and painful break in the treatment. It is the analyst's job to try and detoxify the air of this fear. The same hypothetically holds for the supervisor in the supervision session.

159

We-ness

In clinical practice, Kleinian psychoanalysis and Bion in his Kleinian period – but also Grotstein, for example, despite being a wonderful theorist – all stay within the bounds of a psychoanalysis where the *I/you* split endures, even in its more or less relational permutations, i.e. where they accept greater or lesser degrees of unconscious participation by the analyst in the analytic process. To be clear, I use the term "splitting" instead of simple "division", for example, in order to emphasize the defensive nature that this kind of distinction can have for the analyst. In FT, the surprising viewpoint is often that of *we-ness*. The consequences are varied and substantial.

The function of intuition becomes that of recalling that each interpretation, whether or not it is made explicit to the patient, must have the character of arriving on the wave of NC/F, i.e. passively, as in a dream. In this respect, at least, it is like an intuition in the everyday sense of the term. As such, the concept of intuition serves to return a sort of unity to the various modes of understanding that are available to the analyst. Paraphrasing the line of Kant often quoted by Bion, whatever envelope it comes wrapped in, intuition is still left blind and one-armed if it is not also seen from the vertex of *we-ness*.

In my opinion, we should not understand intuition as an idea, however brilliant and effective, that comes from who knows where; or think that it cannot somehow be attributable to a reverie or transformation in dream or in hallucinosis. How else could it be "disciplined"? What kind of exercises could ever increase the analyst's capacity for intuition? Interventions of this sort, which are sometimes made on the model of intuitions in Bion's sense of the term, have the air of arbitrary interpretations, when they are not frankly outlandish.

If, as Bion writes, intuition is "the knowledge we don't know we have – what we sometimes call 'intuition'" (Bion 1976, 42), our most obvious response is to think in terms of knowledge based on experience, with which dream-thought is impregnated – a semiotic-aesthetic knowledge, not just an abstract one. We always have this knowledge, even during the day when we are awake. If we do not see it, this is because we do not give up the luminosity of focused attention. What wrong-foots us about intuition is that in general we tend to reduce the idea of consciousness to intellectual consciousness only.

160

The fact is, however, that concepts are a necessary but not sufficient component of intuition.

I think the reading of intuition in Bion that I am offering here is endorsed by the image of the poet he uses to talk about it: "It is rather like the poet who is able to express something in a way that draws the attention of the reader to what he might otherwise not be aware of" (Bion 1976, 42). Like poetry, dreaming expresses the ineffable, understood here simply as intentionality or affective intelligence of things and, for this reason, not translatable into words. So, intuiting the truth of what happens in the session means, to use an expression of Freud's, trusting in the mind's poetic function.

Perhaps, we understand a little better why Freud mistrusts intuition, which he likens to divination and revelation, sees as essentially irrational and calmly dismisses to the category of "illusions, the fulfilments of wishful impulses" (Freud 1932, 159). We should not dismiss these doubts as superficial. It is precisely in relation to this other legitimate but unspecific definition that I am trying here to add precision to the particular meaning which the concept of intuition acquires in Bion's thought. That is why I have tried in this paper to extricate intuition from readings that, in my opinion, make it into something excessively vague and undefined.

Obviously, analysts, and all of us in everyday life, could not do without this type of obscurely "normal" intuition. I am making a different point here; what I maintain is the following. First, in order to anchor the Bionian concept of intuition firmly as specific to his thought, we ought to emphasize its reference to the various elements of oneiric sensoriality as *factors* of an essential *function* of the psyche. Second, such a distinction, which Bion himself uses constantly, enables us better to understand the nature of the psychic process of intuition and consequently to increase our capacity for intuiting the significant facts of the analysis.

Third, one of the factors to add to the list of tools already available for improving this capacity for intuiting the emotional truth of what is happening in the here and now of the analysis is to use the vertex of *we-ness* in a radical manner: if intuition is the *function* that is expressed in the act of synthesis with which the analyst consciously monitors the progress of the analytic process, so as to realize its potentialities to the fullest degree, it is better to see the *factors* that prepare the way for them as not exclusive to one or other member of the analytic couple but as co-created, of the field, or intersubjective.

Notes

1 The article consists of an expansion of a short paper presented at the Bion International Online Conference Mexico 2022, "Oneiric Dimensions of the Mind", and subsequently published as such (Civitarese 2023a).

2 "A central part is played by alpha-function in transforming an emotional experience into alpha-elements because a sense of reality matters to the individual in the way that food, drink, air and excretion of waste products matter. Failure to eat, drink or breathe properly has disastrous consequences for life itself. Failure to use the emotional experience produces a comparable disaster in the development of the personality; I include amongst these disasters degrees of psychotic deterioration that could be described as death of the personality" (Bion 1962b, 42).

3 Hereafter FT.

4 I cannot dwell at length on this concept, which I have addressed elsewhere (Civitarese 2019, 2019b, 2020b). Suffice it to say, we can pragmatically understand O as the basic assumption of the group of two: that is, the unconscious emotion which pervades the analyst-patient group at a given moment. If we accept this reading, the consequence is that any intuition can only be directed at grasping the ever-changing nature of O.

5 https://www.treccani.it/vocabolario/eidetico/.

6 Cf. Bion (1962b, 42): "an emotional experience cannot be conceived of in isolation from a relationship".

7 "The intuitive psycho-analytic background is that which I have 'bound' by terms such as pre-conception, definition, notation, attention" (Bion 1965, 138).

8 As is often the case, musical improvisation is the most illuminating model with regard to the concept of intuition. However, in order not to limit ourselves to an obvious and overused analogy, it would be necessary to develop it in terms of an ontology of the body and movement, such as that of Merleau-Ponty. In this respect, see Angelino (2014).

9 The theory of functions is one of the key features of Bion's thought, where it means enabling the construction of provisional models to delineate the psychic elements and their functioning. Despite being uttered in passing, the significance Bion gives to the concept of "function", which appears a total of 965 times in his complete works and mirrors his "processual" rather than substantialist view of the unconscious, is very much worth noting. Bion assigns this concept the task of putting terms from different categories into relation with each other within the same system, as is the case for the mathematical functions:

"'Function' is the name for the mental activity proper to a number of factors operating in consort. 'Factor' is the name for a mental activity operating in consort with other mental activities to constitute a function. Factors are deducible from observation of the functions of which they, in consort with each other, are a part. They can be theories or the realities the theories represent ... Factors are deduced not directly but by observation of functions" (1962, 7).

10 In reality, even though I make it mine here for the sake of simplicity, this view is still too coloured by Cartesianism.

11 In Italian "she" is "lei", which with a capital letter is also the formal way of saying "you". The patient is thinking simultaneously of a safe place being provided by her friend and also by her analyst.

12 Translator's note: there is an untranslatable play here on "porta", which means both a door and the third person indicative of the verb to carry, to bring. The analyst says "qualcosa che la porta ad agire".

6

BION'S O AND HIS PSEUDO-MYSTICAL PATH

The eternal Idea, the Idea that is in and for itself, eternally remains active, engenders and enjoys itself as absolute spirit.

–Hegel

O as Kant's Thing in Itself

Bion introduces the concept of O in *Transformations* (1965) and then uses it extensively in *Attention and Interpretation* (1970). It is a striking concept, because very difficult to define and dangerously close to nonsense. In fact, it is the most misunderstood of Bion's concepts and it has the rare privilege of giving rise to exhilarating interpretations. Nevertheless, we cannot do without it. The reason lies in its pivotal role in Bion's theory of mind and psychoanalysis. It always comes in a group of three with the closely related concepts of *transformation* and *invariance*. But unlike the last two, in Bion's pages, it has so many names that we get easily confused and prone to attribute our dizziness to the author's elliptic and idiosyncratic style. Did he get sick? Or less exact in his thinking? Or was it just ageing that pushed him towards some kind of slippery mystical path? So let's just have a taste of what it means to try to shed some light on the concept of O.

When it makes its first appearance, it is presented as a philosophical concept, basically equivalent to Kant's thing in itself:

DOI: 10.4324/9781003625247-6

The patient enters and, following a convention established in the analysis, shakes hands. This is an external fact, what I have called a 'realization'. In so far as it is useful to regard it as a thing-in-itself and unknowable (in Kant's sense) it is denoted by the sign O. The phenomenon, corresponding to the external fact, as it exists in the mind of the patient, is represented by the sign T (patient) α.

(Bion 1965, 12–13)

So, as a theoretical notion, O points to an X (not a mental thing) that cannot be known in itself but only *indirectly* through the phenomena that represent transformations of it. Importantly, these transformations are mental.

Affirming that a clinical fact, its O or its essence, cannot be known, is a way, as we shall see, to start elaborating an intersubjective, social or pragmatic model of truth. In fact, what is Kant's anxiety about conceptualizing the thing in itself? It is to instantiate the idea that we cannot know reality as it is because each of us, so to speak, cooks it up in his own way. This is an anti-essentialist move. It goes against centuries of ingenuous realism and representationalist speculative theories of knowledge. Of course, the issue remains of how then we can agree on any kind of truth. Kant's answer is that there are *a priori* forms in sensible intuition and in intellect that guarantee the universalism of knowledge. This is the so-called Kantian transcendentalism.

The *a priori* spectacles of space, time, and categories give us the possibility to see things, more or less, in the same way. This conception is not without flaws, as many subsequent scholars harshly pointed out. They say that, in his view, Kant gets either to a new dualism of subject and object or to a new version of idealism. In fact, since logically the thing in itself could only be known by the eye of God, and this being unacceptable in a lay arena, it turns out to be a weak concept. It is so weak that, in the end, we are left with only a mind and without a world. Moreover, in these readings, Kant is not able to explain how the subject gets to have these *a priori* forms and categories. Their genesis stays in obscurity and abstruseness. We can anticipate here that Bion gives a tentative solution to this question that is very similar to Hegel's, i.e. to the latter's radically social understanding and rendering of self-consciousness, nothing less than what he considers to be the essence of humanity.

Invariance

Left with his idea of O as the thing in itself, where do we find Bion now in *Transformations*? We find him struggling to gain a ground on which we can find our truths in psychoanalysis. He says that in the process of transforming O, patient and analyst may each use their own group of transformations, yet they have to arrive to something that is true to both of them. To do this, some "invariants" are needed. By the way, we notice that he borrows these notions of "group of transformation" and "invariance" from mathematics. The fact is that the invariant of a transformation is not easy to define. Could it be something that resides in the thing in itself that is undergoing a process of transformation? No, because this angle would make us fall back into some kind of pre–critical realism; for example, in thinking that the colour "red" in a field of poppies could "confirm" the link between the two terms in a painting of this same subject, and so to give ground to a basic agreement between different viewers on the objectivity of their perceptions.

So the invariant has to be placed somewhere else: if not (only) in the thing itself – otherwise why did we make of it a thing *in itself?* – (also) in the *process* of knowing/transforming. Again, we rediscover the brilliance of Kant's method in withdrawing from the study of the object to the study of the knowing subject. By definition, this process implies the dimension of self-reflexivity, which by itself is nothing but a benefit given by membership in the *intermediate* realm of the symbolic or language. This is sufficient to say that the invariant can only have to do with something that *happens*, it is not a feature of the thing but an event. In the space between two (actually, more) subjects engaged in the act of trying to grasp the truth of what is happening. This truth lies not between the subject and the object of knowledge, but between two subjects that share – Bion would say – the experience of the same (in itself, unknowable) O. In brief, it is an *intersubjective* process. In order to explain how it works, Bion turns to the mother-infant relationship and extracts from it the best model we have to conceptualize subjectivation and, consequently, therapeutic action.

At-One-Ment

Now, before going further, let's resume our itinerary from O as the thing-in-itself (O) to the invariant or factor of truth (I) and to the *at-one-ment* (I') as the function of truth. We can link them as the first three terms of a chiasm. We started with Bion's need to go past the traditional positivistic flavour of psychoanalysis, his intellectual loan from Kant, the effort to give a psychological solution to the aporias of Kantian theory of knowledge, and the introduction of the notions of O, transformation and invariant. Then we argued that he identifies the invariant with a *process* and not with a concrete quality of the thing that has to be known. More precisely not with *any* process, but with an intersubjective process of reciprocal attunement which is naturally based on the development of a certain human brain skill. Freud (1950, 318) would name it the capacity of *"communication"* (Verständigung), Tomasello (2009) the capacity for "joint intentionality".

Thus, in Bion's intersubjective turn, we spot immediately the revolutionary contribution given to psychoanalysis by Melanie Klein, especially with her concepts of unconscious phantasy and projective identification. As a matter of fact, it is almost impossible to look at Bion's thinking as a development of mainstream psychoanalytic theory if we do not do our homework with Klein. On the contrary, in the light of Klein's ideas, Bion becomes quite easy to understand. His new theory of dreaming, unconscious, and affects, directly stems from Klein's equation dreaming = play = activity-of-symbolization, from her view of the mind as the never closing theatre where meaning is constantly shaped by the interplay of unconscious phantasies, from her emphasis on the key role of the emergent anxieties in the here and now of the session; from the original and very fertile concept of projective identification – which is indeed a concept that gave the kick to those Bionian concepts of container/contained, and "normal" projective identification. Above all, these concepts represented the seeds of a proto–intersubjective model of psychoanalysis.

So the first three terms of our chiasm are O as the thing in itself (O) → the invariant (I) → the invariant as at-one-ment (I'). Now let's consider the latter more closely. A frequently biased understanding of at-one-ment assimilates it into an experience of fusion. From this reading, the consequence follows that analysts who use the concept of at-one-ment to mean the path that leads to the final goal of the growing of mind(s) would avoid taking responsibility for the negative transference and would have the tendency to be too "good" with the patient.

What can we say in reply to this criticism? First of all that, strictly speaking, the concept of transference is not an intersubjective one because it belongs to another psychoanalytic paradigm: the unconscious as our regressive and most primitive way of thinking, made of repressed contents, and not the unconscious that has to be conquered in the process of subjectivation and which is the function of the personality that gives the fullest possible meaning to experience. Central to this model, usually characterized as "unipersonal", is the continuous confrontation with the patient and the correction, through timely interpretations, of his *mésalliances*.

Secondly, if Bion chooses the term at-one-ment, it is for its proximity with that of "atonement" – without hyphens! Atonement means "reconciliation" with God: a dimension of conflict distinctively inheres to it. Therefore, at-one-ment can be seen not as the clue to an excessive and inappropriate desire to cure on the side of the analyst, but as a healthy dialectic of identity and difference, in favourable situations as the fly-wheel of mental growth. So fusion, which also can have a role in some moments in the relationship, is not what Bion's concept indicates and prescribes. At-one-ment makes us think more of Stern et al.'s (1998) "moments of meeting" or of Tronick et al.'s (1998) "dyadic expansion of consciousness".

The issue, again, is to explain the nature of *invariants* in the process of knowledge. The solution that Bion proposes – on the model of the mother-child relationship – is to consider the *shared emotion* (O) of the session as the first element for *aesthetic* growth of the mind. But, for this to happen, there must always be at least one developed self-consciousness. It should be stressed that the aesthetic way of attributing a meaning to experience, while on the plane of ontogenesis, it is primary, does not therefore become less important throughout life.

Bion thinks that analysis should serve to make the mind of the patient grow. In this way, he will be able to contain his emotions, give a full sense to experience, and will have less need for the solutions represented by neurotic symptoms. The most effective model to represent the growth of the mind is that of the mother-child relationship. Mother and child understand each other perfectly even when the latter cannot yet speak. Clearly, between the two, there is a communication system based on the intensity of exchanges, their duration, and nonverbal language. More specifically, the event that promotes psychic growth is the emotional *at-one-ment*. There is a meeting of the minds involved in digesting reality (O). A "primordial" concept is created that, before being a true linguistic concept, is rather a "concept" of the body, a *habit*.

But why is the model of infant-mother relationship so precious in the project of theorizing the process of subjectivation? Among other matters, it gives us a way to conceptualize what Kristeva (1975) calls the "chora semiotica", i.e. the level of reciprocal influencing that, while not being excluded from the field of the symbolic, "speaks" to each other − that is, conveys meanings. This is not in words but mainly through their being gesture and sound. The theoretical challenge of psychoanalysis is to explain how a mind can be born from another, more developed mind. Of course, a gradient has to be in place if something has to pass from A to B − when at least for one member of the dyad the semantic meaning of language is not yet available. This amounts to saying that the primordial constitution of the psyche takes place in the *aesthetic* domain of sensations (Civitarese 2016d, 2017a). Rhythms of sound-, tactile, coenaestho-, olfactory-, taste- and picto-grams, all of them continuously accompanied by proto-emotions, confer a first (bodily) organization on the emergent ego of the newborn.

Anticipating Bion, Merleau-Ponty (1945/2012) − as we now know, a thinker who inspired the Barangers' concept of "field" − extends Kantian transcendentalism to the whole expression of life (Ferri 2008). The body exists as a "bodily subject", it has its own "motor intentionality" − hence it knows and understands the world,[1] though in its own way. It has a practical knowledge of things (*praktognosia*). That the body has an intentionality means that it is always *moving towards* something or *distancing* itself from it. Through these (*e*)motions, it organizes spatiality and determines behaviours. Its comprehension of the world is written in body patterns, namely dynamic "systems"/"totalities"/or "fields" of sensory impressions that otherwise would be dispersed. The effect produced by their sum could not be explained by the properties of each of them, if taken in isolation. Clear intentionality, which paradoxically can also be unconscious and therefore latent, is doubled by an opaque intentionality. It is opaque by reason of the procedural matter of its own weaving. If we want to avoid splitting the psyche from the body, we must admit that in the dimension of humanity, that is to say, of language and meaning, the two forms of intentionality (actually, three) are interlaced and continuously influencing each other. Therefore, it would not be correct to think of corporeal intentionality as purely natural, because it is immediately impregnated, at the very birth of each new individual, by social factors.

This means that getting to know something is re-cognition in the sense that any possible knowledge can only take place in the intersubjective field of human sociality, marked by the use of language. Knowing anything is to recognize each other as subjects, to share a belonging to the same dwelling. That's why, at the same time, it is also a *re-birthing*. We get, in Bion, this striking identification of the process of knowledge with the process of becoming a subject. Truth is the food for the mind. Freud's idea of repression reflects a strong etiopathogenic hypothesis about the origin of neurotic symptoms. Repression concerns the removal from the psyche of a *specific* content (a representation) that is at the base of the symbolical expression of a definite symptom. Freeing the foreign body in the psyche would release the symptom. Bion's concept of repression refers to the intrinsically normative character of language and meaning (or better, sense) construction. The link between transgression of, or non-alignment with, the law and symptom is reasserted but becomes *non-specific*. It is mediated by a deficit in the capacity to translate the sense of experience, something that is attainable only by living in the house of consensuality – even in conflict! –, within the rules of the most extensive sociality.

Keeping this point in mind is essential to a modern view of therapeutic action. We no longer aim to discover hidden contents or to offer an intellectual explanation of unconscious conflicts and defence mechanisms. Instead, we aim to expand the capacity of the mind/psychic-container (or group-mind) to give a full, i.e., intellectual *and* emotive, meaning to experience; to dreaming O, so to speak. What is at stake is the primary role of emotions: the way they map and shape the experience, drive to action, and provide a non-verbal language with which to communicate. In other words, in Bion, emotion is a synonym of meaning acquired intersubjectively. As he writes, an emotion cannot be seen disconnected from a relationship. A point that might give rise to misinterpretation is that we sometimes use the words emotion and proto-emotions as if they meant the same thing, which is not the case. Emotion is a proto-emotion (at this level no different from beta-element) that has already been admitted to the social realm of language and human meaning.

In the analytic process, the moments of at-one-ment are fundamental because they generate order out of chaos or, in other terms, they represent the possibility that is given to the couple of negotiating and discovering the truth of what is happening in the living present. We see that aesthetic experience of beauty becomes a preconception of the intellectual concept of truth. As in the most praised lines by Keats, "Beauty is truth, truth beauty – that is all/Ye know on earth, and all ye need to know".

O as the Godhead

But now it is time to get to the fourth and last term of our chiasm. In fact, a problem immediately arises with the conception of at-one-ment as the main therapeutic factor and with the related idea of truth as the food for the mind and truth-drive (Grotstein 2004). What assurance do we have that the emotional and intellectual truth of the couple does not deteriorate into some kind of *folie à deux*? This is an important point because it shows what we might call the epistemological function of the concept of O in Bion's thought. More generally, it shows his theory of humanity, and his conception of what it means to become more human or to grow one's mind. Here is where the other names of O – to our consternation (or amusement!) – finally arrive. In *Transformations* and in *Attention and Interpretation*, Bion calls O: Darkness and Formlessness, Ultimate Reality, Infinite, Infinity – and these still seem understandable as they are close to the thing-in-itself or to the Lacanian "Real" (and in Grotstein 2007: noumenon, Unknown, Other, Ideal Forms, impersonalness of Fate, Eternal Forms, impersonal Reality, unconscious) – , but what about Deity, Truth, Absolute Truth, Person-in-Himself, Eternal Light, Divine Being, Godhead?[2]

We realize here that Bion asks us to cross the traditional demarcation lines of disciplines, or at least to renew the sources from which to gain new models for psychoanalysis. We say: wow, fine! Still, this is the point where our heads start spinning and a sense of vertigo and scepticism come over us. But I think that we can make our way through all of this, strictly following the clues Bion gives us to intuit how he gets there, and not necessarily arguing about the correctness of the use he makes of literary, mystical or speculative concepts. My idea is that Bion uses a certain interpretation of the concept of Platonic form as a bridge that helps him to connect the riverbank of Kant's thing in itself with the riverbank of the intersubjective and pragmatic nature of truth. Let's see.

The turning point in the theorization of O comes with a statement that is a hybridization of Plato and Dante:

The object represented by the term Platonic Form may also be represented in mystical terms such as 'One is one and all alone and ever more shall be so', and those of canto xxxiii of the Paradise [...] 'Eternal Light, that in Thyself alone/Dwelling, alone dost know Thyself, and smile/On Thy self-love, so knowing and so known!'

It seems to me that, in this passage, Bion posits the identity of Kantian category, Platonic form and Godhead. It is as if he read the concept of O as thing in itself through the lens of the concept of O as Platonic form and the latter through the concept of O as the Godhead. How can we then interpret this radical shift towards mysticism? In the first instance, the presence of the capital letter O in the original version of the tercet is worthy of attention: "O luce etterna che sola in te sidi/Sola t'intendi, e da te intelletto/E intendente te, ami e arridi" (Dante, *Paradiso*, XXXIII, 124–126).

Soon afterwards, Bion quotes from the 13th-century Flemish mystic Ruysbroeck, known for having differentiated the concept of God from that of deity: "God in the Godhead is spiritual substance, so elemental that we can say nothing about it" (1965, 139): could this sentence not be taken as a reference to the spiritual substance of language and its being fundamental, in the sense of foundational, for humanity as opposed to animality? And isn't language something that by definition transcends the individual? Couldn't the doctrine of the Incarnation – which describes how from Being (*Sein*) emanates a subject (*Da*) – express the emergence of the single human mind from a collective pre-conception, ultimately, manifesting its cultural or linguistic nature? Could the event of this phenomenon – the subject having the opportunity to grasp, or represent in itself a happy reunion with this pre-individual background of meaning – be called: Deity, God, Language, Unconscious, Thing-in-itself or Person-in-itself, Infinite, Being, etc.? In my view, all of these questions are rhetorical. This can be deduced from Bion's writings and from the implicit interpretations that are discovered in the play of the cross-references of his various definitions of O. If we want to find support *outside* Bion, we could think of the number of places where Hegel asserts, in a non-metaphysical sense, the *divine* nature of language.[3] Even in Merleau-Ponty, we read that "language (like God's understanding) contains the germs of every conceivable signification" (1969, 4).

Dante's verses and the Hegelian quote in the epigraph, so extraordinarily similar, express the inadequacy and impotence of humanity to understand/"intendere" Deity. The literal and theological gloss of the tercet is the following:

> Eternal light, which dwell only in you that only you can understand yourself (and as such you are the Father)
> You are understood by yourself (and as such you are the Son), and
> Understanding yourself you love yourself and
> Rejoice (and as such you are the Holy Spirit).

Such an interpretation has the advantage of recalling the concept of the paternal (the "third" or the social) function as the underlying source of symbolization. Of course, a secular reading would also be legitimate: nothing more than the deep expression of a passionate affection for the object (it is known that love, in itself, is ineffable). Hence, the rhetorical figure, dizzying here, of the *polyptoton*, the repetition of a word at short distances and with slight variations: because certain things can be said only in the way of insistence or tautology.

The meaning of the citation from Dante becomes easy to understand. First of all, I repeat, the capital letter O is placed right at the start, as if Bion had discovered in *The Divine Comedy* a perfect definition of what he meant by O. Next, Bion identified (O) with a non-dominable, non-declarative horizon of sense that is also "divine", since it is rational and human.

In Italian, when the letter O is followed by a name, it indicates a vocative expression; it becomes an invocation to the other. This is another clue that confirms one of O's different meanings: the reference to the intersubjective essence of language and therefore, of the unconscious. Getting in touch with this divine that *solo s'intende e si ama e arride a sé* has the sense of being allowed to enter into the symbolic universe through the mediation of the object.

On this page, Bion's goal is to define O, but no longer solely in Kantian terms. The previous digressions work as interpretative clues and point in this direction. If O is in the order of Platonic forms or in the order of Deity, *it is out of question that it can refer to an idea that we are merely made of inert matter*. On the contrary, it is more logical to suppose that it refers to a first level of organization of the psychic, which is naturally on a trans-individual or social basis. Such organization or structure emerged phylogenetically when humans became capable of cooperative intentionality (Tomasello 2019). Put simply, as the Bible states:

In the beginning was the Word
The Word was with God and
The Word was God

(John 1: 1–3).

Winnicott describes this as "the indwelling of the mind in the body": a space for dreaming reality. Bion (1965, 139–140) writes that

> O is not good or evil; it cannot be known, loved or hated.
> It can be represented by terms such as ultimate reality or truth.
> The most, and the least that the individual person can do is to be it.

O cannot be known, loved, or hated because it cannot be objectified.
    Nietzsche's twofold imperative to become oneself and to become divine – expressed in his *Zarathustra* – comes to mind here. Bion adds:

> The phenomenon does not "remind" the individual of the Form but enables the person to achieve union with an incarnation of the Godhead, or the thing-in-self (or Person-in-Himself).

(1965, 139)

What does this mean? Here, Bion's concern is the same as Heidegger's in theorizing the pre-reflective and pre-categorical background, which is truly *aesthetic*, and from which subjectivity emerges. Bion emphasizes the importance of not shedding the roots that sink so deeply into this ground. All theory of O has to do with this group/social/protomental system from which the subject rises as a separate individual facing up to existence. Heidegger's work drives us towards awareness of being-towards-death – which itself is a theory that could offer us an acceptable interpretation of Freud's concept of the death drive. That is why, in my opinion, in *Transformations* and in *Attention and Interpretation*, Bion gives such importance to O. The parts of these books that are most annoying to readers, because they draw on terms from religion or mysticism, are perhaps the most profound ones. They are meant by Bion to translate into the (scientific) language of psychoanalysis the truth that mystics express in their own, idiosyncratic language. In fact, Bion reminds us that they claim they are able to reach O.

174

O as the Groundless Ground: An Intersubjective and Pragmatic Conception of Truth

Thus, the concept of Deity seeks to locate itself at the sense level which, although culturally conditioned, cannot be translated into words. Rather, is the pragmatic or semiotic level at which the non-verbal mother-child or patient-analyst or social exchange is based. This is an essential step in reaching an aesthetic paradigm in psychoanalysis. The interpretation of Deity as the social, as language, and as the unconscious, is authorized by Bion himself with the play on the many names of O. Indeed, it finds precise counterparts also in philosophy; for example, in some of the most recent interpretations of Hegel's thought by the American contemporary pragmatism offered by the so-called Pittsburgh School.[4] What do I mean? That Bion's definition of O as Deity, God, Godhead, and so on, is born from having met the rocky layer that does not allow us to go further in determining which are the ultimate foundations of our knowledge and our being (Braver 2014). This shouldn't be a reason for giving up our search. It is precisely what Wittgenstein does, for example, with the concept of "language play" (*Sprachspiel*) and "form of life" (*Lebensform*). Hegel, as well, uses concepts such as spirit, idea, self-consciousness. There is nothing mystical in the proper sense of the word. We stay on absolutely rational ground. As synonyms for O, the concepts of Godhead and of deity should not be taken in their theological significance but as expressions of a speculative anthropological truth.

In language, an obscure knowledge is deposited as a sort of survival kit. What matters is that when the individual is subjected to this knowledge, he may or may not accept it, or live in consensuality with it (or not). Consensuality as a result of the intersubjective encounter is therefore understood as bound to the real, although it has ties that we cannot translate into words and concepts. Its roots go much deeper than just the layers of discursive – or non-verbal – mutual understanding. They go beyond subjectivity. A subject isn't merely a whirlpool in the river water. It is organized and individualized and still is influenced by the deep, deep running of the river. (Civitarese 2017c).
According to (the post-Saussurian) Merleau-Ponty, neither the signifier is completely arbitrary.[5] From this point of view, any

175

form of pathology, and not only psychosis, could be seen as a crisis of the pact of consensuality. Of course, the subject could not continue to nourish himself with truth, if the pact were not open to novelty. Novelty is imposed by the ever-changing character of the ultimate reality (O). Deprived of it, the subject would grow into Heidegger's *Das Man*. He would condemn himself to inauthenticity or illness.

As any word is dialectically related to all the other elements of a language, so any speaker always addresses someone else (the vocative O) as the momentary recipient of the "eternal light" of the realm of language. That is why the emotion as a transformation-of-a-proto-self-affection would already imply a relationship, because it is thought as already included in this field of pre-individual sense – indeed it is its first, foundational, expression. The reason is – as Lacan, deeply influenced by Kojève's reading of Hegel's *Phenomenology*, writes incisively in "The Function and Field of Speech and Language in Psychoanalysis" (1966) – that the infant comes to the world already as a member of the symbolic area: this is what the Catholic dogma of original sin translates; no guilt without self-awareness. It should be clear at this point that instead of being a quasi-metaphysical concept of reality, and irrespective of the entity that knows it, O becomes another name for the unconscious, because it is a function of the personality. It also transcends the individual. It is anything but a differentiated part of O. We know it through transformations or narrative derivatives or developments-in-discourse, but we will never know it in its entirety or infinity.

At this point, we have seen, in examining the various terms of our chiasm known as O, that they translate both the Bionian theory of psychic birth and of the development of thought. As a result, we will be less mistaken in considering some of the points in his theory of technique that are spoken by Bion in an unexpectedly assertive manner. The reality (O) to be known (transformed) is the unconscious emotional experience shared by the analytic dyad at a given time. Focusing on this issue (the O of the session) whenever possible, the analyst tries to pass from – (negative) attunement to + attunement.

O as the Unconscious Emotional Experience
and the Object of Transformation in the Session

In Bion's theory, emotion and thought are closely tied. The (alpha) emotion, which is the (beta) experience of proto-sensations and proto-emotions that have met the maternal reverie, is a proto-thought or a "sensible" thought that prepares the ground for "true" thoughts. Yet, it is important to have an idea of what emotions are active at a given moment in the analytical field. It is in the (social) space that the meaning is generated; this may become an actual and fruitful encounter or not. As we can see, the emphasis of the analytic investigation no longer falls on the subject (on the search for psychic *contents*), but on *how* the dyad reaches an intersubjective agreement on the nature of reality, and on the functioning of *containers* or on psychic transformation. *In a positive spiral form, the dreaming favours the unison and the unison produces other dreaming.*

The analytic pair is continuously engaged in a process of mutual recognition or making the other into a subject. In other words, the dyad is constantly in a process of negotiating reciprocal status of *personae* with one another. This is the specific and true field of analysis. There is, therefore, a strong affirmation of the role of emotional and sensory engrams or pictograms in relation to the essential facts of the session. Most notably, Bion speaks of the process of self-construction of the subject and the feeling of self and vitality that follows. This also reflects clinical experience which tells us that what patients are suffering from is their inability to contain (transform) their overwhelmingly violent emotions. *The unknown of O, then, is the emotional position occupied by the patient and the analyst on the map that represents the vicissitudes of their relationship.* This space of engagement demands to be investigated in analysis; everything must be aimed toward the goal of this emotional encounter.

That's why, for Bion, only what is in the view of analyst and of the patient can be known:

> In psycho-analysis, any O not *common* to analyst and analysand alike, and therefore, not available, for transformation by both, may be ignored as irrelevant to psycho-analysis. Any O not *common* to both is incapable of psycho-analytic investigation; *any*

appearance to the contrary reflects a failure to understand the nature of psycho-analytic interpretation.

(1965, 48–49, emphasis added)

This Bion precept is the most widely neglected in clinical practice, often even by analysts who are inspired by his theories: the impulse to cling to the concreteness of reality, whether historic or present is too strong. Bion's assertion is decisive and has a soldierly tone, not unlike the one used when he argues that:

Psychoanalytic "observation" is concerned neither with what has happened nor with what is going to happen, but with what is happening. Furthermore, it is not concerned with sense impressions or objects of sense ... Every session attended by the psychoanalyst *must* have no history and no future ... What is "known" about the patient is of no further consequence: it is either false or irrelevant ... The only point of importance in any session is the unknown. Nothing *must* be allowed to distract from intuiting that ... *Obey the following rules ... Do not* remember past sessions ... *no* crisis should be allowed to breach this rule ... The psychoanalyst can start by avoiding any desires for the approaching end of the session (or week, or term). Desires for results, 'cure' or even understanding *must not* be allowed to proliferate ... These *rules must be obeyed* all the time and not simply during the session ... If this *discipline* is followed, there will be an increase of anxiety in the psychoanalyst at first, but it *must not* interfere with preservation of the rules. The procedure *should* be started at once and not be abandoned on any pretext whatever.

(Bion 1992, 380–382, emphasis added)

Bion also explains why it is so difficult to stick to these principles:

1 Increase of anxiety because there is no barrier against fears of acknowledged dangers.
2 No barrier against guilt because of no substitute for acknowledged and conventional therapeutic aims.
3 Isolation from group basic assumption.

(1992, 296)

The essential task is, therefore, not to inhibit the *evolution* of the session, the evolution, or the emergence of O; where for "evolution" – again – Bion intends the possibility of intuiting through the experience *where* the patient is (what he is really feeling). What can it mean that "In psycho-analysis any O not *common* to analyst and analysand alike, and not available therefore for transformation by both, may be ignored as irrelevant to psycho-analysis. Any O not common to both is incapable of psycho-analytic investigation"?

Indeed, it is assumed that *any subject* of knowledge is accessible because it is *common*, that is, consensual, even when it is perceived by a single individual, in the sense that it can only be perceived through the conceptuality shared by a community of speakers, that is, by many observers. Hence, the idea of a sensible certainty resulting from a pure immediacy would be naïve. In fact, if we ask what this quality of being "the common" can reside in, and if we discard the idea of the *a priori* forms of sensible intuition and intellect, we are forced to consider language as the *common* house of human beings. The fact that there must be something in common, a medium that permits knowledge, is something that transcends the narrow field of psychoanalysis and the facts of the analysis that are linked to the relationship in the here and now. *But then why is Bion so emphatic about this point?* What, in his eyes, is the specificity of psychoanalysis?

If the most effective way of helping patients to gain emotional competence passes through the filter of the current relationship with the analyst, then the truth of what is happening cannot be just intellectual. It is not enough to use one's emotional reaction by identification or as a countertransference response, especially if intended in a unidirectional way. It is, rather, necessary to engage directly in the relationship and thus feel the weight of responsibility for what is happening in it. If it is not something that has happened in the past or happens elsewhere, but it is something that happens *here and now*, the analyst can immediately try to improve the climate of the meeting.

Letting O "evolve" or "becoming O" means not to take refuge in mere abstract decodings of the facts of the analysis, but, rather, to favour the development of an emotional or experiential knowledge: for Bion also a psychoanalytic paper must arouse emotions. All of Bion's work can be seen as a radical attempt to reposition psychoanalysis, theory and practice, in the area of the unconscious and the dream. This is where sensoriality and the raw emotions are transformed into images, which, because of their proximity to the body and the poetic-oneiric ambiguity that characterizes their language – their anti-semantic drive – are the most appropriate means to dream oneself into existence.

Bion often quotes Kant's assertion that concepts without perceptions are empty and perceptions without concepts are blind. In "A Theory of Thinking" (1962a), he writes that with respect to the inner world the emotions fulfil the same function as the perceptions have towards the external world. It follows that if the concepts are deprived of the supply of "sensorial", i.e. emotional, data about the inner world, they remain ineffectual. Then the person, even if things aren't too bad yet, that is, if he still has a sufficiently working contact barrier, sinks in the sea of concreteness. In essence, he is halved. For this reason, the place of the dream, row C of the grid or, with Winnicott's concept of the transitional space, the dimension of dream and of play, is essential to psychoanalysis. It is there that perception-emotions and perceptions *tout court* can both be offered to the mill of intellect.

Psychoanalysis is a method of psychic investigation of the psyche, a theory of how this evolves, and a technique of cure that aims to alleviate the psychic suffering caused by emotional trauma, helping patients to develop emotional competence in relationships. Sensations and emotions cannot be ignored. Above all, this is because they are the primordial form of knowledge that we have of things, and this is immediately *social*, since, as we saw, the child is born into the world as already immersed in the field of the symbolic. Then, the understanding and mastery of emotional states are recognized as the goal of analysis.

Another obvious meaning of this theoretical and practical approach is that the direct and continuous emotional involvement of the analyst arises whenever he brings back the discourse to the dream of the session (Ferro 2009), and therefore to the therapeutic relationship. This process makes available hyper-amplified signals to map their positions in the analytical field. For example, if a patient tells a childhood memory or an event from his current life, the analyst can only have an indirect knowledge and try to empathize with him perhaps by using a conscious identification. If, on the contrary, he reads the same recollection as an unconscious communication about the living emotions of the present relationship, he will have a *direct/lived* cognition of the same fact of the analysis. He will be relying less on transformation in K and more on transformation in

O. Not only: *as every un/conscious transformation – i.e. not limited in its dreamed quotient –, the perspective he will derive will be richer and more "real" than any other confined, even if it is not possible in absolute terms, to conscious experience.* It is not that the analyst cannot know anything about the patient if he values the historical content of his discourse; rather, that for the purposes of the analysis, and in accordance with all the premises listed so far, it is more pertinent to pursue knowledge by taking everything back to the dream of the session in the here and now. In other words, as the scalpel is for the surgeon, so for the analyst the main tool is a radical notion of unconscious functioning of the minds in the living encounter with the patient.

Is Bion a Mystic?

In the light of what we have said so far, it should be clear that Bion's mystical path is simply his passionate search to investigate the essence of humanity. The mystical discourse is for him a source of inspiration, as we saw with the concept of "atonement". This concept is used purely as an allegorical narrative to coin a new *psychoanalytic* concept and to develop a psychoanalytic model in which language as meaning and language as act are not split. Bion is a gifted *bricoleur*, as he finds the material he needs to build up his theories from so many different fields of knowledge – literature, mysticism, psychoanalysis, mathematics, and physics – but especially philosophy. His interest in the *thing-in-self*, Platonic ideas, Faith, etc., and many other concepts borrowed from philosophy, actually conceals a very concrete and psychoanalytic, theoretical, and practical-technical need to find subjectivity on the safe ground of consensuality while at the same time distancing it from any concern of arbitrariness. Deity must be translated as consensuality, sociality, and language, with what makes us human. *In my opinion, this is the most consistent theoretical and "clinical" significance that we can attribute to the concept of O.* Getting in "contact" with Deity is an allegorical tale about getting in contact through the at-one-ment with the object, and metonymically with all sociality.

Let's try now to summarize briefly the results that Bion achieves through the introduction of the concept of O:

a using Kant's concepts of thing-in-itself as a first definition of O immediately characterizes its endeavour as the effort to construct a theory of knowledge;

181

b   this theory will be a sceptical one, as the main principle adopted by Bion is one of a systematic doubt;

c   the fact that he defines O by bringing up a vignette (the patient and analyst shaking hands) demonstrates that his aim is always directed at elucidating the clinical interaction between patient and analyst, at trying to get to a higher formalization of psychoanalysis and at developing a more effective cure for psychic suffering – see for example the linked concepts of transformation in O *vs.* transformation in K and negative capability;

d   the concept of O takes on a central epistemological function in the development of a pragmatic and intersubjective theory of truth;

e   it gives a more subtle account of the aesthetic and intersubjective constitution of the psyche in the process of subjectivation;

f   finally, we end up with a dramatic – and in my view very welcome – shift from the classical to a new paradigm in psychoanalysis: from the archaeologic-evidential to the intersubjective-aesthetic one.

The notion of transformation in O emphasizes the participation of the body in the experience of knowledge and in the process of becoming a subject. In this model, dreaming is not a private affair. It is always dwelling in the house of language and sociality. It follows that we dream either during sleep or when we are awake. Putting aside the fact that it is a mystery still awaiting to be elucidated, the main difference seems to reside in the capacity of attention of enlarging or restricting the field of consciousness while awakened and thus producing the oscillation primary ↔ secondary process in mental functioning. As Vygotski and Luria (1984) write, the main function of language is not the communicative one, but that of a *medium* to control attention. In fact, they distinguish attention driven by natural stimuli from attention driven by language, which they call "artificial" attention. Now, it is vital to understand that we dream also in our body. This is where the concept of O proves most useful. By emphasizing so much the relevance of the analyst's receptivity, it forces us to pay attention to a domain that by definition defies our efforts in theorizing it.

So, the point is that in Bion there is no longer any dualism of subject/object or psyche/body. Finally, the Freudian assertion of the ego as a bodily ego finds a true theoretical realization. The opacity of the Bionian "mystical" attitude, and the usefulness of the mystical discourse as a model of a psychoanalysis of intercorporeality, then finds its justification in the opacity of what we define, precisely, as corporeal intentionality: sense, and not meaning, can only be approached *indirectly* – after all, it is never possible to achieve the possession of a knowledge about anything, since every knowledge is already in itself a transformation and always also has a semiotic side.

From this point of view, Freudian psychoanalysis still appears to be deeply anchored in a psychology of the un/conscious knowledge of consciousness, while Bion's psychoanalysis is anchored in a psychology of knowledge of the body. The shift from one paradigm to another is justified on the basis of the significant weight that, in the genesis of psychic suffering, has gradually been attributed to the traumatic events of the phase in which the primary constitution of the psyche takes place, a constitution that can only be of an intersubjective and aesthetic nature. If, therefore, it is pre-eminently *there* that the damage has occurred, we must have as precise a description as possible of where and how to intervene. Now the essential point to grasp, and not an easy one, is that the dynamics of sense set at the level of the body's functions are indeed "procedural" or implicit, but never outside the area of what is human, i.e. language and meaning.

Notes

1 Cf. Merleau-Ponty (1945/2012, 49). "The movements of one's own body are naturally invested with a certain perceptual signification, they form a system with external phenomena so tightly woven that external perception 'takes account' of the movement of the perceptual organs, and it finds in them, if not the *explicit explanation*, then at least the *motive* for the intervening changes in the spectacle and can thereby understand these changes".

2 It is worth noticing is also the centrality of the letter O in the word God. By the way, in his essay *On the Name,* Derrida (1993b) takes up the same graphic characters used by Angelus Silenius in writing God: G*Ott.*

3 Cf. Hegel (2001, 406): "by *indicating* this piece of paper, 'I' then experience what is, in point of fact, the real truth of sense-certainty: 'I' indicate it as a *here* which is a here of other heres, in other words a here that involves in its self a *simple concatenation* of many *heres.* i.e., a universal. Thus 'I' take it up as it is in truth, and instead of knowing what is immediate, 'I' truly take, I *perceive*". This passage is found

in the first section, almost a kind of prologue, of the *Phenomenology*, which discusses sense-certainty. Hegel's aim is to argue that there is no perception that is not mediated by language. He is by no means talking about any literally "divine" nature of language, but only of its normal functions. Mostly we do not realize it, but these functions are in fact extraordinary. Language is "divine" because it captures the object perceived through concepts (indeed it could not do otherwise) and thus universalizes it: "[...] it would be appropriate to tell those who allege this truth and certainty of the reality of sensible objects that they have to be sent back to the most elementary school of wisdom [...] They mean *this* piece of paper on which 'I' am writing, or rather, have written, *this*, but they do not say what they mean. If they really wanted to *say* this piece of paper that they mean - and that is what they wanted to *say* - then this is impossible because the sensible this, which is meant, is *inaccessible* to language and language belongs to consciousness, to what is, in itself, universal" (2001, 405–406). The clearest and most authoritative commentary on this passage from Hegel that I know is to be found in Heidegger: "Language is divine because [...] it detaches us from one-sidedness and allows us to state what is universal and true [...] This furthest externalization exists only in the nearest internalization [*Erinnerung*] of language" (1980, 64). Now, to return to Bion: even if it is not an explicit reference of his, I think we can treasure the suggestive halo that emanates from these extraordinary passages, if only to direct our intuition of what it might mean when he refers to O and speaks of it in terms of the Deity, Person-in-Himself, Eternal Light, Divine Being, Godhead, etc. Not the eye of God as a supernatural entity that contemplates the thing in itself, but (the most human) device of the concept that rises above multiplicity and makes it thinkable.

4 See Pinkard (1994); and Brandom (2008, 2–4): "I do think of the *Phenomenology* as a large allegory and that what it's an allegory for is a story about conceptual contents, about selves and about the kinds of normative communities that we institute by our re-cognitive relations to one another. I think one of the principal lessons that we can learn from the Phenomenology is indeed the lesson that the classical American Pragmatists learned from it and is what deeply binds together German Idealism and American Pragmatism and Neo-pragmatism. And that is that we'll never understand our interaction with the world if we think in antecedent terms of what subjects are—say the way Descartes did—and what objects are—say the way contemporary natural science tells us they are—and somehow try to clamp those two together to understand subjects as able to know about objects and act on objects so understood. Hegel's recommendation—what was taken up by the

Pragmatists—was that we have to think about our interaction. [...] And it's by thinking about that sort of skillful, practical interaction with our environment that we'll come to understand what knowing subjects and intentional agents really are, that we can then abstract notions of subject and object of mind and world from. [...] Self-consciousness is not something that happens principally between our ears. It's something that happens between our selves; it's a social achievement, a matter of reciprocal recognition. I am what I'm recognized to be by those I recognize as having the authority to determine what I really am".

5 Cf. Kirchmayr (2008, 119): "Therefore, the Saussurian relationship between signifier and meaning implies an anchorage to the natural world and cannot be defined as completely arbitrary. In fact, in Merleau-Ponty's perspective, the thesis of the arbitrariness of the sign would limit the consideration of language to the institutional aspect only, that is to say to the language as code and system (*langue*), losing sight of the concrete use that is made of it (*parole*)".

References

Aenishanslin, J.-F. 2019. *Les Pensées Parallèles: Husserl et Freud*. Lausanne: Antipodes.

Aguayo, J. 2019. Wilfred Bion: On Clinical Method and Intuition during the Late Period in His Clinical Seminars. Presentation for James Grotstein Memorial Lectures, Los Angeles, California, April 18, 2019.

Angelino, L. 2014. *Entre Voir et Tracer. Merleau-Ponty et le Mouvement Vécu Dans L'expérience Esthétique*. Milano-Udine: Mimesis.

Augustine of Hippo, Saint. 1961. *Confessions*. Translated by R. S. Pine-Coffin. Harmondsworth: Penguin.

Aulagnier, P. 1975. *The Violence of Interpretation. From Pictogram to Statement*. Translated by A. Sheridan. Philadelphia: Brunner-Routledge, 2001.

Baranger, M., and W. Baranger. 2008. "The Analytic Situation as a Dynamic Field." *The International Journal of Psychoanalysis* 89: 795–826.

Benjamin, W. 1955. "On Some Motifs in Baudelaire." In *Selected Writings: Volume 4*, edited by Howard Eiland and Michael W. Jennings, 313–355. Cambridge, MA: Belknap Press.

Bergson, H. 1896. *Matter and Memory*. Translated by N. M. Paul, W. Scott-Palmer. London: G Allen, 1913.

Bergson, H. 2002. *Key Writings*. New York, NY: Continuum, p. 85.

Bergstein, A. 2022. "'Truth Shall Spring out of the Earth … ': The Analyst as Gatherer of Sense Impressions." *International Journal of Psychoanalysis* 103: 246–263.

Bion, W. R., and J. Rickman. 1943. "Intra-Group Tensions in Therapy—Their Study as the Task of the Group." *The Lancet* 242: 678–681.

Bion, W. R. 1954. "Notes on the Theory of Schizophrenia." *International Journal of Psychoanalysis* 35: 113–118.

Bion, W. R. 1956. "Development of Schizophrenic Thought." *International Journal of Psycho Analysis* 37: 344–346.

186

Bion, W. R. 1957. "Differentiation of the Psychotic from the Non-Psychotic Personalities." *International Journal of Psycho Analysis* 38: 266–275.

Bion, W. R. 1958a. "On Arrogance." *International Journal of Psychoanalysis* 39: 144–146.

Bion, W. R. 1958b. "On Hallucination." *International Journal of Psycho Analysis* 39: 341–349.

Bion, W. R. 1959. "Attacks on Linking." *International Journal of Psycho-Analysis* 40: 308–315.

Bion, W. R. 1961. *Experiences in Groups and Other Papers.* London: Tavistock.

Bion, W. R. 1962a. *"The Psycho-Analytic Study of Thinking."* Reprinted in Second Thoughts, 110-119, London: William Heineman, 1967.

Bion, W. R. 1962b. *Learning from Experience.* London: Karnac, 1984.

Bion, W. R. 1963. *Elements of Psycho-Analysis.* London: Heinemann.

Bion, W. R. 1965. *Transformations: Change from Learning to Growth.* London: Heinemann.

Bion, W. R. 1967. *Second Thoughts.* London: Karnac, 2007.

Bion, W. R. 1977. *The Italian Seminars.* London: Routledge, 2018.

Bion, W. R. 1970. *Attention and Interpretation.* London: Tavistock.

Bion, W. R. 1975. *A Memoir of the Future: The Dream.* Abingdon: Routledge, 2018.

Bion, W. R. 1976. "Penetrating Silence." In *The Complete Works of W. R. Bion,* edited by C. Mawson, 31–44. Vol. XV, 2014. London: Karnac.

Bion, W. R. 1980. *Bion in New York and Sao Paulo: And Three Tavistock Seminars.* London: The Harris Meltzer Trust, 2018.

Bion, W. R. 1987 [1976]. "Evidence." In *Clinical Seminars and Other Works,* edited by F. Bion, 230–237. London: Routledge, 2019.

Bion, W. R. 1990. *Brazilian Lectures. 1973 Sao Paulo, 1974 Rio de Janeiro/ Sao Paulo.* London: Karnac.

Bion, W. R. 1991. *A Memoir of the Future.* London: Routledge, 2018.

Bion, W. R. 1992. *Cogitations.* Abingdon: Routledge, 2018.

Birksted-Breen, D.2009. "'Reverberation Time', Dreaming and the Capacity to Dream." *The International Journal of Psychoanalysis* 90: 35–51.

Bleger, J. 1967. "Psycho-Analysis of the Psycho-Analytic Frame." *International Journal of Psychoanalysis* 48: 511–519.

Brandom, R. 2008. Transcription of the interview with Robert Brandom (Interviewer: G. Seddone – Leipzig, 30/06/08) (A. L. Shoichet, Ed.). Retrieved from https://www.filosofia.it/archivio/images/download/multimedia/08_Brandom%20Interview_transcription.pdf

Braver, L. 2014. *Groundless Grounds: A Study of Wittgenstein and Heidegger.* Cambridge, MA: The MIT Press.

Bronstein, C., and E. O'Shaughnessy. 2017. *"Attacks on Linking" Revisited: A new Look at Bion's Classic Work.* London: Karnac Books.

Bronstein, C. 2015. "Bridging the Gap." In *The W.R. Bion Tradition*, edited by H. Levine and G. Civitarese, 239–249. London: Routledge.

Brown, L. J. 2005. "The Cognitive Effects of Trauma." *The Psychoanalytic Quarterly* 74(2): 397–420.

Butler, W. M. 1999. "Psychoanalytic Time." *Canadian Journal of Psychoanalysis* 7: 303–319.

Carroll, L. 2003. *Alice's Adventures in Wonderland and Through the Looking Glass*. London: Penguin.

Chantraine, P. 1999. *Dictionnaire étymologique de la langue grecque: Histoire des mots*. Paris: Klincksieck.

Civitarese, G. 2008. "'Caesura' as Bion Discourse on the Method." *International Journal of Psychoanalysis* 89: 1123–1143.

Civitarese, G. 2011. "Exploring Core Concepts: Sexuality, Dreams and the Unconscious." *The International Journal of Psychoanalysis* 92: 277–280.

Civitarese, G. 2013a. "The Grid and the Truth Drive." *The Italian Psychoanalytic Annual* 7: 91–114.

Civitarese, G. 2013b. "Bion's 'Evidence' and His Theoretical Style." *Psychoanalytic Quarterly* 82: 615–633.

Civitarese, G. 2014. "Bion and the Sublime: The Origins of an Aesthetic Paradigm." *International Journal of Psychoanalysis* 95: 1059–1086.

Civitarese, G. 2015. "Transformations in Hallucinosis and the Receptivity of the Analyst." *The International Journal of Psychoanalysis* 96: 1091–1116.

Civitarese, G. 2016a. "On Sublimation." *The International Journal of Psychoanalysis* 7: 1369–1392.

Civitarese, G. 2016b. "Where Does the Reality Principle Begin? The Work of Margins in Freud's Formulations on the two Principles of Mental Functioning." In *Sublime Subjects: Aesthetic Experience and Intersubjectivity in Psychoanalysis*, 107–120. London: Routledge, 2018.

Civitarese, G. 2016c. *Truth and the Unconscious in Psychoanalysis*. London: Routledge.

Civitarese, G. 2016d. "Sense, Sensible, Sense-Able: The Bodily but Immaterial Dimension of Psychoanalytic Elements." In *The W. R. Bion Tradition: Lines of Development—Evolution of Theory and Practice Over the Decades*, edited by H. B. Levine and G. Civitarese, 297–306. London: Karnac.

Civitarese, G. 2017a. *Sublime Subjects: Aesthetic Experience and Intersubjectivity in Psychoanalysis*. London: Routledge.

Civitarese, G. ed. 2017b. *Bion and Contemporary Psychoanalysis: Reading 'A Memoir of the Future*. London: Routledge.

Civitarese, G. 2017c. "Whirlpools, Rhythms, Ideas: Aesthetic Experience and Intersubjective Constitution of the Individual." In *Sublime Subjects: Aesthetic Experience and Intersubjectivity in Psychoanalysis*, 77–82. London: Routledge.

Civitarese, G. 2018. "Traduire l'expérience: le concept de Transformation dans Bion et la théorie du champ analytique." *Revue Française de Psychanalyse* 82: 1327–1386.

Civitarese, G. 2019a. "Bion's O and His Pseudo-mystical Path." *Psychoanalytic Dialogues* 29(4): 388–403.

Civitarese, G. G. 2019b. "On Bion's Concepts of Negative Capacity and Faith." *The Psychoanalytic Quarterly* 88: 751–783.

Civitarese, G. 2019c. "The Concept of Time in Bion's 'A Theory of Thinking'." *International Journal of Psychoanalysis* 100: 182–205.

Civitarese, G. 2020a. "Regression in the Analytic Field." *Romanian Journal of Psychoanalysis* 13: 17–41.

Civitarese, G. 2020b. "The Names of O: Is Bion a Mystic?" *The Italian Psychoanalytic Annual* 14: 9–28.

Civitarese, G. 2021a. "Bion's Graph of "in Search of Existence". *The American Journal of Psychoanalysis* 81: 326–350.

Civitarese, G. 2021b. "Intersubjectivity and Analytic Field Theory. *Journal of the American Psychoanalytic Association* 69: 853–893.

Civitarese, G. 2021c. "The Limits of Interpretation. A Reading of Bion's "On Arrogance"." *International Journal of Psychoanalysis* 102: 236–257.

Civitarese, G. 2021d. "Experiences in Groups as a Key to 'late' Bion." *International Journal of Psychoanalysis* 6: 1071–1096.

Civitarese, G. 2023a. "We-Ness as an Expansion of Bion's Psychoanalytic Function of Intuition." *Fort Da* 29: 7–16.

Civitarese, G. 2023b. *Psychoanalytic Field Theory: A Contemporary Introduction.* London: Routledge.

Civitarese, G. 2024. "Intuition and we-ness in Bion and Post-Bionian Field Theory". *International Journal of Psychoanalysis* 105: 13–39.

Civitarese, G., and C. Berrini. 2022a. "On Using Bion's Concepts of Point, Line, and Linking in the Analysis of a 6-year-old Borderline Child." *Psychoanalytic Dialogues* 32: 17–35.

Civitarese, G., and C. Berrini. 2022b. "The Aesthetic-Rhizomatic Matrix of Thinking: Reply to Caron Harrang." *Psychoanalytic Dialogues* 32: 45–53.

Civitarese, G., and A. Ferro. 2018. *A Short Introduction to Psychoanalysis.* London: Routledge.

Derrida, J. 1993a. *Specters of Marx: The State of the Debt, the Work of Mourning, and the New International.* Translated by P. Kamuf. New York, NY: Routledge, 1994.

Derrida, J. 1993b. *On the Name.* Stanford, CA: Stanford University Press, 1995.

Di Noia, A. 1978. "Enigma." In *Enciclopedia Einaudi*, edited by R. Romano, 5, 439–462. Torino: Einaudi.

Edmunds, L. 2006. *Oedipus*. New York, NY: Routledge.

Elliott, A., and J. Prager. 2015. *The Routledge Handbook of Psychoanalysis in the Social Sciences and Humanities*. London: Routledge.

Ernout, A., and A. Meillet. 1985. *Dictionnaire Etymologique de la Langue Latine*. Paris: Klincksieck, 2001.

Esposito, R. 2015. *Persons and Things: From the Body's Point of View*. Cambridge: Polity Press.

Ferri, G. 2008. *Il problema dell'intenzionalità nella filosofia di Merleau-Ponty*. [The Problem of Intentionality in Merleau-Ponty's Philosophy] Retrieved from https://iris.univr.it/retrieve/e14ff6e2-e314-0209-e053-6605 fe0ad24c/Tesi%20Dott%20Merleau-Ponty%20mod.pdf

Ferro, A. 1987. "Il mondo alla rovescia. L'inversione di flusso delle identificazioni proiettive." *Rivista di Psicoanalisi* 33: 59–77.

Ferro, A. 2009. "Transformations in Dreaming and Characters in the Psychoanalytic Field." *The International Journal of Psychoanalysis* 90: 209–230.

Foucault, M. [1976] 2020. *The History of Sexuality: Volume 1. The Will to Knowledge*. London: Penguin.

Freud, S. 1890. "Psychical (or Mental) Treatment (1890)." *The Standard Edition of the Complete Psychological Works of Sigmund Freud* 7: 281–302.

Freud, S. 1900. *The Interpretation of Dreams*. SE, vol. IV.

Freud, S. 1911. "Formulations on the two Principles of Mental Functioning." SE 12: 213–226.

Freud, S. 1912. *The Dynamics of Transference*. SE, 12.

Freud, S. 1915. "Instincts and Their Vicissitudes." SE 14: 109–140.

Freud, S. 1920. "Civilization and its Discontents." SE 21: 57–146.

Freud, S. 1921. "Group Psychology and the Analysis of the Ego." SE 18: 65–144.

Freud, S. 1925. *A Note Upon the 'Mystic Writing-Pad'*. SE XIX (1923–1925): The Ego and the Id and Other Works, 225–232.

Freud, S. 1932. "My Contact with Josef Popper-Lynkeus." SE 12: 217–224.

Freud, S. 1933. "New Introductory Lectures on Psycho-Analysis." SE 12: 1–182.

Freud, S. 1950 [1895]. "Project for a Scientific Psychology." SE 1: 281–391.

Fusini, N. 2015. "Un'altra Capacità, Negativa." *Rivista di Psicoanalisi* 61: 67–78.

Gallese, V. 2005. "Embodied Simulation: From Neurons to Phenomenal Experience." *Phenomenology and the Cognitive Sciences* 4: 23–48.

Gerson, S. 2004. "The Relational Unconscious: A Core Element of Intersubjectivity, Thirdness, and Clinical Process." *The Psychoanalytic Quarterly* 73: 63–98.

Green, A. 1993. *The Work of the Negative*. Translated by A Weller. London: Free Association, 1999.

Green, A. 1997. "The Intuition of the Negative in *Playing and Reality*." *International Journal of Psycho Analysis* 78: 1071–1084.

Green, A. 1998. "The Primordial Mind and the Work of the Negative." *The International Journal of Psychoanalysis* 79: 649–665.

Grimalt, A., ed. 2022. *Bion, Intuition and the Expansion of Psychoanalytic Theory*. London: Routledge.

Gross, R. 2013. "The Sphinx as Oedipus' Other Mother." In *The Sphinx and the Riddles of Passion, Love and Sexuality*, edited by S. Zwettler-Otte, 39–61. Frankfurt am Main: Peter Lang.

Grotstein, J. S. 2004. "The Seventh Servant: The Implications of a Truth Drive in Bion's Theory of 'O'." *The International Journal of Psychoanalysis* 85(5): 1081–1101.

Grotstein, J. S. (2007). *A Beam of Intense Darkness: Wilfred Bion's Legacy to Psychoanalysis*. London: Karnac.

Hegel, G. W. F. 2001. "Sense Certainty", from the *Phenomenology of Spirit*, Chapter 1 (1807)." *The Philosophical Forum* 32: 399–406.

Hegel, G. W. 1807. *The Phenomenology of Spirit*. Cambridge: Cambridge University Press, 2019.

Heidegger, M. 1927a. *Being and Time*. Albany, NY: State University of New York Press, 2010.

Heidegger, M. 1927b. *The Basic Problems of Phenomenology*. Translated by A. Hofstadter. Bloomington: Indiana University Press, 1982.

Heidegger, M. 1954. *What is Called Thinking?* Translated by J. Gray. New York, NY: Harper & Row, 1968.

Heidegger, M. 1987. *Zollikon Seminars. Protocols-Conversations-Letters*. Translated by F. Mayr and R. Askay. Evanston, IL: Northwestern University Press. 2001.

Heidegger, M. 1980. *Hegel's Phenomenology of Spirit*. Bloomington & Indianapolis, IN: Indiana University Press, 1988.

Herrmann, von F. W. [1981] 1997. *Il concetto di fenomenologia in Heidegger eHusserl* [The Concept of Phenomenology in Heidegger and Husserl]. Genova: Il melangolo.

Hofmannsthal,von U. 1906. *Ödipus und die Sphinx: Tragödie in drei Aufzügen* [Oedipus and the Sphinx: Tragedy in Three Acts]. Berlin: Hofenberg Sonderausgabe, 2017.

Hinshelwood, R. D. 2000. "Foreword Bion, Rickman, Foulkes and the Northfield experiments." In *Advancing on Different Front*, edited by T. Harrison, 7–10. London: Jessica Kingsley.

Hinshelwood, R. D. 2014. "Bion's Paper on Arrogance. Reading His Personal Disaster." In *A Memoir of the Future, Funzione Gamma*, edited by G. Civitarese, R. D. Hinshelwood, and S. Marinelli, 33.

Husserl, E. 1913. *Idee per una Fenomenologia Pura e per una Filosofia Fenomenologica*. Vol. 1. Turin: Einaudi, 2002.

Husserl, E. 1928. *On the Phenomenology of the Consciousness of Internal Time (1893–1917)*. Translated by J. B. Brough. Dordrecht: Kluwer Academic, 1991.

Jaspers, K. [1913] 1997. *General Psychopathology – Volumes 1 & 2*. Translated by J. Hoenig and Marian W. Hamilton. Baltimore and London: Johns Hopkins University Press.

Kaës, R. 2005. "Internal Groups and Psychic Groupality: Genesis and Issues of a Concept." *Revue de psychothérapie psychanalytique de groupe* 45: 9–30.

Kafka, F. 1919. *In the Penal Colony*. Translated by I. Johnstone, GolbalGrey Ebooks, 2019.

Kernberg, O. F. 1996. "Thirty Methods to Destroy the Creativity of Psychoanalytic Candidates." *International Journal of Psychoanalysis* 77: 1031–1040.

Kernberg, O. F. 2011. "Divergent Contemporary Trends in Psychoanalytic Theory." *The Psychoanalytic Review* 98: 633–666.

Kernberg, O. F. 2012. "Suicide Prevention for Psychoanalytic Institutes and Societies." *Journal of the American Psychoanalytic Association* 60: 707–719.

Kirchmayr, R. 2008. *Merleau-Ponty: Una sintesi*. Milano: Marinotti.

Klein, M. 1946. "Notes on Some Schizoid Mechanisms." *International Journal of Psycho Analysis* 27: 99–110.

Klein, M. 2017. *Lectures on Technique: Edited with Critical Review by John Steiner*. London: Routledge.

Kristeva, J. 1975. *Revolution in Poetic Language*. New York, NY: Columbia University Press, 1984.

Lacan, J. 1947. "British Psychiatry and the War." *Psychoanalytical Notebooks of the London Circle* 4: 9–34.

Lacan, J. 1966. *Écrits: The First Complete Edition in English*. Translated by B. Fink. New York, NY: Norton, 2006.

Le Guen, C. 2008. *Dizionario Freudiano* [Freudian Dictionary]. Rome: Borla, 2013.

Lewin, B. D. 1946. "Sleep, the Mouth, and the Dream Screen." *The Psychoanalytic Quarterly* 15: 419–434.

Levine, H. 2022. "Intuition, Construction and Representation." In *Bion, Intuition and the Expansion of Psychoanalytic Theory*, edited by A. Grimalt, 111–116. London: Routledge.

Levine, H., and G. Civitarese, eds. 2016. The W. R. *Bion Tradition: Lines of Development—Evolution of Theory and Practice Over the Decades*. London: Karnac.

López Corvo, R. E. 2002. *The Dictionary of the Work of W.R. Bion*. London: Karnac, 2003.

Magrelli, V. 2002. *Vedersi. Modelli e Circuiti Visivi Nell'opera di Paul Valéry.* Turin: Einaudi.

Mancini, R. 2019. *La fragilità dello Spirito. Leggere Hegel per comprendere il mondo globale* [The Fragility of Spirit: Reading Hegel to Understand the Global World]. Milan: FrancoAngeli.

Marcelli, D. 1986. *Position Autistique et Naissance de la Psyché* [The Autistic Position and the Birth of the Psyche]. Paris: Presses Universitaires de France.

Massey, H. 2015. *The Origin of Time: Heidegger and Bergson.* New York, NY: Suny.

Mawson, C. 2014. "Editor's Introduction." In *The Complete Works of W. R. Bion,* edited by C. Mawson, 117–120. London: Karnac.

McCarthy, C. 2006. *The Road.* New York, NY: Alfred A. Knopf.

Meltzer, D. 1978. *The Kleinian Development – 3. The Clinical Significance of the Work of Bion.* London: Karnac, 2008.

Meltzer, D. 1984. *Dream-Life: A Re-Examination of the Psycho-Analytical Theory and Technique.* Strathtay: Clunie Press.

Meltzer, D. 1986. *Studies in Extended Metapsychology: Clinical Applications of Bion's Ideas.* London: Karnac.

Merleau-Ponty, M. 1969. *The Prose of the World.* Translated by J. O'Neill. Evanston, IL: Northwestern University Press, 1973.

Merleau-Ponty, M. 1945. *Phenomenology of Perception.* Translated by D. A. Landes. Abingdon: Routledge, 2012.

Merriam-Webster. 2021. *"Group." Merriam-Webster.com Dictionary.* Accessed April 3, 2021.

Moran, D., and J. Cohen. 2012. *The Husserl Dictionary.* New York, NY: Continuum International Publishing Group

Nancy, J.-L. 1966. *Being Singular Plural.* Stanford, CA: Stanford University Press.

Nissim-Momigliano, L. 1991. "*Il tè nel deserto*: Further Thoughts on 'The Psychoanalyst in the Mirror'." *Rivista di Psicoanalisi* 37: 772–818.

Nissim-Momigliano, L. [1992] 2018. *Shared Experience: The Psychoanalytic Dialogue.* London: Routledge.

Noel-Smith, K. 2002. "Time and Space as 'Necessary Forms of Thought'." *Free Associations* 9: 394–442.

O'Shaughnessy, E. 1981. "A Commemorative Essay on W.R. Bion's *Theory of Thinking*." *Journal of Child Psychotherapy* 7: 181–192.

Ogden, T. H. 2008. "Bion's Four Principles of Mental Functioning." *Fort Da* 14: 11–35.

Ogden, T. H. 2010. "On Three Forms of Thinking: Magical Thinking, Dream Thinking, and Transformative Thinking." *Psychoanalytic Quarterly* 79: 317–347.

Ogden, T. H. 2015. "Intuiting the Truth of What's Happening: On Bion's "Notes on Memory and Desire". *Psychoanalytic Quarterly* 84: 285–306.

Ogden, T. H. 2019. "Ontological Psychoanalysis or 'What Do You Want to Be When You Grow Up?'." *The Psychoanalytic Quarterly* 88: 661–684.

Orange, D. M. 2009. "The Price of an Open Heart: Book Review Essay on Chris Jaenicke's, 'Das Risiko der Verbundenheit: Intersubjektivitaetstheorie in der Praxis'." *International Journal of Psychoanalytic Self Psychology* 4: 393–397.

Pines, M. 1985. *Bion and Group Psychotherapy*. London: Jessica Kigsley Publishers, 2000.

Pinkard, T. 1994. *Hegel's Phenomenology: The Sociality of Reason*. Cambridge: Cambridge University Press.

Priel, B. 1997. "Time and Self: On the Intersubjective Construction of Time." *Psychoanalytic Dialogues* 7: 431–450.

Ricoeur, P. 1970. *Freud and Philosophy: An Essay on Interpretation*. New Haven, CT: Yale University Press.

Romanyshyn, R. D. 1977. "Phenomenology and Psychoanalysis: Contributions of Merleau-Ponty." *Psychoanalytic Review* 64: 21–223.

Rovelli, C. 2017. *The Order of Time*. Translated by E. Segre, S. Carnell. London: Penguin, 2018.

Rugi, G. 2022. "Intuition in Bion: Between Search for Invariants and Creative Emergence." In *Bion, Intuition and the Expansion of Psychoanalytic Theory*, edited by A. Grimalt, 117–130. London: Routledge.

Sabbadini, A. 1989. "How the Infant Develops a Sense of Time." *British Journal of Psychotherapy* 5: 475–484.

Sandowsky, L. N. 2004. "Heidegger and the Concept of Time – the Turns[s] of a Radical Epoch[é]." *Existentia: An International Journal of Philosophy* 3–4: 213–230.

Segal, H. 1957. "Notes on Symbol Formation." *International Journal of Psycho Analysis* 38: 391–397.

Seligman, S. 2017. *Relationships in Development: Infancy, Intersubjectivity and Attachment*. New York, NY: Routledge.

Sophocles. 1978. *Oedipus the King*. Translated by S. Berg and D. Clay. New York, NY: Oxford University Press.

Sophocles. 1994. *Ajax. Electra. Oedipus Tyrannus*. Translated by H. Lloyd-Jones and Loeb Classical Library. Cambridge, MA: Harvard University Press.

Souter, K. M. 2009. "The War Memoirs: Some Origins of the Thought of W. R. Bion." *The International Journal of Psychoanalysis* 90(4): 795–808.

Stern, D. N., Sander, L. W., Nahum, J. P., Harrison, A. M., Lyons-Ruth, K., Morgan, A. C., … and Tronick, E. Z. 1998. "Non-Interpretive Mechanisms in Psychoanalytic Therapy: The 'something more' than Interpretation." *The International Journal of Psycho-Analysis* 79: 903–921.

Terman, D. M. 2014. "Self-Psychology as a Shift Away from the Paranoid Strain in Classical Analytic Theory." *Journal of the American Psychoanalytic Association* 62: 1005–1024.

Tomasello, M. 2009. *The Origins of Human Communication.* Cambridge, MA: MIT Press.

Tomasello, A. 2019. *Becoming Human: A Theory of Onthogeny.* Cambridge, MA: Harvard University.

Trist, E. 1985. "Working with Bion in the 1040s: The Group Decade." In *Bion and Group Psychotherapy*, edited by M. Pines, 1–46. London: Jessica Kigsley Publishers, 2000.

Tronick, E. Z., Bruschweiler-Stern, N., Harrison, A. M., Lyons-Ruth, K., Morgan, A. C., Nahum, J. P., ... and Stern, D. N. 1998. Dyadically Expanded States of Consciousness and the Process of Therapeutic Change. *Enfant Mental Journal* 19: 290–299.

Vygotsky, L. S., and A. Luria. 1934. "Tool and Symbol in Child Development." In *The Vygotsky Reader*, edited by R. Van Der Veer, and J. Valsiner. Translated by T. Prout, R. Van Der Veer, 99–174. Oxford: Blackwell, 1994.

Vygotski, L. S., and A. R. Luria. 1984. *Strumento e segno nello sviluppo del bambino* [Instrument and Sign in Child Development]. Bari: Laterza, 1997.

Winnicott, D. W. 1945. "Primitive Emotional Development1." *International Journal of Psychoanalysis* 26: 137–143.

Winnicott, D. W. 1949. "The World in Small Doses." In *The Child and the Family. First Relationships*, 52–58. London: Tavistock, 1957.

Winnicott, D. W. 1958. *Through Paediatrics to Psycho-Analysis.* London: Hogarth, 1975.

Winnicott, D. W. 1960. "The Theory of the Parent–Infant Relationship." *The International Journal of Psychoanalysis* 41: 585–595.

Winnicott, D. W. 1965. *The Maturational Processes and the Facilitating Environment.* London: Hogarth.

Winnicott, D. W. 1974 [1963]. "Fear of Breakdown." *International Review of Psycho Analysis* 1: 103–107.

Yuan, Y. 2016. *The Riddling between Oedipus and the Sphinx: Ontology, Hauntology, and the Sphynx.* Lanham: University Press of America.

Zahavi, D. 2001. *Husserl and Transcendental Intersubjectivity: A Response to the Linguistic-Pragmatic Critique.* Athens, OH: Ohio University Press.

Zahavi, D. 2017. *Husserl's Legacy: Phenomenology, Metaphysics, and Transcendental Philosophy.* Oxford: Oxford University Press.

Index

of two 89; intersubjectivity 12;
negative capability and faith
59, 136; O = basic assumption
14; shared dreaming 8;
transformations in hallucinosis
58, 154
Cohen, J. 134–136
common sense 79, 106
common unconscious 29–31, 156
conception 98, 103–109, 114–115,
118, 120, 125
constant conjunction 55, 118, 137
container/contained 148, 167
corporeal intentionality 169, 183
countertransference 18, 179
cruel superego 55, 60, 63
curiosity-stupidity-arrogance 10,
35, 36, 38, 41, 45, 50, 59

Darkness and Formlessness 171
death drive 44, 171, 174
death instinct 37, 47
"deep" interpretation 54
deficiency of the scientific
method 60
Deity 171–173, 175, 181, 184
Derrida, J. 70, 183
destruction of time 99, 106, 110
Di Noia, A. 42
distortion 27, 108
Divine Being 171, 184
The Divine Comedy 173
dream screen 80, 91–92, 96
dreaming 27, 60, 71, 87, 89, 108,
113, 136, 140, 151, 161, 167, 170,
174, 177, 182
dyadic expansion of
counsciousness 168

"early" Bion 4
Edmunds, L. 62
eidetic intuition 135–136
Elliott, A. 33

emotional drive 103
envy 46–47, 50–51, 53, 68, 71–73,
76, 88
epistemophilic instinct 39
epoché 134–136, 141
Ernout, A. 137
Esposito, R. 12
evasion of frustration 110
evolution 50, 60, 130, 143, 157,
179
existence (in search of) 1, 147

facilitating environment 93, 101
faith 30, 31, 59, 125, 134, 156, 181
fear of breakdown 91–93
Ferri, G. 169
Ferro, A. 8, 9, 56, 96, 131, 180
field theory 2, 7–9, 14–15, 26, 33,
96, 131, 151–153, 160
fort and *da* 105
Foucault, M. 61
Freud, S.: *in absentia or in effigie*
144; beam of darkness 137,
141; bodily ego 172; death
drive 174; "Formulations on
the Two Principles of Mental
Functioning" 99, 106, 113–116;
insight 138; intuition 161;
Junktim 6; "Mystic WritingPad"
95; negative hallucination 65,
90–92; "neo-Kantian" vision
126; one-person psychology
9; primary motherinfant
relationship 99–101, 107–109;
psychology of group 13–14, 67;
reality principle 79; repressed
representation 15; senseorgan
for the perception of psychic
qualities 112, 137, 140; theory
of emotion 62, 150; theory
of unconscious 27, 52–53;
transference 25
frustrated couple 48–49, 52

For Product Safety Concerns and Information please contact our EU
representative GPSR@taylorandfrancis.com
Taylor & Francis Verlag GmbH, Kaufingerstraße 24, 80331 München, Germany

www.ingramcontent.com/pod-product-compliance
Lightning Source LLC
Chambersburg PA
CBHW050649280326
41932CB00015B/2832

* 9 7 8 1 0 4 1 0 3 1 2 5 3 *